INCREDIBLE
BASEBALL STATS

The Coolest, Strangest Stats and Facts in Baseball History

BY KEVIN REAVY AND RYAN SPAEDER

FOREWORDS BY WADE BOGGS AND LANCE McCULLERS JR.

SPORTS PUBLISHING

Sports Publishing books may be purchased in bulk at special discounts for
sales promotion, corporate gifts, fund-raising, or educational purposes. Special
editions can also be created to specifications. For details, contact the Special
Sales Department, Sports Publishing, 307 West 36th Street, 11th Floor, New
York, NY 10018 or sportspubbooks@skyhorsepublishing.com.

Sports Publishing® is a registered trademark of Skyhorse Publishing, Inc.®,
a Delaware corporation.

Visit our website at www.sportspubbooks.com.

10 9 8 7 6 5 4 3 2 1

Library of Congress Cataloging-in-Publication Data is available on file.

Cover design by Tom Lau
Cover photo credit iStockphoto

ISBN: 978-1-68358-318-9
Ebook ISBN: 978-1-68358-313-4

Printed in the United States of America

TABLE OF CONTENTS

In Memoriam of the lone major leaguers who lost their lives
serving in World War II, both Hall of Famers in our book:
1st Lt Harry O'Neill (USMC), KIA March 6, 1945
Capt Elmer Gedeon (USAAF), KIA April 20, 1944

ACKNOWLEDGMENTS

Writing this book required the help, encouragement, and support of some really great people:

Wade Boggs and *The Man in the Arena* Lance McCullers Jr. (SIUEFA), for their fantastic forewords, providing statistical insights from a player's perspective.

Mr. Brian Kenny, Edgar Martinez, Tim Raines, Larry Walker, for their kind words about the contents of this book.

Amy McCormick, for helping us edit, fact-check, and research along the way. She's insanely talented with the written word. We owe her forever.

Matt Rappa, for being a dynamo with the odds and ends. His contributions (photos, notes) are all over this.

Sean Forman and his team at Baseball-Reference.com, for helping casual fans and professional researchers alike see through the statistical looking glass of baseball's rich history. The Baseball-Reference play index really helps make this book possible.

Christopher Kamka, for his guidance and great insights regarding everything White Sox.

Julie Ganz, for editing and directing this ongoing project.

Also, a huge thank-you to the following for their invaluable assistance for this book and over the years:

Lane Adams; Tyler Adkison; J.P. Arencibia; Cody Asche; Dan Baker; John Baker; Josh Barnett; Andrew Belleson; Geoff Blum;

Bret Boone; David Branson; Dr. Patrick B. Burrell, PhD; Paul Byrd; Eric Byrnes; Rob Campbell; Will Carroll; Mary Chastain; Julia Morales Clark; Mr. Ned Colletti; Coach Rob Cooper; Loren Crispell; Chris De Luca; Kevin Durso; Anthony Eichler; Ryan Fagan; Marc Farzetta; Diane Firstman; Carlton Fisk; Casey Fisk; Jason Foster; Kevin Frandsen; Jeremy Frank; Joe Frantz; Rob Freidman; Jack Fritz; Peter Gammons; Tom Gatto; "Pop" George; Todd Greene; Leo Gregory; Randy Grossman; Leslie Gudel; Tom Hackimer; Jerry Hairston Jr.; Mitch Haniger; Marshall Harris; Mitch Harris; Tim Hevly; Dan Hirsch; Jason Hirsh; Gregg Hurwitz; Jay Jaffe; Garrett Jones; Adi Joseph; Sunil Joshi; Tommy Joseph; the late, great Harry Kalas; Todd Kalas; Amy Fadool Kane; Hugh Kanter; Len Kasper; Kevin Keating; Bob Kendrick; Jonah Keri; Mike Kirk; Frank Klose; Holden Kushner; Sean Lahman; Ryan Lawrence; Heath Lewison; Scott Lindholm; Ryan Lubner; Mike Lynch; Dan Mallon; Charlie Manuel; Justin McGuire; Glen Macnow; Tom McCarthy; Charlie McNulty; Geoff Nason; Rafa Nieves; Brandon Novak; Andrew Owens; Carl Patterson; Robert Raiola; Joe Rivera; Cameron Rupp; Travis Sawchik; Curt Schilling; Marnie Schneider; Jon Sciambi; Katie Sharp; CJ Shumard; Jon Sikes; Mark Simon; Ryan Spilborghs; Jayson Stark; Brian Startare; Ben Steffen; Larry Stone; Shane Sullivan; Dan Szymborski; Tom Tango "Tiger"; John Thorn; Lucas Tomlinson; Julian Valentin; Hans Van Slooten; Cindy Webster; Chris "Wheels" Wheeler; Dave Williams; Daren Willman; Meredith Wills; Kevin Youkilis; Nolan Ryan's fastball; the National Baseball Hall of Fame and Museum; Negro League Baseball Museum; Canadian Baseball Hall of Fame; Major League Baseball; Baseball Savant; FanGraphs; Retrosheet; SABR; and Statcast.

A note from Kevin: I would like to thank my family and friends—They're the best. I do this stuff to make them proud . . . and also to impress strangers in bars. I grew up wanting to write about greatness, idolizing giants on the field and in the press box. I stand on their shoulders thinking of funny things to tweet during the 7th inning stretch.

A note from Ryan: Mom and Dad—thank you for backing me in everything I do and all of the decisions I make, even if you did *tell me so*; I love you. Georgie, Jenna, Carlie (aka "Oh"), and Jake(man), your support drives me. Finally, thank you to everyone who follows me on Twitter. Without you, I am just a crazy person spouting off statistical nonsense.

FOREWORD

Wade Boggs played the game the right way. His skillset was often underappreciated throughout his career, as he caught the reputation as a Punch-and-Judy singles hitter—but he was so much more than that.

Wins above replacement (WAR), which is relied upon heavily today to measure a player's overall contribution to his team, can only be applied to Wade's career in retrospect. But when looking back on his prime seasons through sabermetric glasses, we can deduce that he was one of baseball's most valuable players. He led American League position players in WAR in 1986, 1987, and 1988 and was second in both 1983, 1985, and 1989. Despite this, he never received a single first-place MVP vote.

Sabermetrics aside, Boggs was a decisive table setter for the Red Sox throughout his Boston tenure (1982–92), during which he maintained an on-base percentage of .428—besting the American League's cumulative OBP by 100 points (.328). He reached base a major-league–best 3,124 times during that same period—381 more than fellow Hall of Famer Tim Raines, who was second—and garnering a mere 470 strikeouts, which ranked 158th most.

Boggs's ability to get on base was emphasized by his ability to hit for a high average. In fact, in just his 58th career MLB at-bat (65th overall plate appearance), he singled to center field off the Tigers' Milt Wilcox, raising his lifetime batting average to .328—a clip he'd never drop below, all the way through to his final big league appearance with Tampa Bay on August 27, 1999.

Unlike Boston's greatest folk hero, Ted Williams, Boggs never batted .400 in a season; however, during his 162-game peak—from June 9, 1985 to June 6, 1986—he maintained a splendid .401 batting average.

Batting average—long used as the key measurement of a player's success at the plate—is now merely a supporting statistic. Boggs played ahead of his time; he knew that getting on base was what mattered most. His new-school approach yielded a .415 on-base percentage, 16th best in baseball history among players with at least 7,000 plate appearances. That's not to say that Boggs's "classic" stats aren't equally as impressive; he would have to return to baseball and go 0-for-854 for his career batting average to officially dip below .300.

In 2016, the Boston Red Sox retired No. 26 forever. What an honor, to have my number up there in right field at Fenway Park with some of the greatest to ever wear the uniform!

It's another tremendously satisfying reward for all the hard work and dedication I put into the game throughout my life. I like to think I played the game the *right way.*

Pete Rose was one of my favorite players growing up, and very well might be the poster boy for leaving it all out on the field. That "Charlie Hustle" persona rubbed off on me, and is everything I preach to the kids I coach at Wharton High School in Florida. Maximum effort and hustle on every play are two things that require zero athletic ability. That's the kind of ballplayer I've enjoyed watching, and that's something I hope to instill in the next generation of players, from Little League on up.

When I played, I always had a plan and tried my best. Statistics weren't at the forefront of my mind, but I knew the stats would be there, if I did my job. Now, more than ever, baseball stats are celebrated and studied in a way that I think really honors the nuances of the game, and the little things that players, past and present, contribute to win games, and ultimately, the World Series.

I wish we had been able to bring home a World Series trophy for Boston during my tenure. Winning one with the Yankees in 1996 probably lost me a few fans, but I truly never wanted to leave Boston in the first place. Jean Yawkey, Sox owner during my career, had hopes that I'd retire a Red Sox, with the likes of Ted Williams and Carl Yastrzemski, and I was thrilled at the thought. Sadly, Mrs. Yawkey, my biggest fan, passed away in 1992, and the front office simply didn't offer me a contract when I was granted free agency shortly thereafter. But I'm proud of what I accomplished in Boston . . . and the same goes for New York, and Tampa Bay, where I still live.

Moneyball, and Billy Beane's philosophies chronicled within, really ushered in a newfound respect for the art of getting on base by any means necessary. I was "Billy Ball" before "Billy Ball." I had a job to do—setting the table for my teammates to knock in some runs. And getting on base 300 times a year was my goal, and my job. Today, that style is celebrated probably more than ever.

Mike Trout, for instance. He's an outstanding example of a player that plays hard and does all the little things on the stat sheet to help his team win. And fans really understand and appreciate everything he does. He's doing a heck of a job against pitchers today that seem to throw harder than ever before. Facing a guy like Aroldis Chapman, who throws impossible heat, has to be nerve-racking, but I'm sure he loves the challenge. I would revel in it.

That's the thing I miss most about playing—the one-on-one battle. That adrenaline rush in the batter's box was my favorite thing, and it's something I just can't get from watching on TV or in the stands. But, it's still exciting to see it in others. Unlike any other competition, there's a chance for history to be made every single day in baseball. The competition, and the history of it all, hooked me when I was young, and it's something that continues to drive my love of the game today.

This book celebrates a lot of that history. There are great stories in here, past and present, all told from a statistical standpoint—a fresh point of view on some of the best players and moments in baseball history. There is no stat for hustle and effort, but I'm sure either Ryan Spaeder or Kevin Reavy is somewhere in a lab right now testing out equations and theories to cook one up!

Baseball is a cool, fun game, in which a lot of cool, fun things have happened. You'll read a lot of that stuff in this book. The authors are big-time baseball fans, and that's the audience I played to. You guys—the fans—made my career.

My hope is that you'll find this plays to you as well. The authors' sole intentions were to put together a fun read, celebrating baseball's history and traditions through stats, and I think they did it the *right way.*

—**Wade Boggs**

Wade Boggs, warming up at Baltimore's Memorial Stadium in 1988. (Ted Straub)

FOREWORD II

I came up in baseball during the *age of analytics*. The availability of all this analytical information allows us to separate players who are dominant from players who are average, or below average. Any pitcher can hide behind a great offense, or a great defense, and collect a bunch of wins—you can't hide behind WHIP, FIP, SO/9, and groundball percentage. These are markers that are able to really prove, on an advanced level, the talent a pitcher might truly possess. That's the goal, whether you're a Major League Baseball GM, fantasy player, or casual fan. You want to have the most accurate information on player value. This kind of stuff wasn't around for most of MLB history, and because of that, players were routinely over- and under-valued.

Even from a player standpoint, if a pitcher is just paying attention to his win-loss total and ERA, he's going to reach a point where his luck is going to run out. When he stops getting six runs of support per outing and line drive double plays with the bases loaded, the losses will pile up and his ERA will soar. But, he's not going to know how to fix it because his attention was focused only on the most basic information. Wins and ERA tell you the result, but not really how things happened, and how things change.

In 2018, I had an outing against the Royals in which Salvador Perez hit a soft fly ball to right. Typically, our right fielder, Josh Reddick, would catch such a ball, 100% of the time. Nevertheless, Josh had been shifted so far into right-center field that the ball just fell in for a hit. Two batters later, Alex Gordon got a broken bat single with two outs. The next batter, Hunter Dozier, hit a three-run homer off me. And those were the only runs they scored all game. Sure, I could have made a better pitch to Dozier, but if I'm going to look at that inning analytically, there were a lot more positives than the three hits and three runs would have you believe. Although I didn't get the win, I still feel like I pitched six strong innings, and the data backed that up. Our *team* pulled out the "W" in the end, 4–3, and though my ERA sat at 4.50 for the game, I feel as though my 2.54 xFIP better represents my effort. Another example of this is my July 29th outing again Texas in which I had a 5.06 ERA, but a -0.96 FIP and a -0.03 xFIP! Sometimes, it is a *game of luck.*

Speaking of the shift—in the Royals' case, it didn't benefit me, with that fly ball to right field. But, that doesn't mean I'm against shifting. The shift, love it or hate it, is a great example of baseball embracing data analytics to get a better result. One thing I've learned is that the shift will get almost no credit when it works, but will get crushed when it fails. While some people want to get rid of it, I think we can do a much better job of using it to our advantage. Personally, it has cost me more than it's given me over the years. Teams right now are using generalized stats and information—they're putting a guy like me, with my unique skill set, in the same category as someone else, who may throw entirely different pitches at entirely different velocities. There's nothing wrong with either pitching style, but the differences change the timing, and the batter's plan, which in turn will affect the outcome. So, if I'm going to get shifted, I want as much information laid out as possible that shows a particular batter's success against pitchers like me, or pitchers that throw pitches similar to the ones I throw. The problem with that is that every pitcher is unique. It's hard to gather enough general data on where to shift fielders at a particular time against me when I'm the only pitcher in baseball that throws exactly like me. All that means is that there are opportunities to improve it.

We can and should hand-craft the shift to each pitcher's repertoire. Does that mean it will take more research, and more man hours? Sure. But, it's worth it to get it right. Putting defenders where the ball is going to be is a good thing! With TrackMan Baseball's pitch evaluation, we can gather enough information on each of my pitches—trajectory, spin, velocity, how close it's released from home plate—and find someone else who throws a similar-enough pitch. If there's enough information there for those particular pitches against specific batters to warrant a shift, it makes perfect sense. Just, from a pitcher's standpoint, it can be frustrating when the pitch you want to throw in a specific situation doesn't really align with the defensive positioning. The shift has only really been around a couple of years, though, so it still has to evolve—like all stats and analytics have over the years. One of the great things about this book is that it uses some of those tools to give a fresh perspective on players from the past who never got their due credit because people didn't know what to look for.

Guys like Miguel Cabrera, Bryce Harper, and Mike Trout would have gotten called up immediately 100 years ago, 50 years ago, 20 years ago, or today, at the age of 19 or 20, because they are just really special players. No amount of advanced analytics would matter because the eye test and the basic stats tell you all you need to know.

On the other hand, the reliance on analytics helps to bring in guys like my teammate Tony Kemp, who, in terms of size maybe at first glance doesn't look like a big leaguer. Despite tremendous ability, he didn't get a shot in the majors until his age 24 season— same as Wade Boggs. But when you give these guys an opportunity, and watch them play every day, with the benefit of the information we have now... you start to understand that these guys belong, and there's so much more to being a big league ball player than eye-test stuff and basic stats. The lack of more nuanced information is the reason Boggs—one of the greatest hitters ever—didn't get a shot for so long. Analytics give guys like Kemp and Jose Altuve a chance to show what they can do when, 20 years ago, they might have had to wait it out for a lot longer in the minors, like Boggs had to. If Boggs played today, he'd get called up from the get-go and be in the running for MVP every single year. Analytics highlight the seemingly smaller things that might make all the difference.

During our World Series run in 2017, it seemed like a million little things went our way, and we came through when we had to, winning one of the best World Series in recent memory, by the tightest of margins. It really is a game of inches, and all the data you get before, during, and after the game can give you the edge you need when one pitch could be the difference between winning and losing. It's so hard to repeat in baseball because there is so much information to consider, and then it all comes down to execution. Throughout the playoffs in 2017, we felt like we constantly had our backs against the wall. Thankfully, we were prepared and we executed; but if a few key plays didn't go our way, it could have turned out differently. In 2018, we could have been in the World Series again—and maybe the Red Sox were just a better team—but it seemed like, that time, the ball was bouncing *their* way, not ours. And because analytics can make all the difference, every team in baseball has fully bought in. They have to, to win.

It seems like, nowadays, probably 95 percent of players are studying things like TrackMan and looking at launch angles, spin rate, groundball rate, etc. These weren't conversations that took place two decades ago—it was all about, "do you throw hard and/ or hit the ball far?" Kids are being exposed to it at an early age now, and that's a good thing.

For me, this book and some of the stats and information in it, continues to open my eyes. I think the fans are drawn to it for the same reason—we are all passionate about baseball, past and present. It puts into perspective how great some of these players were, in ways we maybe hadn't considered before, with numbers. Ryan will send me crazy stats all the time. It's great because it helps us appreciate players from baseball's past, through analytics. It helps us understand why this numbers game is so important—not just to evaluate players now and the ones coming up, but to also give due credit to the greats that have come and gone. I think what Ryan and Kevin are doing is a little bit groundbreaking, as far as giving people one source to be able to discover all these cool stats, stories, and perspectives that we are really just now beginning to understand.

—Lance McCullers Jr., 2017 World Series Game 3 Winner

MLB greats, past and present: Wade Boggs (right) and Lance McCullers Jr. (Lance McCullers Jr.)

INTRODUCTION

Baseball can be romanticized in any number of ways. As America's pastime and sporting tradition since the mid-1800s, the game offers sights, sounds, and smells that are deeply entrenched in our culture and personal lives.

For some, the experience may be less visceral.

Just as a computer programmer lives and breathes the binary 1s and 0s, and *http gigabyte gobbledygook* that operate in anonymity within a quarter-inch thick tablet computer, we obsess over baseball statistics. Stats give the game historical context, and measurables for past, present, and predictive analysis. The numbers may not always be what we see and experience at the ballpark, or through our television screen, but one thing is certainly true: stats tell stories.

In 2000, Pedro Martinez tied for just the eighth-highest win total in baseball. Dig deeper and the numbers tell us that, if Martinez had been charged a run for every time he walked or hit a batter on the season (46 times total), he would still have the lowest ERA in the league.

Sure, the Los Angeles Angels won the American League Rookie of the Year Award by putting up great statistics both as a batter and a pitcher in 2018, but did you know that he was the first player with double-digit home runs and victories on the mound in a season since Babe Ruth in 1921? That's a fun story.

Those are the kinds of stories we tell in this book—through stats.

America's fascination with baseball stats gave birth to fantasy sports, exciting home run chases, and thrilling pilgrimages to Cooperstown, New York, to visit the Baseball Hall of Fame and Museum—a building built on the historical records and statistical achievements of the game's greatest players. The numbers are a very critical part of the story.

We scoured the records for untold tales, and looked at familiar ones from new statistical contexts. There's a monstrous pile of data and satiating sabermetric goodies in this book, if that's what you're into. But also, there are some really incredible stories.

STATS INCREDIBLE!

Every team chapter in the book ends with a collection of some of our favorite stats pertaining to that team, labeled, "Stats Incredible!" You can shoot to those sections for quick-hit stats, or just dive into the whole thing.

Overall, you'll find a brief team history for each franchise, along with a few subsections, with stats on some of their greatest players, moments, and achievements.

If you see a stat you don't know or understand, don't freak out. Check the glossary of terms in the back of the book.

I. AMERICAN LEAGUE

AMERICAN LEAGUE EAST

BALTIMORE ORIOLES

Est. 1901

The Orioles were victorious over the Twins in their 2018 opener, besting Minnesota, 3–2, in extra innings on a walkoff home run by Adam Jones in the bottom of the 11th inning—making Baltimore the first team in baseball history with a walk-off win in three consecutive season-opening games.

The Baltimore Orioles are a storied franchise, but a complicated one. The original eight American League teams in 1901 featured a Baltimore Orioles, but not *the* Baltimore Orioles we know today. The modern O's squad is a descendant of the original Milwaukee Brewers of 1901, but not *the* Milwaukee Brewers we know today. Get it?

Deep breath . . .

The O's of today began as the Milwaukee Brewers in the American League's eight-team formation in 1901. One of the other eight was the Baltimore Orioles, but that franchise folded, opening a spot for the New York Highlanders, which would be renamed the Yankees we know today, ten years later. The Brewers moved from Milwaukee to Missouri in 1902 and became the St. Louis Browns. Fast forward 52 years, when the team was sold and moved to

Baltimore, where the current Orioles started fresh and still reside. Ultimately, the team originally known as the Brewers became the Browns and finally the Orioles in less than 55 years.

The modern O's may prefer to promote their Hall of Fame Baltimore brethren of Cal Ripken Jr., Jim Palmer, Frank Robinson, et al, but that half-century in St. Louis is impossible to ignore.

St. Louis Browns

Third baseman Scott Rolen, upon being traded to the St. Louis Cardinals in 2002, remarked that he felt as though he had "died and gone to baseball heaven." Surely, the city today regards its lone baseball team as divine, stuffing the Busch Stadium cathedral to capacity with regularity. But perhaps the greatest example of St. Louis's reputation as a historically great baseball town is how the fans wrapped their arms around the Browns—a historically dreadful franchise.

After their first season in Missouri in 1902, the Browns finished second in the eight-team American League (78–58), but would fail to finish higher than fourth for the following 18 seasons. The NL Cardinals were having a rough couple of decades themselves, with just two third-place finishes over the same span. The early part of baseball's Modern Era would seem to paint a

The 1915 St. Louis Browns, managed by Dodgers front-office legend Branch Rickey (suited). (Author unknown; PD)

particularly hellish picture of the situation in St. Louis, but the fans persevered.

One of the few true gems of the Browns franchise was first baseman George Sisler, who ranks among the greatest pure hitters in baseball history, and was a true one-man show for the club.

In 1920, Sisler had 240 runs produced, accounting for 30.11 percent of his team's scoring that season—and the Browns finished third in the league in runs (797).

Sisler's greatest campaign was his 1922 MVP season, in which he led the league in batting average (.420), hits (246), runs (134), and stolen bases (51). He had more than twice as many games with three hits or more (36) as no-hit games (17). His .420 clip is good for third highest during the Modern Era of baseball (since 1901) and second highest during the Live Ball Era (since 1920) only to the .424 posted by his roommate at Sportsman's Park, Cards great Rogers Hornsby, in 1924.

Today, we wonder if there will ever be another .400 hitter. Tony Gwynn was the closest with the Padres in 1994 (.394). But from May 4, 1920 to April 17, 1924, spanning 425 games and parts of four MLB seasons, Sisler maintained a .402 average.

Zany owner Bill Veeck purchased the Browns in 1951 and immediately set his sights on making the Browns the top show in town, by any means necessary.

He famously signed Eddie Gaedel, a 3-foot-7 dwarf with the jersey number "1/8", and actually put him into a game to pinch hit. Gaedel's microscopic strike zone aided the inevitable walk, and pushed Major League Baseball toward a void of his contract the following day, instilling new discretionary disqualification rules based on height.

Veeck's fan-friendly style was a big hit. He signed former Cards greats to work for the team and generated a dizzying array of promotions to keep interest high. He even once allowed fans to pick a lineup and vote on managerial decisions during a game. It was all part of his master plan to drive the Cardinals out of town and lay sole claim to St. Louis and its fans.

And he would have gotten away with it too, if it weren't for those meddling Brew makers . . .

Browns Out, Baltimore-Bound

In 1953, the Cardinals were sold to the local Anheuser-Busch brewery with the intent of staying put and having significant financial backing to do so.

Veeck could no longer compete, so he sold the stadium to the Cards and the Browns to Clarence Miles, and the Miles group moved the team to Baltimore. Success would soon follow.

Since the move, the Orioles did what the Browns couldn't in St. Louis—win the World Series. The Orioles won it all three times (1966, 1970, 1983), totaling exactly one more championship than the Philadelphia Phillies (established in 1883) have to date.

Jim Palmer, who tossed a Live Ball era record 11 shutouts in which he allowed three or fewer baserunners, played on all three of Baltimore's championship teams. The owner of three Cy Young

Awards over the span of four seasons (1973–76), he might be one of the most underappreciated hurlers of all time.

He ruled the 1970s, leading the decade in both ERA (2.58) and wins (186). Over the past 100 seasons, no other American League pitcher has had more sub-2.50 ERA seasons than Palmer.

Palmer also led the famed 1971 rotation that featured four 20-game winners. With Dave McNally, Pat Dobson, and Mike Cuellar, the quartet totaled 81 wins and registered a 1.131 WHIP, the best in baseball's Live Ball Era (1920–present).

Palmer was "the man" in the early years of Baltimore baseball, but the "Iron Man" would eventually unseat him as the face of the franchise.

Cal Ripken Jr.

Ripken was a revolutionary shortstop, bringing unheard-of offensive production to a predominantly defensive position.

Cal Ripken Sr. & Jr. during Junior's 1982 Rookie of the Year season.
(Baltimore Orioles / MLB)

He holds the AL record for All-Star appearances (19), making every squad from his second full season in the majors until his last. For traditionalists, he ranks first in home runs (345) and RBIs (1,328) in history among shortstops; for the more modern, saber-metric-minded fan, he is tied with Honus Wagner for most 10-plus WAR seasons at shortstop (two). Overall, Ripken is one of just a dozen players in history to have multiple seasons with 10 or more WAR—Tony Gwynn, his Hall of Fame contemporary, did not have a single season with even 9.0 WAR.

While Derek Jeter gets a lot of credit these days as one of the greatest Yankees and maybe the best shortstop in the game's history, consider this:

In terms of WAR, one full season played by Ripken (162 games) is worth nearly 197 games played by Derek Jeter. Sure, Jeter could return to baseball, have an 0-for-1,376 skid, and still not see his career batting average fall below Ripken's, but the overall game—specifically when looking at the numbers beyond their baseball cards—sways decidedly in Ripken's favor.

Ripken had 180.7 career DRS (Defensive Runs Saved), 11th most overall and third among shortstops, while Jeter ranks last with -243.3. Amazingly, he won just two Gold Glove awards to Jeter's five. One of Ripken's non-wins is considered one of the greatest fielding seasons ever, as he committed just three errors in 680 chances, tallying 22.0 DRS, playing, of course, every game in 1990. But shortstops were supposed to be short, quick fellas named "Pee Wee," and Ripken was tall, strong, and slowed by all that iron.

Famously, Ripken earned the "Iron Man" moniker, playing in 2,632 straight games. Only 38 players in the game's history have played 2,632 games *total*.

The Human Vacuum Cleaner

Eighteen-year-old Brooks Robinson debuted for the Orioles in 1955 and retired as an Oriole at age forty in 1977. He's tied with Carl Yastrzemski (Boston Red Sox) as the longest-tenured single-franchise player in MLB history (23 seasons).

The slick-fielding third baseman won a Gold Glove every season during a 16-year stretch, from 1960–1975. During that time, he was selected to 15 All-Star games, and received MVP votes 12 times, winning the AL honor in 1964.

He tallied 13 seasons with at least a dozen DRS, most all time and two more than The Wizard himself, Hall of Famer Ozzie Smith, who ranks second. Robinson's 293.1 total DRS ranks first among all players in baseball history, 52.4 more than his under-appreciated teammate of 13 years, Mark Belanger, who is sandwiched between Robinson and Smith on the all-time leader list, though Belanger averaged nearly three more DRS-per-162 games played than Robinson.

STATS INCREDIBLE!

56: Brian Roberts's total doubles in 2009, the single-season record for a switch hitter. José Ramírez (Cleveland Indians) tied the record in 2017.

5: Postseason RBIs by Dave McNally in 1970. Ranks him tops (with Kerry Wood, 2003) among pitchers for a single postseason.

.332: Roberto Alomar's home-field batting average at the O's Camden Yards, the highest mark in park history. Alomar also owns the top OBP (.400) and OPS (.907) there.

1.65: Zach Britton's ERA in 2014, making him the first pitcher in franchise history with a sub-2.00 ERA, sub-1.000 WHIP, and 25+ saves. He repeated the feat in 2015 and then again in 2016.

31: Outfielder Brady Anderson's stolen base total in 1994. He finished ninth in baseball in stolen bases, and tied for 208th in caught stealing (one).

58: Home runs hit by the 1986 St. Louis Cardinals. The 1987 Orioles hit 58 home runs just in May.

53: Home runs hit by O's first baseman Chris Davis in 2013. The 1954 Orioles hit 52 home runs as a team.

61: Davis's home run total over a 162-game span, from August 18, 2012 to August 23, 2013.

51: Davis's age during the last year that he will receive a paycheck from the Orioles.

2,632: Cal Ripken Jr.'s "Iron Man" streak began on May 30, 1982 and ended on September 20, 1998. The day prior, Ripken did play, but missed the second of Baltimore's twin bill, playing in the first. His Iron Man streak spanned 2,632 games and 5,957 days.

11.5: Ripken's best single-season WAR, in 1991. Babe Ruth had an 11.5 WAR in 1926, hitting .372 with 47 home runs and 153 RBIs.

.520: Outfielder Mark Devereaux's batting average with the bases loaded in 1992, collecting 38 RBIs.

10.69: ERA of O's starter Brian Matusz in 2011. It is the highest single-season ERA ever recorded (40 innings minimum).

3: The number of players in baseball history with at least 2,000 hits, 200 home runs, and 200 DRS: Brooks Robinson, Roberto Clemente, and Adrian Beltre.

3x3: On August 7, 2016, Manny Machado became the first player to homer in each of the first three innings of a game since Carl Reynolds (Chicago White Sox) on July 2, 1930.

4: On May 8, 2018, Dylan Bundy became the first starting pitcher ever to allow at least four home runs without recording an out.

Longtime Oriole Chris Davis conversing with eventual Boston Red Sox World Series MVP Steve Pearce at Oriole Park at Camden Yards in August 2018. (Keith Allison, CC BY-SA 2.0 [https://creativecommons.org /licenses/by-sa/2.0], via Flickr)

BOSTON RED SOX

Est. 1901

Pedro Martinez had a 228 ERA+ from 1999 to 2003. His ERA+ over that five-year span tops the career-bests of Roger Clemens (226 ERA+ in 2005), Cy Young (219, 1901), Randy Johnson (197, 1997), Clayton Kershaw (197, 2014), and Nolan Ryan (195, 1981), to name a few.

Two thousand and eighteen World Series champions! Red Sox franchise history is quite remarkable. An 86-year championship drought, from 1918 to 2004, defined who they were—a cursed team with a seemingly inescapable impediment to glory. It was illogical, but consistent for almost a century. Since 2004, their story—not unlike certain time-specific statistical baseball books—has been drastically updated.

The drought lasted about seven years longer than current American life expectancy estimates (78.8). With four championships over the last 15 years, there's now an entire generation of kids—and adults!—that have no significant personal perception of the Red Sox as anything other than a perennial winner. That's quite a shift, but this kind of success is actually nothing new for the 118-year-old club.

The Boston Red Sox, established in 1901, weren't always the "Red Sox," nor did they always wear red socks.

More recently, the Sox have won four World Series in 15 years from 2004–2018 (2004, 2007, 2013, 2018), making the playoffs nine times in that span. They won a franchise-record 108 games in 2018. Famously, however, the Sox have not always had the ball bounce their way.

In 1918, Babe Ruth was ninth in the league in ERA (2.22), and second in WHIP (1.046), while also leading all of baseball in home runs (11). He had 170 Ks in 1916 without giving up a single home run, which is still a franchise record.

Ace pitcher Babe Ruth, warming up for the Red Sox (between 1914 and '19). (Frances P. Burke)

In 1917, Ruth led the league in complete games, going 24–13 with a 2.01 ERA. Ty Cobb, during the only season in which he led the majors in at-bats (588), struck out 34 times; 11.8 percent of those came from pitches thrown by the Great Bambino.

This was the guy Boston traded to the rival Yankees for $100,000 in 1919. Boston had won three of the previous four World Series with Ruth on the roster, while the Yanks were still searching for their first World Series victory.

In 2004, when Boston lifted "The Curse of the Bambino" by finally winning another championship, New York had twenty-six under its belt.

Cy Young

Cy Young (SP, 1901–08), in his day, was perhaps the game's greatest pitcher. Since he has been immortalized beyond even Cooperstown, as the namesake of Major League Baseball's award for each league's top arm. The name "Cy Young" is alive and well, but is most routinely associated with the accomplishments of other players.

Lest we forget—

Young joined the upstart American League and Boston Americans in 1901 with a stellar reputation, racking up 286 wins in just 11 seasons with Cleveland and St. Louis in the National League. He led the league in victories his first three seasons with Boston, and averaged 24 wins, with a 2.00 ERA during his eight-year stint with the team. His ERA was over a full run higher in the NL (3.06).

He had four seasons with at least 20 wins, a sub-2.00 ERA, and a sub-1.000 WHIP; only Walter Johnson had more (seven). Remarkably, he seemed to get *much* better with age, pitching a career-best 1.26 ERA at the age of forty-one in 1908. If he stopped pitching at the age of forty-three in 1910, he would have had an ERA below 2.00 (1.95) through 1,100 innings in his forties. Still, his 2.14 ERA as a quadragenarian is an MLB record (200 IP minimum), which he shares with Eddie Plank. Consider—*when Young was born in 1867, life expectancy was around 40 years!*

The Cyclone had uncanny control of his craft, and remains the only pitcher in baseball history to throw consecutive seasons with

200+ strikeouts and 30 or fewer walks (1904–05). In fact, only Roy Halladay (2010), Cliff Lee (2012), and Clayton Kershaw (2017) have done it in a single season since.

Ted Williams

Teddy Ballgame was a baseball savant long before Daren Willman was born. He hit 521 home runs, with a .344 career average, despite missing three full seasons to serve in World War II, and nearly two more to the Korean War. He famously batted .406 in 1941, won the Triple Crown in 1942 (.356, 36 HRs, 137 RBIs), served in the Marine Corps, was named MVP his very first season back in 1946, and then won another Triple Crown in 1947.

Teddy Ballgame being sworn in to the US Navy—May 22, 1942.
(PD-USGOV-MILITARY-MARINES)

[H-E-R-O: *During the Korean War, Williams flew 39 combat missions. He was struck by enemy fire on three different occasions, and was awarded three air medals . . . and, yeah, he also played 43 games for the Sox, batting .406/.508/.901.*]

Ruth once remarked to Williams that he hoped the Splendid Splinter would make a run at his career home run record. Henry Aaron eventually became the man to do it, and it's odd that Williams (1939) and Aaron (1954) both share the anniversary of their first home run—April 23.

Aaron's 755 home runs may have dwarfed Wiliams's total, but if every one of Teddy's home runs (521), and doubles (525) were changed to strikeouts, his career on-base percentage (OBP) would still be 0.00087 higher than Aaron's.

His .450 career OBP against the Chicago White Sox was his worst against any other team, but is still higher than the OBP of baseball's current all-time home run champion, Barry Bonds (.444).

Williams also had five seasons in which he had at least 100 more walks than strikeouts. Bonds had two such seasons, while the Great Bambino had nary a single one.

There have only been 19 separate .500+ OBP seasons in baseball history, yet Williams *averaged* a .505 mark from 1941–49. Here is a breakdown of his OBP in select 162-game stretches:

First 162 games: .435

Worst 162 games: .404*

Best 162 games: .549

Last 162 games: .442

*Hall of Famers Cal Ripken Jr., Dave Winfield, Ernie Banks, Yogi Berra, and Jim Rice, among them, never once registered a single .404-or-higher OBP season.

In Williams's final season in 1960, he compiled an OPS+ of 190, at the age of forty-two. In 2013, thirty-year-old Miguel Cabrera had a career-high 190+ and won the AL MVP.

Williams batted an impressive .361 at Fenway Park, but he's not the park's all-time leader. That honor, at .369, belongs to . . .

Wade Boggs

Wade Boggs (3B, 1982–92) hit .338 in eleven seasons with Boston, winning five batting titles—four of which were consecutive, from 1985–88. But whether he got his bat on the ball or not, Boggs was simply one of the best ever at getting on base. Some facts and figures about Boggs that support this assertion:

- He led the American League for five straight seasons in on-base percentage, from 1985–89.
- He led all of baseball in times he reached base safely for *seven* straight seasons, from 1983–89.
- His .463 OBP from 1986–88 is the same as Joe DiMaggio's OBP during his famous 56-game hit streak in 1941.
- In games in which Boggs had at least one strikeout, his OBP was still .341. Cal Ripken Jr. had a .340 OBP for his entire career.
- He's the only player in history to have four straight seasons with at least 200 hits and 100 walks (1986–89).
- He had four seasons with at least 200 hits, including 50+ for extra bases, and 100+ walks. Babe Ruth had only three such seasons.
- Roger Maris had a 167 OPS+ the year he hit 61 home runs in 1961. In 1988, Boggs hit just five home runs and had a 168 OPS+.
- He had two seasons with at least 150 singles, 50 extra-base hits, and 100 walks. Every other player in history, combined? Zero.
- Boggs reached base safely in 152 games in 1985—most in a season in baseball history.

Perhaps the ultimate sign of respect for the scrappy hitter: Boggs led the league in intentional walks for six straight years, from 1987–92. He totaled just 53 home runs during that span.

New Millennium, New Results

The Sox have completely shed their reputation as the hard-luck loser, which hung like a fog over the franchise after Ruth's departure.

Boston is the first and only team to successfully come back from an 0–3 deficit in a playoff series, discarding the rival Yankees in a dramatic 2004 ALCS. They rode the high to a quick victory over the St. Louis Cardinals in the World Series, and suddenly the hex was gone.

Future Hall of Famer **Curt Schilling** *(P, 2004–07)* was a big part of the solution, going 21–6 with a 3.26 ERA in 2004 and finishing as runner-up for the AL Cy Young. He faced 910 batters that season and got ahead in the count 0–2 against 240 of them without surrendering a single walk. He averaged a 4.383 strikeout-to-walk ratio over his 20-year MLB career, second only to Tommy Bond (5.036 K/BB), who last pitched in 1884—during a time when as many as *nine* balls were required for a walk—among pitchers with at least 1,500 innings pitched.

Schilling is probably best remembered as a *gamer*, as evidenced by his career +4.092 WPA (Win Probability Added) in the postseason, the highest ever for a starting pitcher. He was instrumental in two of Boston's championship runs (2004, 2007), compiling a 2–0 record, with a 0.79 ERA in World Series starts for the Sox.

One of his predecessors, **Pedro Martinez** *(P, 1998–2004)*, was 16–9 with a 3.90 ERA in '04, but he was much, *much* better than that overall during his Red Sox career. In his five seasons prior, Martinez was a combined 82–21 with an ERA of just 2.10. He had four qualified seasons during that stretch with an ERA below 2.30, and had five such seasons total throughout his career. No other pitcher since 1915 has had more.

In 1999, he faced 314 batters with runners on base, and did not allow a single home run to any of them. The following season, Pedro tossed an AL-best 1.74 ERA that was a ridiculous 35.4

percent of the league average. *He would have still led the league in ERA if his ERA were doubled.*

Pedro was a first-ballot election to the Hall of Fame in 2015, and it was a no-brainer. The 1999 Triple Crown winner (23 Ws/ 2.07 ERA/ 313 Ks) had a 2.20 ERA through seven straight seasons, from 1997–2003. Hall of Famers Nolan Ryan, Bob Feller, Warren Spahn, Lefty Grove, and Phil Niekro all only had just one season in their careers with an ERA that low.

On the offensive side, **David Ortiz** *(DH, 2003–16)* was a mainstay at first base/DH for the Sox. He earned All-Star and Silver Slugger honors in three of Boston's championship seasons (2004, 2007, 2013).

Big Papi, after a 38-homer campaign in 2016, had ten career 30-home run seasons (all with Boston), two more than Ted Williams (eight). He is the all-time leader among DHs in home runs (485) and slugging percentage (.559). However, the 2013 World Series MVP seemed to make his greatest contributions on the game's biggest stage.

Ortiz compiled a career slash line of .455/.576/.795 in World Series play, the best batting average, on-base percentage, and slugging percentage ever among players with at least 35 plate appearances.

Stats Incredible!

.304: Outfielder Carl Yastrzemski's "diminutive" batting average over a six-year span in which he won three batting titles (1963–68).

12.5: Yastrzemski's WAR in 1967, making him the only player not named Babe Ruth with a single-season position player WAR that high. He reached base 5,305 times in his career—more than the Babe, and fifth-most all-time.

.476: Boggs's on-base percentage in 1988, the highest OBP by a player with single-digit home runs since Tris Speaker's .483 (with 8 HRs) in 1920.

80%: The percentage of games in which Boggs reached base—according to his Hall of Fame plaque. This is an error. He reached base safely in 85.2 percent.

12: The Red Sox selected Nomar Garciaparra 12th overall in 1994. He accumulated a 44.2 WAR for his career, while selections 1–11 combined for just a 34.7.

.406: Ted Williams's batting average in 1941, the last .400 batting average season in baseball. His 1.287 OPS that year was the highest in baseball history for a .400 season.

.1433: The differential of Williams's 1941 batting average to the league average. This was the largest batting average differential during the Live Ball Era.

9: Home runs allowed by Pedro Martinez through 213⅓ innings in 1999. Each one was just a solo shot.

1942: The year shortstop Johnny Pesky led the AL in hits, as a rookie. He served three years in the Navy from 1943–45, and came back to lead the AL in hits in both 1946 and 1947.

13: The number of home runs hit by Babe Ruth in games he pitched from 1914–19. He surrendered just nine home runs in those games.

.00087: If all of Ted Williams's 521 home runs and 525 doubles were outs, he would still have a .00087 higher on-base percentage than Henry Aaron.

.323: Red Sox Dom DiMaggio's batting average at Fenway Park—higher than brother Joe DiMaggio's average at Yankee Stadium (.315).

50/50: Red Sox center fielder Tris Speaker became the first player in baseball history with 50 doubles and 50 stolen bases in the same season in 1912. The only player to do it since was Craig Biggio in 1998.

Boston Red Sox right fielder Mookie Betts, playing in the third full season of his career, high-fiving teammate first baseman Mitch Moreland during an April 2017 game against the Baltimore Orioles at Oriole Park at Camden Yards. (Keith Allison, CC BY-SA 2.0 [https://creativecommons.org/licenses/by-sa/2.0], via Flickr)

NEW YORK YANKEES

Est. 1901

The Yankees were never sub-.500 during any span of 162 games played by Derek Jeter.

L ike it or not, the Yankees are "America's Team" in Major League
Baseball. With a record 18 division titles, 40 American League
titles, and 27 World Series championships, it's hard to argue other-
wise. But, it didn't always look like things were going to turn out so
great for the Yanks.

The Yankees actually started as the Baltimore Orioles in 1901,
but not the modern Orioles we know today. They were initially
denied access to the Big Apple by the National League's New
York Giants in 1901 and had to set up shop in Baltimore instead.
Perhaps fortuitously for the franchise, things went very wrong,
very quickly.

It was a horrifically mismanaged franchise its first two seasons,
and was given up to league control after a 50–88 showing in 1902.
Before the start of the 1903 season, the league was able to overrule
the Giants' objection and get the franchise moved to Manhattan,
with new owners, as the New York Highlanders. But, because the
franchise essentially folded, and was then sold to a separate location
and ownership group, it's unclear whether the *team* was sold, or just
the team's designated spot in the American League. Currently, most
baseball historians consider the two completely separate franchises,

especially since only five players (13 percent) remained on the club after the move. Either way, it was a shaky start.

The Highlanders/Yankees were unspectacular their first 17 years, averaging a 72–76 per season record over the stretch, while never reaching the World Series. Then came Babe Ruth—it was really just that simple.

Ruth had been one of the game's best pitchers, and part-time hitters, while with the Red Sox before being sold to New York. The acquisition turned the fortunes of both franchises, "cursing" the Sox into an 86-year World Series drought, all the while handing the Yankees one of the most dominant figures in American sports history. Of course, Ruth had some help.

In 1920, with Ruth hitting more home runs by himself (54) than any other *team* in the American League, maybe he didn't need help. But, over a 12-year period (1921–32), the Yankees really were one of the most dominant, and balanced, teams in history, reaching seven World Series and winning four (1923, 1927, 1928, 1932). After all, one single player doesn't explain a near-century of consistent excellence.

The Yankees have always been masters of reloading. You know the names—after Ruth and Lou Gehrig came Joe DiMaggio, Whitey Ford, Mickey Mantle, Reggie Jackson, Don Mattingly, Derek Jeter, Mariano Rivera . . . and now Aaron Judge and Giancarlo Stanton. Just to name a few. There's a legend (or two . . . or five) for every era of Yankees baseball, and each one adds to the lure. But it all started with The Babe.

The Team that Ruth Built

When the Boston Red Sox famously shipped George Herman "Babe" Ruth to New York for the paltry sum of $100,000, the Yankees weren't just getting one of the game's best hitters *and* pitchers. They were also reeling in one of their most formidable opponents.

The Great Bambino's slash line against the Yankees to that point was .337/.438/.663 in 194 plate appearances. For comparison's sake, if not for Jose Altuve's .341 batting average, each one of those numbers would have been tops in all of Major League Baseball in 2014.

In addition, as a pitcher, Ruth compiled a 17–5 record and 2.21 ERA in 23 career starts against the Yanks. Again, for comparison, AL Cy Young Award winner, Corey Kluber, was 18–4 with a 2.25 ERA in 2017.

Ruth only pitched in five regular season games after joining the Yankees, so it's easy to forget he was one of the game's best hurlers. He led the league in ERA with the Red Sox in 1916 (23–12, 1.75), and his career 2.28 ERA (min. 1,000 innings pitched) has been bested just once since 1927—by future Hall of Famer, and lifetime Yankee, Mariano Rivera (2.21). Of course, the Babe didn't accrue nicknames like the Sultan of Swat and the Colossus of Clout without doing some pretty incredible things with a baseball bat.

Ruth is famous for his 714 home runs, good for third all-time, and he's the career leader in slugging percentage (.690), OPS (1.164), and OPS+ (206). But did you know . . . ?

- Ruth is the single season WAR leader amongst all MLB players for ages 25, 26, 28, 29, 31, 32, and 35.
- He batted .401 through a 255-game stretch from April 24, 1923 to August 8, 1924.
- His single-season best was 60 home runs, but Babe hit 71 in 162 games from July 24, 1927 to July 30, 1928.
- Babe mashed a record 365 home runs with runners on base. That is nine more than Henry Aaron, and 53 more than Barry Bonds.
- Qualified seasons with a slash line of at least .350/.500/.725: Babe Ruth, 5.
   Everyone else combined, 4.

Babe Ruth, in 1920, his first season with the Yankees.
(Paul Thompson, 1920)

- For nine separate seasons, Ruth managed a slugging percentage of at least .700. That is more than Barry Bonds, Ted Williams, Stan Musial, Mickey Mantle, and Sammy Sosa combined.
- If Ruth did the truly impossible and resurrected, returned to baseball, and struck out in 3,187 straight plate appearances, he would still have a slugging percentage of .500. This is the same mark as—and actually percentage points ahead of—Hall of Famer Ernie Banks. Additionally, Babe Ruth would have to resurrect, return to baseball, and go 0-for-1,147 for his slugging percentage to drop below Barry Bonds's .6069.
- Ruth averaged 10.49 WAR per 162-games played—the highest in baseball history. Mike Trout, one of today's biggest stars, ranks second at 9.78. Remarkably, this does NOT factor Ruth's 20.4 WAR as a pitcher.
- He would have to resurrect, return to baseball, and go 0-for-1,501—or 0-for-three full seasons—for his career OPS to dip below 1.000.

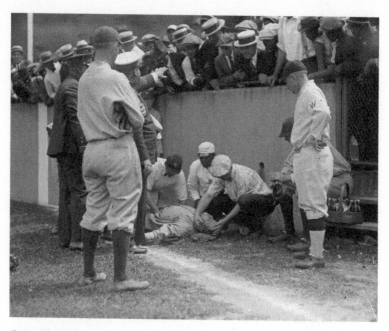

Babe Ruth, laying unconscious after colliding headfirst with the Washington Senators' outfield wall, at full speed. Ruth finished the game 3-for-3, with two RBIs, and then played the second game of the doubleheader. He homered the following day. (LOC, nocc.11744)

- He had 10 career steals of home. That is more than Rickey Henderson, Lou Brock, and Tim Raines had combined (nine).
- He had three qualified seasons in which he batted at least .375/.500/.750. No other player in baseball history has even one.
- His 182.5 combined pitcher and position player WAR is exactly what Derek Jeter and Tom Seaver had combined in their careers.
- Of his 714 career home runs, 84.5 percent (603) were record-breaking.

56 in '41

Joltin' Joe DiMaggio picked up where Ruth left off, joining the Yankees in 1935, and matching the Babe's four World Series wins . . .

Joe DiMaggio, in an offseason photo-op, kissing the bat that got him hits in 56 straight games in 1941. (The Sporting News Pub. Co., LOC)

in just four years. He had a .341/.391/.622 slash line during that period to start his career, in addition to winning the four straight rings. Historically, that was his *second*-most famous streak.

DiMaggio's 56-game hit streak is one of the most storied accomplishments in sports history, and when it ended on July 17, 1941, the Yankee Clipper began a 16-game hit streak the very next day. In those 73 games, he batted .408.

Willie Keeler's 45-game hit streak in 1896–97 sits well behind in second place, but interestingly, Joe's brother Dom holds the 16th-best streak at 34 games in 1949. Even older brother Vince managed a 12-game streak in 1941 for Pittsburgh, the same season as Joe's.

In all but two seasons that DiMaggio and Boston rival Ted Williams played together from 1939 to 1951, there was not a single MVP election that did not feature one of the two, or both, in the top three in balloting, and they'd split five MVPs between them, with Joe taking home the lion's share (three). In many ways, the argument still exists over who was better, but for the record, while DiMaggio racked up a .463 on-base percentage during his hit streak, Ted Williams put up a .482 OBP for his entire career.

[Just for fun—Pitchers Ted Lyons and Lefty Grove both surrendered a home run to Babe Ruth during his 60-home run season and a hit to Joltin' Joe during his tremendous streak.]

Next Verse, Same as the First

The Yankees are unlike any other franchise in sports because of their dominantly successful history. For seemingly every generation, they played best and had the best players. The Yanks appeared in 22 World Series during a 29-year period, from 1936 to 1964. But, considering the tremendous parity and continuous turnover that exists in the game today, it's *almost* as impressive that they haven't finished under .500 in any of the previous 26 seasons. Derek Jeter,

Yankee captain Derek Jeter's iconic batting stance, 2008. (Keith Allison, KeithAllisonPhoto.com)

Mariano Rivera, and a host of other recent Yankee greats have helped keep the legacy going.

Jeter, easily the Yankees' best shortstop, and in the argument for best player not named "Babe" in franchise history, leads the team all-time in hits (3,465), at-bats (11,195), doubles (544), and stolen bases (358).

In 2005, he clubbed a major-league record 66 opposite-field hits. The next season, he hit 64—the second-most in recorded history.

Hall of Fame shortstop Ozzie Smith would have to return to baseball and hit 294 consecutive home runs to edge past Jeter in slugging percentage. Of course, Smith had 485 more defensive runs saved over the course of his career (+238.7 to -246.3), but I think Greg Maddux and Tom Glavine put it best:

"Chicks dig the long ball."

On the pitching side, it's hard to quantify the impact that MLB saves leader, 2019 Hall of Fame inductee, Mariano Rivera, had on nearly two full decades of Yankees baseball—but we will try.

Rivera, who owned 20.4 percent of all saves in Yankees history at the time of his retirement in 2014 (652 of 3,190), had 366 more saves than walks surrendered in his career. Only ten players in history have more than 366 saves alone (Jeff Reardon, Jonathan Papelbon, Joe Nathan, Dennis Eckersley, Billy Wagner, John Franco, Francisco Rodríguez, Lee Smith, Trevor Hoffman, and Rivera).

His career adjusted ERA+ (1,000 IP minimum) is staggeringly ahead of every other pitcher in baseball history. Rivera (205), is well ahead of runner-up Clayton Kershaw (159). But it's what he did in the postseason that might make him the best Yankees hurler of all time.

In 141 career postseason innings, Rivera racked up an ERA of just 0.70, which ranks tops in history (25 IP minimum). He faced 527 postseason batters and only surrendered two home runs. The number of runners (earned) who have scored on Rivera in the postseason (11) wouldn't even fill a jury pool.

The Yankees of today have taken a Murderer's Row approach, with a lineup that could make The Bash Brothers blush, as the 2018 team clubbed an all-time single-season record 267 home runs. Veteran newcomer Giancarlo Stanton led the way with 38 home runs and four more Yankees—Didi Gregorius, Miguel Andujar, Aaron Hicks, and Aaron Judge—paid homage to the 1927 Yankees, each with 27 home runs of their own.

In all, a dozen Yankees hit at least ten home runs in 2018, most ever by a team in a single season.

Rookie sensations Andujar and Gleyber Torres became the first rookie duo in baseball history to hit at least 20 home runs in a season while primarily playing second base, third base, or shortstop.

Aaron Judge, who won the Rookie of the Year Award in 2017 batting .284/.422/.627, set rookie records for home runs (52), walks (127), and slugging percentage (.627), adding a 1.049 OPS—the best by a rook since "Shoeless" Joe Jackson put up a 1.058 OPS for the Indians in 1911, long before OPS was ever even a thought. He experienced a sort of "sophomore slump" in 2018, missing time with injuries and batting only .278/.392/.528 with 27 home runs, losing 50 games to injury.

Aaron Judge during his American League Rookie of the Year Award-winning 2017 season, in which he led the AL in runs scored (128), home runs (52), and walks (127), while striking out a MLB-most 208 times. (Keith Allison, CC BY-SA 2.0 [https://creativecommons.org/licenses/by-sa/2.0], via Flickr)

Stats Incredible!

32.9%: The percentage of all World Series games through 2018 (225 of 684) in which the Yankees have been participants.

4: The number of seasons Lou Gehrig had at least 15 triples, 15 homers, and 100 walks. Every other player in history who achieved this mark did so twice. Both were Yankees—Babe Ruth in 1921 and Charlie Keller in 1940.

55: Times Yankees shortstop Frank Crosetti was hit by a pitch from 1932–38, most in the American League. With just under half as many during the same period, Lou Gehrig (27 HBP) was second in the AL. A study on the effects of concussions in 2010 left open the possibility that Lou Gehrig may not have actually had "Lou Gehrig's Disease" (ALS) when he died in 1941. Instead, frequent beanballs to the head (pre-helmet era) may have mimicked ALS symptoms.

14.7%: Percentage of Lou Gehrig's 102 career stolen bases that were steals of home (15).

.350/.470/.640: In a season with at least 700 plate appearances, only Lou Gehrig has slashed this high. And he did it four times.

.314: Joe DiMaggio never had a career batting average below .314 at the end of any given day throughout his Hall of Fame career.

206/122: For his career, Babe Ruth had a 206 OPS+ hitting, and 122 ERA+ pitching. Context: Mickey Mantle had a 206 OPS+ in 1961 with a career-high 54 home runs, and Nolan Ryan had a 123 ERA+ in 1973 when he set the modern-day strikeout record.

379: The number of times Ruth reached base safely in 1923, most ever. In 1957, Mantle reached base safely 319 times, most ever for a switch-hitter.

115: The number of home runs hit by Yankees teammates Mantle (54) and Roger Maris (61) combined in 1961. The Red Sox, as a team, hit 112 that year.

40: RBIs by Mickey Mantle in World Series play, an all-time record.

21: Mickey Mantle's career high in stolen bases in 1959. This was the most ever by a player under Casey Stengel (managed 25 seasons).

90/40: In 2002, Alfonso Soriano became baseball's only player with at least 90 extra-base hits and 40 stolen bases in a single season.

5: Number of qualified seasons in which a catcher had more home runs than strikeouts since 1940. They all belong to Yogi Berra.

56: Giancarlo Stanton had 56 batted balls with an exit velocity of at least 115 MPH between 2017 and 2018, most in baseball and 20 more than his new teammate Aaron Judge (second place). Judge's 36 are 20 more than Rangers slugger Joey Gallo, who is third in the category.

3: In 2018, Aaron Judge became the first player to homer in each of the Yankees' first three games during a single postseason since Hank Bauer in 1958.

1,699: Lou Gehrig's RBI total over a 1,698-game period from September 19, 1926 to September 29, 1937.

2: Didi Gregorius now has two seasons with at least 25 home runs. Every other Yankees shortstop in history has zero.

72: Joe DiMaggio famously owns the 56-game hit-streak record. He encored that streak by beginning a 16-gamer, hitting safely in 72 of 73 games from May 15 to August 2, 1941.

8: Times Aaron Judge struck out during a doubleheader on June 4, 2018. Joe Sewell struck out just seven times in his final 277 career games.

23,225⅔: Career innings fielded by Derek Jeter, all of them at shortstop . . . perhaps the Yankees might have benefited by letting him check out right field on occasion.

1.214: Babe Ruth and Lou Gehrig both had a career 1.214 OPS during postseason play, highest in baseball history. The Iron Horse edges The Great Bambino by percentage points.

425: Mariano Rivera received 425-of-425 votes for the Hall of Fame. He is the first player ever to be unanimously inducted into the Hall of Fame . . . having said that, this fact better not waste space on his plaque.

TAMPA BAY RAYS

Est. 1998

On August 7, 1999, Wade Boggs became the 23rd member of the 3,000 hit club and the first ever to homer for hit number 3,000. Perhaps even more amazing is the fact that Tony Gwynn became the 22nd member just one day earlier.

While the Rays, formerly the Devil Rays until the 2008 season, have a dogged reputation for terrible attendance figures—the team has only twice finished in the top ten in AL attendance—its performance, overall, has been impressive. The Rays averaged 92 wins between 2008 and 2013. In 50 seasons, the Kansas City Royals have only managed five *total* seasons of 92 wins or more.

What the team needs most is time. Wade Boggs was the initial face of the franchise and he finished his career with Tampa Bay, but the Rays currently have no team-associated Hall of Famers, and no significant historical tradition on which to fall back. Contrary to the mystical whispers in *Field of Dreams*, just building a major-league franchise is not enough. Winning is attractive and impossible to ignore: if they keep playing well, people will most definitely come.

The Devil's Rays

What's in a name? Tampa Bay secured its first winning season in franchise history and reached the World Series during its first season as the sun-centric "Rays." Until then, the "Devil Rays" were actually quite putrid. Then-owner Vince Naimoli picked the original name from over 7,000 fan suggestions in 1995, but managed just a .399 win percentage before the team's deviled logo turned sunny side up.

[*Fun Fact: The now-defunct Maui Stingrays, of the Hawaiian Winter League, held a copyright which prevented Tampa from using the same name. At the time, religious fanatics had protested the use of the word "devil" in the team's alternative, so it was seemingly a doomed, and perhaps cursed, idea from the start.*]

Swan Songs

In the early years of the franchise, Tampa Bay was a popular stop for big-name players whose careers were coming to an end.

Wade Boggs was one of the first, joining the team at its inception in 1998. He is still the only Hall of Famer to don the uniform, and a very lonely list of team HOFers on the Rays' website backs this up. But Boggs's final 727 farewell at-bats in Tampa were anything but sad.

He's currently ranked fifth in franchise history in batting average (minimum 700 plate appearances), and managed a slash line of .333/.430/.442 in his final 50 games.

"Crime Dog" Fred McGriff was another MLB great that finished his career in Tampa, but those final 72 at-bats in 2004 do not adequately tell the story of his Rays career. He batted just .181 that year, and finished seven jacks short of the 500-homer club. It was a poor finale, but McGriff was brilliant in the franchise's first four seasons (1998–2001), before being dealt to the Cubs on July 27, 2001.

Coming in, Boggs was the future Hall of Famer, but McGriff was that team's most productive player. He earned All-Star honors in 2000, mashed 99 home runs (seventh all-time in franchise history), and at .864, still has the team's highest career OPS (minimum 1,000 plate appearances). Of course, if one were to drop the plate appearance minimum to 700, the franchise leader would be Jose Canseco (.898 OPS, 766 PA)—and it starts to become clear that Tampa Bay may not have had a flawless organizational plan from the start.

Canseco's .563 slugging percentage in 1999 is still the best in team history for a right-handed hitter, but he epitomized what was wrong with the Rays' plan. In 2000, the meat of the Rays batting order was McGriff, Canseco, and newcomers Greg Vaughn and Vinny Castilla. They are all members of the 300 career home run club, sure, but they were also decidedly old (average 34.25 years) and slow (13 collective stolen bases) compared to the average ballplayer at that time. Tampa's power push led to a mere 69 wins in 2000 and did nothing to push the franchise forward.

On a Brighter Note

We did mention the Rays have done some good things too, right?

This past season, the franchise turned 21, finally able to join Wade for a drink. It's tied with the Diamondbacks as the youngest franchise in baseball, but the team still owns the single-season postseason record for stolen bases—24 in 2008.

The Rays floundered a bit from 2014–2017, failing to finish .500 or better in any season. Then, Tampa proved to be Ahead of the Curve in 2018, taking a page out of Brian Kenny's book as they introduced "The Opener."

They failed to make the postseason, but Tampa won 90 games despite playing in the juggernaut AL East.

On May 19, they shifted to "bullpenning," with the team sitting at just 21–22 in the standings. They went on to finish 69–50, a span during which their starters—rather openers—led the AL with a 3.34 ERA. Their pitchers overall sported a 3.50 ERA during that 119-game stretch, third in baseball only behind the Dodgers and Astros. Their .288 wOBA against represented the best of any AL team.

Ryne Stanek, who will perhaps go down as baseball's first true opener, became the first pitcher to make at least 25 starts and 25 relief appearances since Hugh Mulcahy (Philadelphia Phillies) in 1937.

In all, Stanek made 29 starts, and in what one might view as a radically crude manipulation of the record books, joined Jake Arrieta and Jacob deGrom as the only pitchers in history to allow three or fewer runs in 29 consecutive starts. Stanek totaled just 40 innings pitched in those opens.

In just 21 seasons, the Rays have evolved more than many teams have over more than a century. The team has shifted its approach from relying on old, slugging ballplayers past their prime; to young starting pitching that includes the likes of David Price, Alex Cobb, Jake Odorizzi, and Chris Archer; to a concept unknown even during the "Moneyball" heyday: bullpenning.

Ironically, as the baseball gods would have it, pitching amongst the Rays' countless number of openers in 2018 was one of the best conventional starters in baseball—Blake Snell. Snell was baseball's first 20-game winner since 2016 (21 W) and the youngest pitcher with at least 20 victories, 200 strikeouts, and an ERA under 2.00 since Dwight Gooden in 1985.

Eventual American League Cy Young Award-winning southpaw Blake Snell wearing a Mother's Day uniform before his ninth start of the season on May 13, 2018, against the Baltimore Orioles at Oriole Park at Camden Yards. Snell led the majors that season in wins (21), ERA+ (219), and H9 (5.6). (Keith Allison [CC BY-SA 2.0 [https://creativecommons.org/licenses/by-sa/2.0)], via Wikimedia Commons)

STATS INCREDIBLE!

271: Strikeouts for David Price in 2014, with the Rays and Tigers. Most by a traded pitcher since Randy Johnson had 329 Ks in 1998.

1,221⅓: Babe Ruth's career innings pitched, with a sparkling 122 ERA+. Through David Price's first 1,221⅓ innings, he compiled a nearly-identical 121 ERA+.

104: Strikeouts for relief pitcher Brad Boxberger in 2014, who became the first Tampa Bay pitcher in history with at least 100 Ks without making a single start.

30/10: Ben Zobrist is the first and only player in team history with 30+ doubles and 10+ homers in four consecutive seasons (2011–14).

31: Jose Canseco's home run total through 81 games in 1999, before his season was derailed due to injuries.

15/15/50: In 2006, outfielder Carl Crawford became the only American Leaguer *ever* with a 15+ triple/ 15+ home run/ 50+ stolen base season.

14.29: Kevin Kiermaier had the fastest inside-the-park home run of 2014, rounding the bases in under 15 seconds.

105: On July 25, 2018, Sergio Romo became the first pitcher to record a save during a game in which he also played third base since Joe Gedeon did so 105 years earlier, in 1913. Joe was the uncle of Elmer Gedeon, one of the gentlemen to whom this book is dedicated.

2,028: Jonny Venters returned to baseball, facing one batter for the Rays on April 25, 2018, after 2,028 days and three (plus one partial) Tommy John surgeries since his last appearance, on October 5, 2012, during the postseason.

TORONTO BLUE JAYS

Est. 1977

In 2000, Carlos Delgado had a 1.134 OPS—the highest ever single-season mark by a player to appear in at least 162 games. His 181 OPS+ is also tops.

The Blue Jays are the only Canadian team in Major League Baseball, and are still relatively new in the scope of the game's storied history overall. However, baseball has deep roots in Canada that extend as far back as the game itself.

There is evidence to suggest that the very first recorded game—albeit a very crude version that included five bases and an undefined fair/foul territory—took place in Ontario in 1838. Canada also lays claim to the first home run of Babe Ruth's professional career.

On September 5, 1914, Ruth, playing for the minor-league Providence Grays, hit his first homer at Hanlan's Point Stadium in Toronto. It was a three-run shot to go with his complete game, one-hit shutout of the Maple Leafs.

Canada was actually a hotbed for minor-league teams for much of the twentieth century, and while Toronto had to wait until 1977 to land a major-league squad of its own, it wasted little time building a contender. Sure, the team finished dead last in five of its first six seasons, but by 1983, the Jays started an 11-year run in which the team would never finish fewer than five games above .500.

Toronto won its first World Series in 1992 with a good mix of young stars (Roberto Alomar, John Olerud) and ageless vets (Dave Winfield, Jack Morris). Joe Carter then capped the Blue Jays' successful run with a walk-off World Series–winning homer in 1993 to repeat as champs, and, really . . . that has been about it.

The Blue Jays had a brief surge of success beginning in 2015 (93–69), completing their first 90+ win season in 22 years. In 2016, they reached the ALCS for the second consecutive year, but failed to eclipse .500 the following two seasons. The window has closed on Toronto's most recent postseason run, but the game is primed for quick turnarounds and the Jays certainly have a championship pedigree from which to draw.

The Championship Run

Pat Gillick, the Hall of Fame GM for the Blue Jays at the time, gets a lot of credit for building a contender in Toronto, and for good reason. Both of the Jays' championship squads featured predominantly traded-for players or free agent signees (aside from John Olerud). Gillick was an ace at picking from other teams' talent.

The list of key contributors from those squads is certainly a roll call of some of the game's best, though they're not always players most fondly remembered as Blue Jays.

John Olerud *(TOR 1989–96):* Selected in the third round of the 1989 draft by Toronto, Olerud was a pillar of the team's offense for several years. He was a major contributor during the team's 1992 WS run, but wouldn't become its brightest star until the following season.

That year, Olerud captured that batting title at .363, setting the Blue Jays franchise mark for single-season batting average. Olerud, who was 15–0 as a pitcher for Washington State University just five years earlier, torched American League pitching, posting 186 OPS. The great Willie Mays never had a single-season OPS+ that high, mustering "just" a 185 in 1965.

Olerud also flirted with .400 late into the season, eclipsing the mark as late as August 2, but finished the year out batting just .290 the rest of the way.

He's one of the greatest Blue Jays of all time, and despite boasting a better OBP than 81 percent of all position players enshrined in Baseball's Hall of Fame, Olerud garnered just four votes in his first, and last, year on the HOF ballot.

Roberto Alomar *(1991–95):* Toronto pulled off a wonderful trade in 1990, landing Joe Carter and future Hall of Famer Alomar from the Padres for Fred McGriff and Tony Fernandez.

Alomar was an All-Star and Gold Glover each of his five seasons in Toronto, and holds the second-highest career batting average in team history (.307), second only to Paul Molitor (.315).

In 1993, Alomar became just the fourth player since MLB began tracking caught stealing in 1951 with at least a .400 OBP, 55 stolen bases, and more home runs than times caught stealing—a feat that no one has accomplished since. Simply put—Alomar was an all-around threat and incredibly efficient.

Jimmy Key *(1984–92):* Key was only 13–13 his final season in Toronto, but he pitched to a 1.50 ERA in postseason play, earning two wins, including a relief W in the deciding Game 6 of the '92 World Series.

Key was a finesse pitcher with tremendous control. He led the league with just 1.1 BB/9 in 1989. In 1990, he threw a first-pitch strike to 254 batters and did not issue a walk to a single one of them.

Jack Morris *(1992–93)* and **Dave Winfield** *(1992):* Morris was a key free agent acquisition for the Jays prior to the 1992 season, leading the team (as well as the league) with 21 wins despite, at age thirty-seven, being the second-oldest player on the team. The oldest? Winfield (forty), who was just the sixth player with a 26-home run season after age thirty-nine.

Individual Champs

Since 1993, the Jays haven't won much team hardware, but they haven't been short on individual accomplishments.

Roger Clemens, winning consecutive Cy Youngs for Toronto in 1997 (21–7, 2.05 ERA, 292 Ks) and 1998 (20–6, 2.65 ERA, 271 Ks), became just the fourth hurler in MLB history to achieve pitching's Triple Crown (league leader in wins, ERA, and strikeouts) in two straight seasons. He was the first and last AL pitcher to do it in consecutive seasons since Lefty Grove in 1930–31.

Hall of Fame inductee **Roy Halladay** (2019) was the last Cy Young winner for the Blue Jays (2003), and accumulated the second-most wins in team history (148; Dave Stieb, 175). He is the last pitcher to toss consecutive shutouts for Toronto (September 25

It never translated to postseason berths, but, at times, the Jays had the best pitcher in baseball in Roy Halladay. (Keith Allison, KeithAllisonPhoto.com)

and 30, 2009) and is the only pitcher in MLB history to have five seasons with at least 200 strikeouts and 40 or fewer walks. No other pitcher has even four such seasons.

"Doc" Halladay's career numbers are, in fact, even better than they appear. He had 88 career no-win quality starts, and he was 0–38 with a 2.59 ERA in those games. He finished with a 203–105 career record. He went at least seven innings in 40 of those losses and had fifteen career complete games losses.

The individual stars seemed to have converged with Toronto in 2015, as sluggers Jose Bautista (40 HRs), Edwin Encarnacion (39 HRs), and Josh Donaldson (41 HRs) combined for 120 home runs in 2015—as many as all 51 players to swing a bat with the Marlins that season.

Bautista hit almost as many home runs his first full season in Toronto (54; 2010) as he did his first six seasons in the big leagues combined (59; 2004–09). But his rise to power, which lasted a good six seasons, saw a steep drop, as he batted just .216/.333/.402 in his final two seasons with the Jays in 2016–17. The end of his career now looks a lot like the beginning, as he played 122 total games for three teams in 2018, batting just .203/.348/.378.

Jays fans, though, will likely always recall the Joey Bats decade fondly. His infamous bat-flip after his go-ahead home run against the Rangers in Game 5 of the 2015 ALDS was iconic—whether you loved or detested it.

Since, Toronto's faithful has had little to cheer about. The team squandered the 2016 ALCS in just five games to the Cleveland Indians—the 2018 home to former Jays Josh Donaldson (2015 AL MVP) and perennial 40-homer/110-RBI man Edwin Encarnacion.

Despite their downward trajectory, there appears to be some hope on the horizon. Toronto, and all of the Americas, impatiently await the debut of nineteen-year-old phenom Vlad Guerrero Jr., who batted .381/.437/.636 in 95 minor-league games in 2018.

In 2018, Blue Jays center fielder Kevin Pillar became the first center fielder to steal second, third, and home on a single time on base since Devon White on September 9, 1989. (Keith Allison, CC BY-SA 2.0 [https://creativecommons.org/licenses/by-sa/2.0], via Flickr)

STATS INCREDIBLE!

43.77%: The amount of hits that went for extra bases for Toronto in 2010, the highest percentage in baseball history. Oddly, the struggling 2018 team ranks second, at 41.39%.

.470: Carlos Delgado's OBP in 2000. It's the highest ever single-season mark for a player who appeared in at least 162 games.

4: Home runs hit by Carlos Delgado in a single game on September 25, 2003. He's the only player in history to hit four home runs in a game in which he had just four plate appearances.

3: The number of players on the 1991 Blue Jays with 40+ doubles and 20+ stolen bases (Roberto Alomar, Devon White, Joe Carter). Only seven other teams in baseball history even had two such players.

50/25: The 2001 Blue Jays were the only team in baseball history to have all three of their outfielders reach 50 extra-base hits and 25 stolen bases.

42: Jose Bautista pulled 42 consecutive home runs to left field, from September 28, 2009 to August 16, 2010.

55/20: The '85 Jays team was the first in history to get 55+ extra-base hits and 20+ stolen bases from each of its three starting outfielders (Jesse Barfield, George Bell, Lloyd Moseby). The only other team to accomplish the feat was the 2001 Jays (Jose Cruz, Raul Mondesi, Shannon Stewart).

10.64: ERA of two-time Cy Young winner Roy Halladay in 2000, his third year with Toronto. From 1871 to today, it is the highest single-season ERA of any pitcher with at least 50 innings pitched.

3: Halladay had three seasons in which he averaged at least 6.25 strikeouts-per-walk over at least 220 innings. It's the most since Tommy Bond had his fourth in 1884. Six balls were required for a free pass in 1884, and Bond pitched in seasons when as many as nine were required.

20: Vladimir Guerrero Jr. was born on March 16, 1999. Twenty days later, his father hit a home run in his first plate appearance of the 1999 season—his first ever as Vlad Sr.

88: Career quality starts by Roy Halladay in which he did not "earn" a victory. He was 0–38 with nine complete games and a 2.59 ERA in those starts.

AMERICAN LEAGUE CENTRAL

CHICAGO WHITE SOX

Est. 1901

From July 27, 1954 to June 25, 1959, Nellie Fox played 741 games. He was hit-by-pitch more times (60) than he struck out (59).

The Chicago White Sox were one of the eight charter franchises of the upstart 1901 American League, and were a powerhouse from the onset, with an average record of 82–66 (.554) their first ten seasons of play.

Chicago won the American League pennant in 1900—the year before the AL reached major-league status. They repeated in 1901 as a major-league entity, but the World Series wasn't a thing until 1903. They won one of those in 1906; that team was known as the "Hitless Wonders," a team that finished last in the AL in batting average (.230) and slugging percentage (.286). They went on to defeat the heavily favored 116–36 Cubs anyway. They won another in 1917 with the only 100-win team in franchise history, but would reach just three World Series over the next 101 years (L, 1919; L, 1959; W, 2005). Why the sudden, dramatic drop-off? A conspiracy, maybe?

Several key members of the 1919 squad took bribes and conspired to throw the World Series during a 5–3 series loss to the Cincinnati Reds in a rare best-of-nine-games format. Commissioner Kenesaw "Mountain" Landis ordered lifetime bans for eight of the reported conspirators, including Ed Cicotte and "Shoeless" Joe Jackson, two would-be Hall of Famers who remain banned to this day. With the team gutted of eight of its best players following the 1920 season, the "Black Sox" began a long journey back to glory.

In 2005, staff ace Mark Buehrle and slugger Paul Konerko led the team to its first world championship in 88 years—which is a mighty leap. Things like frozen food, microwaves, and television were all invented between White Sox championships—which made eating a TV dinner and watching them win a title on the tube a surely new and exhilarating proposition in 2005. But the in-between "Shoeless" Joe–to–Konerko era also had its fair share of exciting moments and players.

Just to name a few: Hall of Famers Ted Lyons, Luke Appling, Nellie Fox, Goose Gossage, Carlton Fisk, Harold Baines, and Frank Thomas all made baseball interesting between championships on the South Side of Chicago. From 1951 to 1967, the club had a franchise record string of 17 straight winning seasons, mostly under the ownership of the enigmatic and inventive Bill Veeck (see Baltimore Orioles). They reached the ALCS in 1983 and 1993 before wild-card playoff expansion, and won the AL Central in 2000.

Things could have been different, and the White Sox might have given the Yankees some good competition over the years, if not for the Black Sox scandal. Still, it's hard to ignore the great—though abridged—careers of the players responsible.

The Black Sox

The moniker given to the 1919 club plays like the stain of an old, ugly tattoo on the franchise. The players were great, and just as

A 1920 newspaper collage after the Black Sox scandal broke.
(Underwood & Underwood, via *The Sporting News*, October 7, 1920)

the movie *Eight Men Out* advertises quite literally in the title, only eight of them were responsible. Whether guilty or innocent of throwing ballgames, some incredibly talented ballplayers wore the uniform.

Banned: Joe Jackson, an outfielder who earned the nickname "Shoeless Joe" after hitting a triple while barefoot in the minor leagues, was arguably the most talented of the lot. His career batting average (.356) ranks third all-time, and his .383 average in 1920 is the highest ever for a player in his final season. His application for reinstatement was most recently denied in 2015, despite convincing evidence that he did nothing to throw the Series.

Cleared: Eddie Collins, who would be inducted into the Hall of Fame in 1939, didn't take part in the fix, and, in an ironic juxtaposition to Jackson (whose brilliant career was cut short), played 25 MLB seasons, which ties him with Rickey Henderson for the most by any single position player.

His 3,315 hits are tops among primary second basemen, and good for 11th overall on baseball's all-time list. He rarely missed the ball, striking out just 205 times in his White Sox career (1915–26). By comparison, ChiSox second baseman Yoan Moncada struck out 217 times in a single season in 2018.

Banned: The Black Sox ace, Ed Cicotte, sits fourth in team history in ERA (2.25) and eighth in wins (156). He pitched three sub-2.00 ERA seasons his last five years in the bigs before his lifetime ban. He is one of just eight players in history with five qualified sub-2.00 ERA seasons, tied with Ed Walsh, his rotation mate for five years, who finished his career with an MLB-record 1.82. The "Eight Men Out" combined for 31.1 wins above replacement in 1919, and in 1920 seven of the eight players (Chick Gandil left after 1919) combined for 26.0 WAR. Imagine a team today losing a cluster of talent all at once . . . without any compensation. It took years for the White Sox to recover.

Best Bats

The White Sox have reached the World Series just twice since 1919, but they have fielded some of the best players in baseball over the years.

Luke Appling, who is generally considered among the top five shortstops in the game's history, played 20 years in his MLB career, all for the White Sox. He is the franchise leader in career WAR (74.4), and holds the club record in single-season batting average (.388, 1936). His .399 on-base percentage is, among shortstops, second only to the .406 posted by Pittsburgh Pirate Arky Vaughan, whose 14 years in baseball were played opposite Appling in the National League.

Appling played consistently well into his forties, playing three full seasons as a quadragenarian before retiring at age forty-four. He joins Cap Anson and Sam Rice as the only three players in history to maintain a batting average of .300 or better over at least 1,000 plate appearances after age forty (.301, 1,930 PA).

Nellie Fox, a scrappy, Hall of Fame second baseman, played 14 seasons with Chicago (1950–63) and was, stylistically, an Eddie Collins clone.

Like Collins, Fox, nicknamed "Mighty Mite," didn't have much power (35 career home runs), but he was relentless in the batter's box, and one of the toughest hitters in the history of the game to strike out. In each of his 19 seasons, five of which he led the league in plate appearances, he never struck out more than 18 times. Fox had 15 qualified seasons with less than 20 strikeouts, which is the most in the Modern Era. Only 26 times (among 17 players) since Fox's retirement in 1965 has a player finished a qualified season with fewer than 20 strikeouts.

In 1951, **Orestes "Minnie" Miñoso** became the first black player in White Sox history. His dazzling combination of power and speed made him one of the most exciting players of the 1950s, and his ability to get on base made him a complete offensive package. Only five players during the 1950s had at least 3,000 plate appearances with a .300 batting average and a .400 on-base percentage—Ted Williams, Jackie Robinson, Stan Musial, Mickey Mantle, and Miñoso. They called him the "Cuban Comet" and "Mr. White Sox" and was a beloved White Sox ambassador all the way to his death in 2015.

Harold Baines, a 2019 Hall of Fame inductee, was the first overall pick in the 1977 draft. He played 22 MLB seasons—14 of them with the White Sox. He missed a chunk of time in both 1981 and 1994 due to strikes, and that may have cost him a chance at 3,000 hits (he had 2,866), 500 doubles (he had 488), and 400 home runs (he had 384)—a fact that, according to Tony LaRussa, the Today's Game Era Committee took into consideration when selecting Baines for induction. Hopefully this fact will lead to the induction of Fred McGriff, who is now off the ballot, having fallen just seven home runs shy of 500, impacted by the 1994–95 strike. He is one of four players in MLB history to collect 100 RBI in his age-forty-or-older season (with Cap Anson, Dave Winfield, and David Ortiz) and is the only one of those four to also have a 100-RBI season in his age-25-or-younger season.

Carlton Fisk is perhaps best known for his dramatic walk-off home run for the Red Sox in Game 6 of the 1975 World Series, but he played more than 300 more games with the White Sox than the Red Sox. Pudge is one of two players who spent at least 50 percent of their career at catcher to hit 300 home runs and steal 100 bases, and the other one shares the same nickname (Ivan Rodriguez). Fisk is second to only Barry Bonds in career home runs after age 40 with 72, which is the number the White Sox retired in his honor.

Frank Thomas (6-foot-5, 240 lbs), the Big Hurt, was a mountain in the batter's box. When he joined the team in 1990, Thomas was the tallest batter in team history, and the heaviest, taking the Burger King crown from Bob "Fatty" Fothergill (5-foot-10, 235 lbs), a corner outfielder for the ChiSox in the 1930s. Like a Fatty Fothergill silhouette, the Big Hurt's game was well-rounded.

Thomas, a first baseman, has five seasons that rank in the franchise's top 10 in offensive WAR (1991–94, 1997), and is the White Sox career leader in total oWAR (75.0). He also holds career franchise records in on-base percentage (.427), slugging (.568), runs scored (1,327), doubles (447), home runs (448), and RBIs (1,465)—just to name a few.

He has the highest on-base percentage (.419) of any right-handed batter since 1946. He reached base in 87.9 percent of his

2,322 career games. The only two players to reach base at a higher frequency than Thomas (.452) in their first eight seasons were Babe Ruth (.467) and Ted Williams (.488).

Arms Race

The argument over who could be considered the best pitcher in team history is a good one, because a number of players make a very solid claim to the title. Not a single player appears twice in the top spot for the franchise lead in pitching WAR (Red Faber, 68.4), ERA (Ed Walsh, 1.81), wins (Ted Lyons, 260), WHIP (Hoyt Wilhelm, 0.935), and strikeouts (Billy Pierce, 1796).

The cases for Faber and Lyons, White Sox teammates from 1923–33, are based on the same factor—longevity. Lyons played 21 years in the big leagues, all with Chicago, while Faber lasted 20, also all with Chicago. While Lyons leads the franchise in wins, he also leads in losses (230), and Faber is second in both categories (254–213).

Three pitchers in MLB history logged at least 4,000 innings, doing so all with the same team: Walter Johnson and White Sox greats Faber and Lyons. Faber was one of the 17 pitchers legally able to throw the spitball (due to a grandfather clause) and was the second-to-last active major leaguer allowed to do so (Burleigh Grimes was the last). Faber's finest moment was collecting three wins in the 1917 World Series (one in relief). Lyons, a knuckleballer, is the only Hall of Fame pitcher with more career walks (1,121) than strikeouts (1,073). He lightened his workload as he got older, but his work improved. From his age 37 season on, he posted a 3.08 ERA (141 ERA+) while completing 94 (79.7 percent) of his 118 starts.

Ed Walsh may have had only seven full major-league seasons, but he made them count. He'll almost certainly end up the last pitcher ever to win 40 games and top 400 innings, both of which he did in 1908 (40 wins, 464 innings). His 1.82 ERA is a major-league career record, and he had a four-year stretch where he pitched to the tune of a 1.43 ERA, which adjusting for league and ballpark, is still excellent (165 ERA+).

However, the best career ERA+ of any White Sox pitcher with at least 500 innings is not Ed Walsh. It's Hoyt Wilhelm, who posted a 171 ERA+ (71 percent better than league average) from 1963–68. The Old Sarge had a truly unique career, leading the NL in ERA in 1952 with the Giants despite not making a start. Then he led the AL in ERA in 1959 with the Orioles, making 27 starts in 32 appearances. By the way, no other pitcher since 1916 has had more relief appearances of 3+ innings than Wilhelm (197).

Mark Buehrle doesn't lead the franchise in any meaningful pitching category; however, during the 2005 World Series—their only championship of the Live Ball Era—Buehrle was the team's best pitcher.

He was a marvel of consistency, averaging 14 victories with a 3.81 ERA in his 11 full seasons with Chicago. His 14 seasons of at least 200 innings pitched are the 13th-most in MLB history—and he pitched them all consecutively, from 2001–14. Buehrle would fall just 1⅓ innings shy of 200 in 2015, his final season, in which he led the AL with four complete games, pitching for the Toronto Blue Jays. There may never be another one like Buehrle, who somehow led the AL in WHIP in 2001 (1.066) despite ranking 26th among 35 qualified major-league pitchers with 5.1 strikeouts per 9 innings.

Chris Sale, an All-Star his final five seasons in Chicago, was traded to Boston in 2017. While Sale never saw his 28th birthday in White Sox pinstripes, his prowess on the pitching mound still made its mark on the franchise record books. His K/BB rate each year from 2013–2016 (4.91, 5.33, 6.52, 5.18 respectively) are the top four in franchise history. Each year, from 2012–2015, Sale set a new ChiSox record for strikeout percentage (24.9, 26.1, 30.4, 33.29, respectively).

Erected in 2008, this statue depicts key moments in Chicago's 2005 championship run. Geoff Blum, Joe Crede, Orlando Hernandez, Paul Konerko, and Juan Uribe are among the players prominently featured. (Ken Lund [CC BY-SA 2.0 (https://creativecommons.org/licenses/ by-sa/2.0)], via Wikimedia Commons)

The Future

Disappointing seasons have led to the dismantling of a once promising squad, comprised of Sale, Jose Quintana, and leadoff man Adam Eaton. These personnel losses contributed to a bottoming out, as they went just 62–100 (.383) in 2018, their worst season since 1970 when they went 56–106 (.346). But now, the Sox boast some of baseball's best young talent, both on the major-league roster and in the minor leagues.

The Eaton trade brought Chicago Dane Dunning, Lucas Giolito, and Reynaldo Lopez from Washington—all top-100 prospects.

The Sale deal cost the Red Sox Yoan Moncada—baseball's No. 10 prospect in 2018 and No. 2 prospect in 2017—and Michael

Kopech, a promising former first-round draft pick that will be out until 2020 recovering from Tommy John surgery.

Sending Quintana to the North Side of Chicago brought south a package of four, highlighted by outfielder Eloy Jimenez, MLB's fourth-ranked prospect, who batted .337/.384/.577 split between AA and AAA in 2018.

So perhaps Volume III of *Incredible Baseball Stats* will read as favorably for the White Sox as this version does for the Cubs . . .

STATS INCREDIBLE!

.424: Frank Thomas's on-base percentage with two strikes in 1994.

54: Outfielder Minnie Miñoso's age during two games in which he appeared for the White Sox, becoming the third-oldest position player in modern baseball history, and joining Nick Altrock as the only players in MLB history to play in five decades.

5: The number of White Sox players to hit at least 25 home runs in 2012, none of whom had 100 RBIs. The 2012 Sox is the only team in history with five 25+ homer, sub-100 RBI batters.

35: In 2014, outfielder José Abreu joined Albert Pujols (2001) and Hal Trosky (1934) as the only players to hit 35+ doubles and 35+ home runs during their rookie season.

200/1.000: In 2014, Chris Sale became the first White Sox pitcher since Ed Walsh in 1910 with 200+ strikeouts and a sub-1.000 WHIP.

CLEVELAND INDIANS

Est. 1901

In 1948, Lou Boudreau won the American League MVP Award. He had 10.4 WAR to just nine strikeouts. He was both the starting shortstop and the manager of the 1948 world champion Indians.

The Cleveland Indians were one of the original eight charter franchises of the American League in 1901. They started out as the "Bluebirds" and wouldn't become the iconic "Indians" we know today until 1915. But, for a 12-year run in between, Cleveland's major-league ball club would actually be named after its team captain.

Star second baseman Napolean "Nap" Lajoie had just batted .426 for the AL's Philadelphia Athletics in 1901—a Modern Era MLB record that still stands—but the young phenom was not long for Philly. Due to being "poached" from the Athletics' National League counterpart, the Philadelphia Phillies, Lajoie was suddenly the primary object of desire in a brutal city turf war. The courts eventually ruled that the Phillies were the only team in Philadelphia that Lajoie could legally join for the 1902 season, and so A's owner Connie Mack threw *brotherly love* out the window and sold his rights to Cleveland. By 1903, the Cleveland Naps were born.

Lajoie was an instant hit in his new digs, leading the AL with a .378 average, and helping improve the club's record by 15 games from the previous season. A newspaper write-in contest locked in

"Naps" as the new nickname in 1903, and Lajoie certainly did his best to earn the title.

In his 13-year stint with Cleveland, Lajoie batted .339 (third-best in franchise history) and even had a five-year turn as player-manager. The Naps' average record from 1903 until Lajoie's departure following the 1914 season was just 78–79, but it was enough to build upon toward a prosperous future.

Local baseball writers decided on "Indians" for the club starting in 1915, and the franchise's first championship in 1920 (5–2 over the Brooklyn Robins/Dodgers) helped make the moniker stick.

World Series appearances have been historically scarce for the ball club, as Cleveland has made it there just six times, with wins in 1920 and 1948. That's a long drought, but the Royals', Cubs', and Astros' recent championship runs have proven that all bad things eventually come to an end.

Napolean Lajoie, leading the team that bore his name, the Naps of 1903.
(*Chicago Daily News*, LOC)

Regardless, just as Lajoie was the spark to keep the Cleveland franchise chugging along at the dawn of the twentieth century, the Indians have always had Hall of Famers in the mix to keep things interesting.

Nap vs. "Shoeless" Joe

Despite what the team's nickname might intimate, the Naps era of Cleveland baseball was not a one-man show. Nap Lajoie was the leader, but "Shoeless" Joe Jackson was, at least for a time, the team's best player.

Jackson racked up a .375 batting average during his six seasons with Cleveland, and .381 with a 1.000 OPS during the five years he played with Lajoie. His .408 average in 1911 and .395 in 1912 are the top two marks in team history.

He accumulated more triples (26) than strikeouts (19) in 1912, becoming one of just seven men in the Modern Era to hit 20 or more triples with fewer than 20 strikeouts in a single season. And Jackson is the only one to accomplish this twice (1920, CHW; 20 3B, 14 Ks).

With some of the greatest legends in baseball history in Walter Johnson, Ty Cobb, Tris Speaker, and Eddie Collins dominating the league, the Naps needed Jackson and Lajoie at their best, but Jackson missed significant time in 1910 and Lajoie missed 107 games between 1911–12. Unfortunately for Cleveland, Lajoie's prime never really matched up with Jackson's.

His first three seasons with the team, Lajoie batted .366, winning two batting titles. His play was a bit spotty after that, perhaps due to added responsibilities that came with taking on the skipper role (1905–09) and various odd injuries—including blood poisoning from the dye in his red socks in 1905. Still, he won his fifth batting title in 1910 (.384), and was surely one of the game's all-time best.

Among second basemen in MLB history, only Rogers Hornsby had more qualified seasons (nine) than Lajoie (six) with a .350+

batting average. For all second basemen, he also had the most seasons (seven) with at least 40 doubles and 20 stolen bases.

So who was the best Nap/Indian of the first half-century of Cleveland baseball—Nap, "Shoeless" Joe, or . . . neither?

The legendary "Shoeless" Joe Jackson, with his "Black Betsy" bat, 1913. (Charles M. Conlon)

The Rest of the Tribe

In 1915, the Indians traded both Lajoie and Jackson and put up just a 57–95 record.

*Enter **Tris Speaker**.*

Speaker, after batting .337/.414/.482 over nine years with Boston, was traded to the Indians in 1916 to help get Cleveland back to .500 (77–77). Over the next 10 seasons with Cleveland, Speaker put up a .354 average and an all-time franchise-best .444 on-base percentage.

Speaker ranks sixth all time with a .345 career average. He was truly a contact king, once batting .489 for a month—July—in 1923, reaching base 81 times over 137 at-bats *without striking out once.*

Addie Joss batted .144 over his nine-year MLB career—but that's because he was a pitcher. Yes, during the Naps years, Cleveland actually had one of the game's best starting pitchers.

Joss owns Major League Baseball's second-best ERA all time (1.89), pitching almost exclusively in the "Naps era" from 1902 to 1910. "The Big Train" Walter Johnson (6-foot-1), who broke into the big leagues in 1907, might more accurately go by "The Caboose," as Joss (6-foot-3) was arguably the first "big man" to dominate the mound. Joss, with four complete individual seasons with a sub-1.75 ERA, is second only to Johnson, with eight.

Lou Boudreau was the MVP of the league, and team manager, when the Indians won their last World Series in 1948. The Hall of Fame shortstop had career highs in runs (116), hits (199), home runs (18), RBIs (106), batting average (.355), and probably high-fives (?) that year.

Incredibly, he struck out just nine times that season, averaging 75.1 plate appearances per strikeout, a mark no one has bested since. [Fun perspective: Tony Gwynn's career best mark was one strikeout per 38.5 plate appearances in 1995. Boudreau nearly doubled that during his MVP season.]

Bob Feller was one of the best young pitchers baseball had ever seen, winning more games (31) in his teenage years (seventeen to nineteen) than anyone else in the Modern Era. He had 14 more wins than runner-up Dwight Gooden. The twenty-two-year-old was the best in baseball and was paid $113,300 ($1,737,545 in 2018 dollars) for his efforts during his first six seasons. He was coming off his third straight season leading the league in victories and innings pitched and his fourth straight leading the league in

Bob Feller had led the league in wins each season from 1939–41. He was up for a new contract. Instead, he signed on with the Navy and was the first American pro athlete to enlist in WWII. (US Navy Photograph)

strikeouts and was looking at an even bigger payday the upcoming season.

During an offseason drive to Chicago to discuss his contract for the upcoming season with the Indians, Feller was listening to the car radio when he had heard the news—that day was December 7, 1941—the Japanese had bombed Pearl Harbor.

"I was angry as hell," recalled Feller, who was not only the best pitcher in baseball, but also had a family-related draft exemption (meaning, he had no requirement to leave baseball for the service, but he did nonetheless, exchanging what would likely be about $7,000-per-month in season salary for what would initially be roughly $50-per-month as an enlisted man in the United States Navy).

Amazingly, Feller led all of baseball with 1,174 strikeouts from 1939 to 1946, despite serving in the US Navy for over three years, from December 1941 to August 1945.

Jim Thome and **Manny Ramirez** were two of baseball's brightest stars of the past 20 years, and got their start with Cleveland.

Both players played their first full season in 1995 for the Indians, and were nearly identical in their ability to dominate for a long period of time. Ramirez batted .319 with a 36-homer average and 1.017 OPS in six full seasons with Cleveland, while Thome batted .293 with 38 homers per season and a 1.013 OPS for seven full seasons with the Tribe.

Thome hit 337 of his 612 career home runs with Cleveland, while Ramirez knocked out 236 of his 555 career homers with the Indians. Babe Ruth and Barry Bonds are the only players in baseball history to have had more games (107 each) than Thome (99) and Ramirez (97) with both a home run and a double.

The Next Generation

The Indians have found success of late, winning three straight division titles and an American League pennant in 2016, falling just one game shy of a World Series Championship.

Corey Kluber has been historically dominant over his last five seasons, posting an 83–45 record with a 2.85 ERA, 152 ERA+, 2.84 FIP, and 1.016 WHIP, averaging 10.13 strikeouts-per-nine. He has had more than 220 strikeouts in each of those five seasons, making him just one of nine pitchers with five straight 220+ strikeout seasons. He averaged better than 5.00 strikeouts-per-walk in four of those seasons; Kluber and Chris Sale are the only pitchers in history with four career seasons of at least 220 strikeouts with 5.00 or more strikeouts-per-walk. He had a stretch of 26 straight starts without allowing more than three runs from August 3, 2017 to June 10, 2018, posting a 20-3 record and a 1.72 ERA during that span.

Kluber is complemented by what is quickly becoming one of the greatest left sides of the infield in history in Francisco Lindor

Cleveland Indians second baseman Jason Kipnis batting in April 2018 at Progressive Field. Later that season, on September 19, he would become the first player to hit a walk-off home grand slam with his team trailing 1–0 since Ron Santo on September 25, 1968. (Erik Drost, CC BY-SA 2.0 [https://creativecommons.org/licenses/by-sa/2.0], via Flickr)

and Jose Ramirez. In 2018, the duo became the first teammates in history with at least 35 doubles, 35 home runs, and 20 stolen bases each. They both tallied 7.9 WAR last season, making them the first shortstop-third base duo to post at least 7.0 WAR in a season since Hughie Jennings and John McGraw of the 1898 Baltimore Orioles.

Lindor, 25, and Ramirez, 26, have both seen a marked increase in production over each of their last three seasons, as they head into the prime of their careers. It's one of the strongest foundations in baseball, leading a team that, really, has as likely a chance to win the World Series in 2019 as any other club.

STATS INCREDIBLE!

0: The home run total of Nap Lajoie in 1906. His 170 OPS+ that season easily tops Sammy Sosa's 63-homer 1999 campaign (151) and is the highest of the Modern Era for any player with zero home runs.

.402: "Shoeless" Joe's combined batting average from 1911–12.

114: Joe Sewell's impossibly-low strikeout total during his 14-year MLB career, spent mostly with Cleveland. The Hall of Fame shortstop owns the lowest career strikeout percentage of all time (1.4 percent; minimum 3,000 PAs).

1,075: From May 14, 1923 to May 26, 1930, Joe Sewell played 1,075 consecutive games without multiple strikeouts. He totaled just 54 strikeouts in 4,744 plate appearances during that time.

4.6: Francisco Lindor's WAR in 2015, the highest by an Indians rookie since Sewell in 1921. He's the first rookie shortstop with double-digit home runs, stolen bases, and defensive runs saved since Nomar Garciaparra in 1997.

6: The number of Indians batters with a qualified .397+ on-base percentage in 1999. The Boston Beaneaters last had six such batters in 1894.

13: Jim Thome's career walk-off home run total, a major-league record. He's the only player in history to hit a walk-off home run for his 500th.

612: Thome's MLB-leading home run total among left-handed batters/right-handed throwers.

7.0: Corey Kluber and Michael Brantley (2014) became the first Indians pitcher/position player combination since 1920 to each have at least 7.0 WAR.

200: In 2015, Corey Kluber and Carlos Carrasco became the first Indians teammates with at least 200 Ks each since Sam McDowell and Luis Tiant in 1968.

.397: Six different members (Vizquel, Lofton, Justice, Alomar, Thome, and Ramirez) of the 1999 Indians had an OBP of at least .397, the most on a team since 1894.

325: Kenny Lofton had 325 stolen bases, compared to just 324 strikeouts, from 1992–96.

1: In 2016, Andrew Miller became the first pitcher ever to win an LCS MVP Award without either starting a game or entering a game in the 9th inning. He has three career postseason relief appearances with at least five strikeouts, most all time. His 11 postseason relief appearances with three or more strikeouts are tied with Mariano Rivera for most ever.

1968: On September 19, 2018, Jason Kipnis became the first player to hit a walk-off grand slam in a game with his team trailing 1–0 since Ron Santo on September 25, 1968.

4: Pitchers Trevor Bauer, Carlos Carrasco, Mike Clevinger, and Corey Kluber each struck out 200-plus batters in 2018. They are the first teammate quartet in history with at least 200 strikeouts each.

111: In 2018, Michael Brantley had 176 base hits to just 111 swings and misses.

5: On September 3, 2017, Jose Ramirez became the 13th player in history to have at least five extra-base hits in a game (since joined by Matt Carpenter). Ramirez is the only switch-hitter ever to accomplish the feat.

DETROIT TIGERS

Est. 1901

Ty Cobb won the American League Triple Crown in 1909. He batted .377 with nine home runs and 107 RBIs. All nine of his home runs were inside-the-park.

The Detroit Tigers, the AL's oldest one-city, one-name team, began in 1894 as part of the Western League, a minor league that would eventually become the major American League (1901) we know today. Those formative years as a minor-league franchise perhaps prepared Detroit for quick success in the majors, as the Tigers earned three straight trips to the World Series by 1909.

Detroit wouldn't win its first championship until 1935—of four world titles to this point—but, historically, it has been a steady franchise. Detroit is one of just six current American League teams with an all-time record over .500 (9,085–8,806, .508; behind the Yankees, Red Sox, and Indians, respectively). The addition of Ty Cobb in 1905 certainly spurred the Tigers to long-lasting success.

The Georgia Peach played his first 22 years in Detroit, and for most of that period—at least until Babe Ruth's offensive game exploded in 1919—he was, arguably, the greatest hitter the game had ever seen. With an MLB-best .366 lifetime average, one could argue Cobb's might have been the game's sweetest stroke.

The Cobb era ended in 1926, but Hank Greenberg and Mickey Cochrane carried the offensive torch for the Tigers into the 1930s, leading them to a 1935 world championship, and lefty ace Hal Newhouser dominated the mound to help Detroit take a title in 1945. Lean years would follow, but from 1961–89 the Tigers would average 86 wins (excluding the strike-shortened 1981), and take two more championships (1968, 1984).

Right-hander Denny McLain and backstop Bill Freehan may have been the best battery in team history and played with, undeniably, the greatest player who sounds like a battery in Al Kaline (apologies, Doug Nickle). Thankfully, the Hall of Fame outfielder didn't play in today's media-centric era, or similar bad jokes and puns would follow Kaline like a lithium ion on a positive electrode.

More recently, the Tigers have had a modern-day marvel in Miguel Cabrera. His career is waning, but the Triple Crown winner in 2012 (.330, 44 HR, 139 RBI) is maybe the franchise's greatest hitter since . . .

Ty Cobb

Cobb's reputation is that of a mean, abusive, hateful bully. To what degree is speculative, but clearly there is enough evidence to suggest Cobb was not an easy fellow to get along with.

His .366 lifetime batting average is still tops in baseball history, and at the time of his retirement in 1928, he was leading a slew of offensive categories as well, including hits (4,189), extra-base hits (1,136), and runs scored (2,244). His home run total (117) is scant by today's standards, but home runs would not become an important part of the game until the end of the Deadball Era and the emergence of the Babe in 1919. Consider:

Cubs slugger Sammy Sosa hit 66 home runs in 1998, and Cobb hit just 65 during a 13-year stretch in which he won 12 AL batting titles (1907–19)—finishing in the top seven in all of baseball in homers four times in that period, including a home run crown in 1909. Overall, Cobb actually had more league top- ten finishes in home runs (11) than Mark McGwire (10) and Ken Griffey Jr. (9).

Home run totals aside, the stats and feats of Tyrus Cobb's tremendous career are incredible:

- His seven seasons with at least 200 hits and 45 stolen bases are the most in baseball history. No other player even has five such seasons.
- Every year from 1907 to 1919, Cobb had a higher batting average than the league slugging percentage. He then did it again in 1922, during baseball's third season of "Live Ball" play, besting Babe Ruth and the rest of the American League, .401 to .398.
- Was the first player to record consecutive .400 batting average seasons (1911, 1912), and maintained a .402 average over a four-year stretch from 1910 to 1913.
- At age thirty-nine in 1926, his final season in Detroit, Cobb batted .339 and struck out just twice in 273 plate appearances. He closed out the season with 59 straight games without a strikeout—a streak that extended another 19 games into the next season, when he was forty.
- In 2014, Astros second baseman Jose Altuve became just the second player ever to record 225 hits, 55+ extra-base hits, and 55+ stolen bases in a single season. Ty Cobb accomplished this in 1911 . . . and 1912 . . . and 1917.
- He would have to resurrect, return to baseball, and go 0-for-2,530 for his career batting average to fall below .300.
- Pete Rose eclipsed Cobb for the top all-time hits total (4,256 to 4,189), but, in terms of WAR, one full season (162 games) played by Cobb is worth nearly 361 played by Rose.
- Cobb has 16 qualified seasons with at least a .350 batting average. No other player has 10.
- Rickey Henderson had a 189 OPS+ with 65 stolen bases during his 1990 MVP campaign. The only other player with at least that was Cobb, who did it three years in a row (1909 to 1911).
- Ty Cobb stole home eight times in 1912. Rickey Henderson and Lou Brock stole home seven times in their careers, combined.

A gifted baserunner with a keen eye at the plate, Cobb was baseball's most complete pre-Live Ball Era player. (Sliding: National Photo Company, 1924; Standing: Bain News Service, 1910.)

Cobb's career covered 79 percent of Detroit's MLB franchise existence upon the time of his retirement from baseball in 1928, but over the years, there have been plenty of players that have helped define the franchise and share the spotlight.

Tiger Greats

Hank Greenberg was one of the first Tigers to follow Babe Ruth's lead out of the Deadball Era and into the age of prolific long balls.

He only played nine full seasons (eight of which came with Detroit), but made his mark, exiting with a franchise-leading 306 homers—67 more than any other Tiger at the time of his departure, after the 1946 season. He is still fourth on Detroit's all-time list, which is remarkable considering he lost nearly five seasons serving in World War II; in fact, with 47 months served, no ballplayer lost more time during World War II (other than the gentleman to whom this book is dedicated).

Every season seemed like a gem for Greenberg, who certainly made the most of his relatively short Hall of Fame career.

In 1935, Greenberg led the league in homers (36) and RBIs (168), while leading the Tigers to their first ever world championship.

In 1937, he set an AL record for RBIs by a right-handed hitter that still stands (184), and reached 280 runs produced—fourth best all time and a mark that hasn't been topped since.

His 58 home runs in 1938 are not just a team record—they are a record for the entire *modern* AL Central division.

In 1940, Greenberg (.340, 41 HRs, 150 RBIs) was just .012 away from the batting title, and the franchise's second Triple Crown. The *Quadruple* Crown is ambiguously defined, but Greenberg was close to a version of that as well, leading the AL with 50 doubles.

Greenberg was selected to serve in the United States Army on May 7, 1941, but was discharged a few months later on December 5, 1941. He would voluntarily reenlist in the US Army Air Forces after Japan bombed Pearl Harbor and serve until July 1, 1945, when, after nearly four years, he led the Tigers to a World Series championship. And despite missing four and a half of his prime seasons serving his great country, he is one of just six players in history with a career slugging percentage of at least .600.

Al Kaline shouldn't get lost in the mix of such early talent in Tigers history, as he, too, was a dominant figure for the franchise.

He got off to a fast start, becoming the youngest player (20) to win a batting title (.340), besting Cobb by one single day.

Kaline didn't put up a ton of big, gaudy single-season numbers—by his own admission, he "was never meant to be a superstar." However, the 10-time Gold Glove winner and 15-time All-Star spread his production out well through a 22-year career (1953–1974) spent entirely in Detroit, amassing club records in home runs (399) and walks (1,277) that still stand today.

Of course, not all the best Tigers did their best work with the lumber.

Hal Newhouser, one of those old timers, should probably be a more recognizable name, but his dominance as a starting pitcher was in perhaps too short a period of time.

Amazingly, in three full seasons from 1944 to 1946, Newhouser averaged a record of 27–9 and a 1.99 ERA. Sandy Koufax, during his three infamously dominant Cy Young seasons, averaged a 26–7 record with a 1.94 ERA. Hal led the AL in wins all three seasons, winning the Triple Crown in 1945 (25 Ws, 1.81 ERA, 212 Ks). Both pitchers won a Triple Crown in their respective stretches, but Newhouser one-upped Koufax, winning two MVP awards to Koufax's one.

Justin Verlander (24 Ws, 2.40 ERA, 250 Ks) was the most recent Tiger to pull off the rare feat of a Triple Crown and an MVP from the pitching mound in 2011, and did so on the 100th anniversary of Cobb winning the first-ever AL MVP in 1911. In 2009, Verlander became the first qualified pitcher in team history with more strikeouts than innings pitched.

For an encore, **Miguel Cabrera** (.330, 44 HRs, 139 RBIs) won both the Triple Crown and MVP on the offensive side in 2012. In terms of OPS+, it was only his fifth-best season.

Though he has tailed off a bit from his prime, due in large parts to wear and tear, Miggy has batted .318/.395/.556 since joining the Tigers in 2008. He ranks second in franchise history in slugging and OPS (.954). He ranks third among Tigers sluggers in home runs (327), OPS+ (155), and wRC+ (154).

Miguel Cabrera, against the Chicago White Sox, ripping one of 34 home runs in 2009. (Kevin Ward, CC BY-SA 2.0 (https://creativecommons.org/licenses/by-sa/2.0), via Wikimedia Commons)

STATS INCREDIBLE!

.402: Second baseman Placido Polanco's batting average after an 0–2 count in 2007.

117: Ty Cobb's career home run total. Babe Ruth hit 123 home runs just against the Tigers.

4: In 672 plate appearances in 1917, Cobb struck out just 34 times. One pitcher was responsible for four of them—Boston's ace, Babe Ruth.

.380: (Ty who?) Outfielder Harry Heilmann's batting average from 1921–27, leading to four batting titles.

50%: In 1937, first baseman Rudy York hit 18 of his 35 home runs (51.43 percent) in August; in 1943, he hit 17 of his 34 homers (50 percent) in August.

75/75: Cobb's 79 extra-base hits and 83 stolen bases in 1911 make him the only man with 75+ XBH and 75+ SB in the same season.

3: In 2013, Detroit had three 200+ strikeout pitchers (Justin Verlander, Max Scherzer, Anibal Sanchez), tying the record for most in a season (1967 Twins, 1969 Astros) . . . until Cleveland fielded *four* 200+ strikeout pitchers in 2018.

1: Second baseman Charlie Gehringer's strikeout total in 90 career World Series plate appearances.

32/42: Catcher Victor Martinez had 32 home runs and 42 strikeouts in 2014. No other player in Tigers history had more home runs and fewer strikeouts in the same season.

19,068: Career innings played by Lou Whitaker on defense, all of which came at second base.

3/2: On May 16, 2017, J. D. Martinez—then with the Tigers—collected three walks and hit two home runs, which amazingly was a feat never accomplished by Barry Bonds.

2,264: Miguel Cabrera has played 2,264 career games, tallying 1,635 RBIs. All-time RBI leader Henry Aaron had 1,621 RBIs through as many games.

250: Ty Cobb could have gone an additional 0-for-250 and he would have still been the all-time leader in batting average.

KANSAS CITY ROYALS

Est. 1969

From 2014–15, Wade Davis became the first pitcher in baseball history with a sub-1.00 ERA over the span of two seasons (with at least 100 total innings pitched).

The Royals were a huge surprise to make the World Series in 2014. Their win in 2015 was a momentous boon for the franchise, but success proved unsustainable, as they floundered to just 58 wins by 2018. The Royals' top hitter/pitcher combo, in terms of WAR, in 2015? Outfielder Lorenzo Cain and relief pitcher Wade Davis—not exactly Mantle and Whitey, but it worked! Without the benefit of superstars, the Royals defied the odds and won with balanced production.

In 2015, the Royals won a league-best 95 games, despite finishing just sixth in the AL (of 15) in runs per game (4.47), seventh in OPS (.734), third in ERA (3.73), and sixth in WHIP (1.282). Superstar Zack Greinke, who owns the fourth-highest pitching WAR in club history, including the top single-season mark (2009; 10.4), averaged 16 wins per season with a 3.08 ERA since Kansas City traded him to Milwaukee in 2010. No big deal, the Royals won 22 postseason games after dealing him away—one more than the Brewers have won in their entire 50-year history.

The Royals will forever be remembered for their championship accomplishment in 2015, but it was truly two years in the making.

To put it mildly, 2014 was a breakout year for the Royals. After an unfathomable 28-year playoff drought, the Royals finally broke through to the MLB postseason. And what a postseason it was.

The San Francisco Giants just narrowly edged the American League champion Royals, 3–2, in Game 7 of the World Series. Though they came up a hair short, the 2014 KC squad restored honor to the proud forty-seven-year-old franchise.

In the beginning, the Royals were fast learners. The upstart franchise, named after the American Royal, a livestock and rodeo show in Missouri, eclipsed .500 in just its third season (85–76, 1971), and reached three straight AL Championship Series (1976 to 1978), only to lose to the "Evil Empire" in each of them, by the time it had logged a decade in KC.

The team averaged 90 wins per year from 1975–85, excluding the strike-shortened 1981. The common denominator of the seven playoff appearances and one championship in that span was the great George Brett (1.023 OPS in postseason play), but a lot of great players passed through Kansas City—just never enough to get back into contention.

Until . . .

2014

Wade Davis had the greatest win-loss percentage (.818, 9–2; minimum 10 decisions) in team history, and did so entirely out of the bullpen. Despite pitching just 72 innings on the season, Davis's output was historically dominant.

Davis's 109 strikeouts were the most without surrendering a home run since 1919 (Walter Johnson, 146 Ks). Aside from Davis and Johnson (who did it twice—in 1916 and 1919), only two other players recorded 100 or more strikeouts without surrendering a home run in a single season over the past 100 years: Terry Forster (1972) and one George Herman Ruth, known by some as "Babe" (1916).

Davis and bullpen mate Kelvin Herrera became the first team-mates to pitch at least 70 innings each without surrendering a home run since Lefty Williams and Reb Russell of the Chicago White Sox managed the feat in 1918.

The dynamic KC duo also became the first teammates EVER to each toss at least 70 innings, record a 20.0+ K percentage (strike-outs per plate appearance), and allow zero home runs—and this is even true since the innings-pitched minimum dropped to 20!

Not surprisingly, Kansas City's pitching staff was the story of its 2014 season, registering the franchise's second-best team ERA since 1986 (3.51; 3.45, 2013). Great pitching and a little good for-tune helped Kansas City become the first team in MLB history to win three consecutive playoff games in extra innings.

The 2015 squad, for the most part, picked up right where it had left off the season prior. Davis never skipped a beat, somehow dropping his 1.00 ERA in 2014 to 0.94 in 2015. In his four sea-sons with the Royals, he never surrendered more than two runs in any relief appearance. As a team, they shined brightest in the postseason.

First baseman Eric Hosmer led all postseason batters with 17 RBIs, and outfielder Ben Zobrist tied an MLB record with eight playoff doubles. Clutch play in all facets of the game helped Kansas City outscore their opponents by a cumulative 40 runs after the sixth inning of play in the 2015 playoffs (51–11; credit: Christopher Kamka, CSN Chicago).

The Kansas City Bretts

George Brett played 21 seasons in the majors, all of them with the Royals. Even though he retired in 1993, he is still widely consid-ered the face of the franchise.

Brett is currently the franchise leader in hits, home runs, RBIs, doubles, triples, (deep breath) runs scored, walks, games played, plate appearances, and All-Star Game appearances. Just to name a few.

Overall, glory years have been slim outside of Brett's tenure with the team, but it shouldn't detract from the amazing things he was able to accomplish with the Royals.

Brett (1979) and Jim Bottomley (1928, St. Louis Cardinals) are the only players in MLB history with at least 40 doubles, 20 triples, and 20 home runs in a single season.

George Brett's statue on display inside Kauffman Stadium. (Flickr Mr.Konerko, CC BY-SA 4.0 [http://creativecommons.org/licenses/by-sa/4.0])

In his 1980 MVP season, Brett had the highest batting average (.390) above the MLB average (+.1252) of any recorded since Ted Williams in 1957 (+.1306). Tony Gwynn was a close second (.394, +.1241) in 1994.

Speaking of most valuable—the Royals were 73–40 (.646) with Brett in the lineup in 1980 and just 24–25 (.490) without him that season.

From May 8 to May 13, 1976, Brett had six consecutive three-hit games, batting a stout .692 over that stretch.

Good company: Brett, Lou Gehrig, Roberto Clemente, Stan Musial, and Robin Yount are the only one-team players each with at least 400 doubles, 100 triples, and 200 home runs.

Since 1920, only Stan Musial has more 3-for-3 (or better, e.g. 4-for-4) games (44) than Brett (40).

Kansas City Royals INF/OF Whit Merrifield led the American League in stolen bases in both 2017 (34) and 2018 (45), as well as in hits (192) in 2018. (Keith Allison, CC BY-SA 2.0 [https://creativecommons.org/ licenses/by-sa/2.0], via Wikimedia Commons)

STATS INCREDIBLE!

5: 2015 rookie outfielder Paulo Orlando (great name) was the first Live Ball Era (1920+) player with five triples through his first seven career games. No other player even had four.

36: The Royals' single-season home run record, which stood for 33 years. It wasn't held by Brett, Hal McRae, Frank White, Mike Sweeney, or Carlos Beltran. Career .229 hitter Steve "Bye-Bye" Balboni set the mark in 1985. Mike Moustakas broke the record with 38 in 2017.

28: Herrera did not allow a single earned run in any eighth inning during the 2014 season. He pitched a total of 28 innings in the eighth that season, which are the most ever by a reliever with a 0.00 ERA.

2,287-to-1: The Royals threw 228,700 percent more 97+ MPH pitches in 2014 than the Minnesota Twins.

1st: 2014 rookie hurler Brandon Finnegan became the first player to pitch in the College and MLB World Series in the same year.

0.97: Wade Davis's ERA from 2014–15. It is the lowest ERA for a pitcher over a consecutive season span.

9: Davis's career World Series innings pitched. He allowed zero earned runs, six hits, zero walks, and 18 strikeouts.

1: The lone plate appearance (a strikeout) for rookie Adalberto (then Raul) Mondesi in 2015, during Game 3 of the World Series. He became the first player to debut in the championship series since Cincy's Bug Holliday on October 17, 1885—though championship series back then were considered exhibitions.

.400: George Brett's batting average during the 1980 season as late as September 19. He would bat just .304 over his final 13 games, dropping his average to a *lowly* .390 clip.

79: Peter Moylan went 0–0 with no saves in 79 appearances for the Royals in 2017—the greatest number of games ever in a season with no wins, losses, or saves.

96.8: Yordano Ventura averaged 96.8 MPH on his 1,667 fastballs in 2016. No pitcher with even 1,250 fastballs thrown averaged harder heat that season.

16: The franchise single-game strikeout record, set by Danny Duffy on August 1, 2016. He dominated, throwing eight innings of one-hit shutout baseball, a 3–0 win over the Rays.

MINNESOTA TWINS

Est. 1901

Torii Hunter, who played 12 of his 19 seasons in Minnesota, had 353 home runs, 195 stolen bases, and nine Gold Glove Awards in his career. Only one player, Willie Mays, had more of each.

The Twins franchise is a tale of two cities, and no, that's not a weak play on their namesake derived from the "Twin Cities," Minneapolis and St. Paul, but a weak play on all of that, mixed with the fact that they have actually played more seasons as a franchise (60 to 58) in Washington, DC, as the Senators.

Founded in 1901 as one of the original eight teams of the American League, the Senators were lousy their first 11 seasons of play, compiling just a .377 winning percentage, with an average record of 55–92. Then, Walter Johnson (career Senator, 1907–27) helped change everything for the team, blooming into one of the game's all-time greatest hurlers. He carried the Senators into respectability at a time when continued failure could have spelled the end for baseball in Washington.

They eventually won their lone championship in the DC era in 1924, Johnson's 17th overall season and his second MVP season—though probably only his 11th best season overall. After a short stretch of success in the 1930s, the Senators were dreadful again—so dreadful, people referred to Washington as "first in war, first in peace, and last in the American League." They were so dreadful that someone made a movie about it (*Damn Yankees*, 1958). The Senators got so bad for so long, they had to pack up and leave.

The team that found itself in Minnesota in 1961, for its first season as the Twins, actually showed glimmers of hope. The Senators managed just five seasons of .500 or better in their final 25 years in Washington, but they had a young Harmon Killebrew in tow, and enjoyed the best of his Hall of Fame seasons in Minneapolis.

The Twins wouldn't win a title until 1987, and would recapture that glory in 1991, but with the contributions of Killebrew, Rod Carew, Bert Blyleven, Kirby Puckett, Johan Santana, and most recently Joe Mauer, they've been a consistent contender across multiple decades.

Joe Mauer played his final game on September 30, 2018, following a 15-season career, all of which were spent with the Minnesota Twins. The six-time All-Star finished a winner of three Gold Glove awards, five Silver Slugger awards, three American League batting titles, and the 2009 American League Most Valuable Player award. (Keith Allison, CC BY-SA 2.0 [https://creativecommons.org/licenses/by-sa/2.0], via Flickr)

The Big Train

When you look back, Walter Johnson (417–279, 2.17 ERA) was so good for the Senators, it kind of makes up for how terrible the whole stretch in Washington was.

Johnson is the only pitcher to win the AL pitching Triple Crown (league leader in wins, ERA, and strikeouts) three times, and it's only been accomplished 16 times in American League history.

In 1924, at the age of thirty-six, he won a championship, his second league MVP award, and his last Triple Crown, which, along with 23 wins and 158 strikeouts, included a 2.72 ERA. A sign of the times—the Big Train didn't have an ERA above 2.22 in any of his 13 pitching-friendly, Deadball Era seasons.

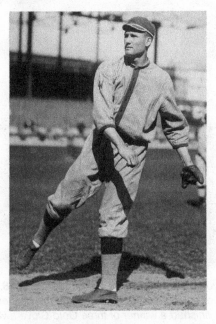

Walter Johnson averaged 34 complete games over a seven-year period, from 1910–16. Zack Grienke has only once ever made 34 starts in a single season. (Charles Conlon)

In a ten-season stretch from 1910–19, Johnson averaged 27 wins and a 1.59 ERA. The American League has not seen a *single* season ERA champion with an ERA that low since Johnson himself finished with a 1.49 in 1919.

He is one of just four players over the past 100 seasons (including Babe Ruth) to pitch at least 250 innings in a season without surrendering a home run, and he did it twice (1916, 1919). In each of those seasons, Johnson managed a home run of his own, with a whopping 369⅔ innings pitched in 1916.

So adept at keeping the ball inside the park, Johnson actually had more career complete-game shutouts (110) than home runs allowed (97). Randy Johnson, just during the stretch in which he won four straight Cy Young Awards (1999–02), surrendered 98 home runs. Walter Johnson is still the most recent player with at least 200 strikeouts and zero home runs allowed in the same season (1916) and the only pitcher to lead the majors in strikeouts without allowing a home run since Candy Cummings danced his way to the feat in 1875—Johnson did so twice, in 1916 and 1919.

Classic Twins

Harmon Killebrew ushered in the Twins age with a bang—475 bangs in a Minnesota uniform, to be exact (573 homers in all, including 84 in Washington and 14 in Kansas City).

Killebrew accrued the third-most home runs in MLB history (272) through 1,000 career games, behind only Ryan Howard (279) and Ralph Kiner (277).

He retired in 1975, but, on the Twins franchise (Senators included) single-season home run list, Killebrew still ranks first, second, third, fourth, fifth, sixth, and t-seventh.

Playing alongside Killebrew for the first nine years of his career, fellow Hall of Famer **Rod Carew** was the perfect complement, with a completely different style.

Carew had a smooth stroke that led to a .328 career batting average, but only 92 home runs. He is the Twins' single season (9.7, 1977) and career (63.8) WAR leader, and the single season (.388, 1977) and career (.334) batting average leader.

In 1977, Carew batted .401 at the halfway point. He finished at .388, but with 16 triples and 23 stolen bases, he became the first .380/15/15 man since George Sisler in 1922, and no one has done it since.

We rarely see it today, but of his 19 stolen bases in 1969, seven were steals of home.

A hybrid of the thunder and lightning combo that was Killebrew and Carew, **Kirby Puckett** led the charge toward Minnesota's last two championships (1987, 1991). A fan favorite who helped put a spotlight on baseball in Minnesota, Puckett was a career Twin, playing 12 seasons before bowing out due to injury. He won six Gold Gloves, played in 10 straight All-Star Games, and is second to only Carew in team batting average in a Twins uniform (.318).

Puckett was drafted by the Twins with the third pick in the January part of the 1982 draft, and finished his career with a 51.1 career WAR. The rest of the players selected in the first round that year finished with a combined WAR of -0.7.

Puckett was diagnosed with glaucoma in 1996, which led to his early retirement from baseball. He seemed to be well on his way to joining baseball's 3,000-hit club. Through his first decade in the big leagues he tallied 1,996 hits over the span of 1,538 games. Hit King Pete Rose had 1,922 hits in 1,537 games over his first ten seasons.

No Walking in Minneapolis
Two pitchers in Twins history have pitched recently with absurdly accurate results.

From August 3, 2003 to May 10, 2007, a time spent mostly with the Twins, right-hander Carlos Silva made 99 consecutive starts without surrendering more than two walks.

In 2005, he was superhuman, recording the best single season K/BB ratio (7.89) of any pitcher with fewer than 100 strikeouts since 1884. To put it in perspective, consider: On May 5, 1970, Twins great Luis Tiant walked nine batters in a single five-inning start. Silva walked nine batters in 188 innings for the *entire 2005 season*.

Phil Hughes may have upped the ante in 2014, walking just 16 batters in 209⅔ innings. He registered an 11.63 K/BB ratio that season, the best qualified mark since Candy Cummings (20.5) in 1875, when nine balls were required for a walk.

Silva's 2005 is the best BB/9 innings ratio in baseball's Modern Era. In fact, the only pitchers in the game's history to best that mark played during a time when eight or nine balls were required for a walk; most recently George Bradley accomplished the feat in 1880.

STATS INCREDIBLE!

.358: The Twins were 29–52 on the road in 1987, a year they won the championship.

0: The Twins were on the good and bad side of two of the greatest World Series Game 7 pitching performances of all time—Sandy Koufax's three-hit shutout of Minnesota in 1965 for the Dodgers, and Jack Morris's 10-inning 1–0 shutout of the Braves in 1991. Twins great Tony Oliva was blanked by Koufax in the first game, and was Minnesota's hitting coach for the second.

127.3: Walter Johnson's JAWS (a Hall of Fame–worthiness value statistic, see page 305). The only other players over 100 are Cy Young (123.6) and the man who won the most Cy Young awards, Roger Clemens (102.8).

18: Innings pitched by Johnson in a complete-game shutout of the White Sox on May 15, 1918.

3: The number of no-hit bids Joe Mauer has ended in the ninth inning.

.365: Joe Mauer's batting average in 2009, the highest batting average in baseball history by a catcher with at least 100 games caught in a season. His .444 OBP was *only* third best—Mickey Cochrane topped it in 1935 (.452) and 1933 (.459).

19th: Johan Santana's place on the all-time career K/9 list (8.83). He only has one qualifying entry on the single season top 100 (64th, 10.46).

41: The number of games it took rookie Miguel Sano to hit his first 10 home runs in 2015, making Sano the fastest player to 10 homers in franchise history.

9: Torii Hunter assisted nine double-plays from 1999 to 2001. He committed just eight errors during that same span.

6: During his six-year peak from 2003–08, Johan Santana had a 156 ERA+ with 9.4 K/9—the same ERA+ and K/9 that Hall of Famer Sandy Koufax registered during his five-year peak from 1961–66.

96: Rod Carew could have gone an additional 0-for-96 and still won the AL batting title in 1977.

1877: In 2017, Chris Gimenez became the first player with at least six games pitched and 40 games caught in a season since Cal McVey in 1877. That season, he became the first player in history with at least five games caught, five games pitched, and five home runs hit in a single season.

7: On September 12, 2017, the Twins beat the Padres by a score of 16–0, homering in each of the first seven innings. They are the first team to homer in seven straight innings since the Cincinnati Reds on September 4, 1999.

167: Rod Carew may have never had that .400 season, but he maintained a .400 batting average over the span of 167 games from May 8, 1977 to May 21, 1978.

AMERICAN LEAGUE WEST

HOUSTON ASTROS

Est. 1962

Lance McCullers Jr. did not allow more than three runs in any of his first 27 career home starts, the best such streak to begin a career in baseball history. It bested the streak of his late, great friend Jose Fernandez, who did not allow more than three runs in any of his first 25 career starts. Lance now uses a Jose Fernandez-model glove, to honor his fallen brother.

The Astros began as the Colt .45s as part of MLB expansion in 1962. The name and logo, though cool and probably inappropriate, would be short-lived, as everything was re-branded Astro-centric in 1965 in an homage to the Houston center of the NASA space program. The team became the "Astros"; the mammoth new dome stadium, coined the Eighth Wonder of the World, became the Astrodome; even the new synthetic turf, which made its debut in Major League Baseball that year, transitioned from "ChemGrass" to "Astroturf."

The team struggled out of the gate, with over half of the franchise's worst 13 seasons occurring in its first seven years of play (1962–68, .418 W–L%). The uniforms were routinely colorful and cool, even now as a retro-hipster throwback, but that's really all the team had going for it until the 1980s.

Probably not coincidentally, the Astros' first postseason appearance came in 1980, after the offseason acquisition of Nolan Ryan. Ryan had established himself in eight prior seasons with the Angels as one of the hardest-throwing, hardest-to-hit power pitchers in the game's history. It was an important turning point, as the Astros had begun to define their franchise from the pitching mound.

Ryan (1980–88, 3.13 ERA), Bob Knepper (1981–89, 3.66), Mike Scott (1983–89, 3.19), and Joe Niekro (1980–85, 3.18) solidified the Astros rotation for much of the decade. The 1985 and 1988 Astros were the only two squads in the '80s to have four starters with at least 20 quality starts.

First baseman Jeff Bagwell and jack-of-all-trades Craig Biggio headlined the "Killer B's" offensive eruption for the 'Stros in the 1990s and 2000s, culminating in the franchise's first World Series appearance, then representing the National League, in 2005 (L, 4–0 vs. Chicago White Sox).

In 2015, the 'Stros, now in the American League, made their first playoff appearance since that World Series loss, and suddenly, the tide had shifted. This Astros squad was set on a much loftier trajectory.

In 2017, the Astros won their first championship in franchise history. Quite a leap considering just four years prior, Houston stumbled to just 51 victories, their lowest single season win total to date.

They fielded the youngest team in Major League Baseball in 2014, the first of four straight seasons that second baseman Jose Altuve would lead the league in hits.

However, it was 2017 World Series MVP George Springer who put them over the top. Springer batted .379/.471/1.000 during the thrilling seven-game series, becoming just one of three players in baseball history to hit five home runs in a single Series (Reggie Jackson, 1977; Chase Utley, 2009).

The 2018 'Stros showed no signs of decline, setting a new franchise-best win total (103)—*more than twice as many wins as their 2013 total!* In five short years, they built a juggernaut from rock bottom. Ultimately, the world champion Red Sox, and their franchise single-season-record 108 regular-season wins in tow, bested Houston in the ALCS, but the 'Stros will be back. The franchise has quickly turned hopes of glory into very serious championship expectations.

The Ryan Express

Nolan Ryan, at 3.13, is the Astros' franchise leader in ERA (minimum 800 innings). He overwhelmed hitters with power, striking out more batters (1,866) than any other Astro. It was his resiliency over time, however, that made this strikeout artist a legend.

Ryan came from the California Angels having won seven of the previous eight AL strikeout titles, with the single-season strikeout record in tow (383; 1973), but it was with Houston that Ryan proved his skills were seemingly impervious to aging.

During the seasons when he was thirty-seven to forty years old, Ryan actually improved his WHIP to 1.185—it had been 1.218 during the seasons when he was thirty-three to thirty-six years old. During Ryan's final two seasons with Houston (ages forty and forty-one) he actually posted a better ERA (3.15), WHIP (1.191), and K/9 (10.4) than he did during his seasons in California (ages thirty-one and thirty-two—3.19/1.374/10.1).

He's only the fourth pitcher of the Modern Era to lead the league in ERA as a quadragenarian (2.76), joined by fellow Astro Roger Clemens, who in 2005 became the oldest player (forty-three years old that August) in MLB history with a qualified ERA under 2.25 (1.87).

The Killer B's

In 1996, the Astros acquired third baseman Sean Berry to add to their offensive core of Jeff Bagwell, Craig Biggio, and Derek Bell. They finished in the top six in WAR that season, and the "Killer B's" was born (and used ad nauseam on SportsCenter). Really, the Killer B's had just two consistent members—Bagwell and Biggio.

Hall of Famer **Jeff Bagwell** (1B, 1991–2005): A career Astro, he is Houston's all-time leader in WAR (79.9), OPS+ (149), home runs (449), and RBIs (1,529), doing so all while sitting down on the job—sort of.

Bagwell was diabolical throughout the 1990s in how he subliminally convinced a small, but potent, faction of youth baseball players that a batting stance should begin as though you're sitting on a tiny, invisible chair. He was crouched so low, looking impossibly silly, one could wonder if the whole thing was part of an elaborate double dog dare. But, it worked.

Bagwell put up two seasons (1997, 1999) with at least 30 doubles, 40 home runs, 30 stolen bases, and 100 walks. No other player in baseball history has even one such season. He is the only player to reach base safely in 150 games in multiple seasons, doing so 151 times in both 1996 and 1999. In 1994, he became just the second player in history to slug .750 or better while stealing at least 15 bases, joining Babe Ruth, who did so in both 1921 and 1923.

Craig Biggio (C/2B/OF, 1988–2007): The first of two Houston Hall of Fame "B's" is the only player in baseball history with an All-Star nod at both catcher and second base, and he also played significant time in center field (288 games). He's the only player in MLB history to play at least 200 games as a catcher, middle infielder, and outfielder, but it's what he did in the batter's box that really set him apart.

A lifetime, 20-year Astro, Biggio leads the franchise by healthy margins in hits (3,060), runs scored (1,844), and total

Jeff Bagwell's impossibly low crouch. (Barbara Moore, CC BY-SA 2.0
[https://creativecommons.org/licenses/by-sa/2.0], via Wikimedia Commons)

bases (4,711). He was a pesky batter, and a furiously tough out,
leading baseball's Modern Era with 285 hit-by-pitches. Add sacrifice flies and sacrifice bunts to that number, and Biggio "sacri-
ficed" his body or his at-bats more times than any other player
during the Live Ball Era (467). He and Barry Bonds are the only
players in baseball history to amass at least 600 doubles, 250
home runs, and 250 stolen bases. And Biggio owns baseball's only
ever 50-plus doubles, 20-plus homers, 50-plus stolen bases season, doing so in 1998.

And then there was **Lance Berkman** *(OF/1B, 1999–2010).*
Though not an original "B," Berkman was a buzzworthy addition
to the club from the onset, hitting a franchise rookie record 21
homers in 2000. He sits third in club history in runs scored (1,008),
total bases (3,053), and RBIs (1,090) behind the original B's, but first
in on-base percentage (.410) with a .406 wOBA, actually besting
Bagwell by one point. Perhaps the most impressive statistic about
B3 is that his 144 OPS+ ranks third all-time among switch-hitters,

behind only Mickey Mantle (172) and Roger Connor (153), a guy who last played in 1897.

Astro Arms

Astros pitchers had 1,687 strikeouts in 2018, most ever in a season by a team. Their 10.44 strikeouts-per-nine are also tops, and their 1.099 WHIP was the best of the Live Ball era and the top overall mark since the 1917 New York baseball Giants had a 1.085 WHIP.

Jose Altuve, 2015. (Eric Enfermero, CC BY-SA 4.0 [http://creativecommons.org/licenses/by-sa/4.0], via Wikimedia Commons)

Justin Verlander, acquired seconds before the waiver trade deadline in 2017 (in a package deal with Kate Upton), made an immediate impact for the Astros. He had a 1.53 ERA through his first 10 appearances (including postseason), leading Houston to a 10–0 record in those games, and capturing the 2017 ALCS MVP Award.

Lance McCullers Jr. broke out in May of 2017, posting a 0.99 ERA in six starts, en route to being named Pitcher of the Month. In the postseason, however, it was as a reliever that he made his biggest impact. He finished off the Yankees in dramatic fashion, tossing the final four innings of Game 7 in the ALCS, earning a save with six strikeouts—just the second six-plus-strikeout save in postseason history (Lefty Grove; Philadelphia Athletics, Game 2 of the 1929 World Series)—recording six straight outs, four by way of strikeout, closing out the game on 24 straight *bangers*.

Dallas Keuchel won the American League Cy Young Award in 2015, making 18 starts in total at Minute Maid Park . . . of which, he lost none—a single season record for most home starts in a season without a defeat.

Charlie Morton, at thirty-four years old, was a first time All-Star in 2018. In 55 starts with the Astros, he sported an ERA+ that was 21 percent above league average, striking out 10.44 batters-per-nine, with a WHIP of just 1.176.

Gerrit Cole, in his first season with Houston in 2018, had five games with at least a dozen strikeouts, which is two more than Nolan Ryan had in any season with the Astros. In all, he struck out 276 batters. Coupling that with Verlander's 290 strikeouts, the duo was just the third pair of teammates ever with at least 275 strikeouts in a season (Randy Johnson and Curt Schilling, Arizona Diamondbacks, 2001, 2002; Tim Keefe and Jack Lynch, American Association New York Metropolitans, 1884).

And you thought the pitching was good ...

The 2017 world champion Astros had a 123 OPS+ as a team, the best by a team since Babe Ruth and Lou Gehrig led the 1931 Yankees to a 125 OPS+ in 1931.

Second baseman Jose Altuve, standing at just 5 feet, 6 inches tall (in cleats), captured the 2017 MVP Award over Aaron Judge, who has an entire foot on him. At the close of the 2018 season, Joey Two Bags is batting .316/.365/.453 with 1,419 hits through 1,119 games, outpacing The Hit King, Pete Rose, who was batting .308/.370/.437 with 1,393 hits through his first 1,119 games and was actually 272 days older than Altuve at the time of their respective 1,119th games.

Altuve set the tone for the would-be world champion Astros during the 2017 postseason, smashing three homers in Game 1 of the ALDS. He is tied with eight others for second all-time in three-homer postseason games, and Babe Ruth is the only player with a pair.

Shortstop Carlos Correa hit the ground running, totaling 4.3 WAR during his 2015 rookie season; at just twenty years old, he became the youngest shortstop with at least that many WAR since John McGraw in 1894. In the postseason, Correa already has eight home runs over his young career, his eighth coming at just 24 years and 16 days old, making him the youngest ever with as many postseason homers—no other player has even seven at his age.

In addition to his 2017 World Series MVP Award, George Springer is already the Astros' all-time leader in postseason home runs with 11.

To bring things full circle, in 2018, fourth "B" Alex Bregman, twenty-four, became just the second player in history with at least 50 doubles, 30 home runs, 90 walks, and 10 stolen bases. The first: Lou Gehrig in 1927.

STATS INCREDIBLE!

8: Carlos Beltran's (another B!) home run total through his first nine career postseason games with the Astros in 2004. Over 12 games that postseason, Beltran batted .435 with 14 RBIs.

16: The number of wild pitches thrown by Nolan Ryan in 1981, with a 1.69 ERA. In the Modern Era, it's the lowest ERA by any player who led the league in both categories.

220: The number of batters that Roy Oswalt faced after an 0–2 count in 2006. He walked none of them.

225: In 2014, Jose Altuve became the shortest player (five-foot-six) in baseball's Modern Era with a 225-hit season.

285: Times Craig Biggio was hit by a pitch during his career, effectively raising his career on-base percentage from .348 to .363.

14: Jeff Bagwell totaled 446 home runs through his first 14 career seasons—one more than Barry Bonds had through his first 14 seasons.

331: In 1999, Bagwell reached base safely 331 times—the most by a right-handed batter in baseball history.

0: In 1997, Craig Biggio led the NL with 744 plate appearances. He grounded into *zero* double plays (78 double play chances).

4: Jose Altuve had four straight seasons with at least 200 hits (2014 to 2017), making him the shortest player to do so since "Wee Willie" Keeler (eight straight, 1894 to 1901).

14: Gerrit Cole had his second 14+ strikeout performance in an Astros uniform in his seventh game wearing one. Nolan Ryan had two 14+ strikeout performances in 282 career games with Houston.

2: Number of players in baseball history who have homered on Opening Day and in Game 7 of the World Series in the same season: Yogi Berra (New York Yankees; 1956) and George Springer (2017).

1: The Astros are the only team in baseball history to win both a National League pennant and an American League pennant.

2/6/2: Lance McCullers Jr. is the only pitcher in baseball history to throw at least six innings in each of his first two postseason appearances, allowing two or fewer hits.

85: Career no-win quality starts for Roy Oswalt. He was 0–36 with a 2.66 ERA in those games.

LOS ANGELES ANGELS

Est. 1961

Mike Trout played 1,065 games during his first eight seasons. He batted .307/.416/.573 (175 OPS+) with 64.3 WAR, 240 home runs, and 189 stolen bases. Through his first eight seasons, Mickey Mantle played 1,102 games, batting .314/.430/.577 (176 OPS+) with 61.4 WAR, 249 home runs, and 77 stolen bases.

The Angels have always seemed to be a team at war with itself. They began as the Los Angeles Angels (1961–64), playing most of their home game games at Dodger Stadium. By 1965, they switched to the all-inclusive *California* Angels, tweaked to account for their thirty-one-mile move southwest in 1966, to Angel Stadium in Anaheim, California. From 1997 to 2004, they shifted to the aesthetically-agreeable *Anaheim* Angels, before ruining a great thing, and taking up their moniker, the Los Angeles Angels of Anaheim. Which is kind of silly.

Alas, since 2016, the team began to identify simply as the "Los Angeles Angels."

Surely, that kind of waffling naming history speaks of internal struggles within the franchise—and that may well be because of the team's external struggles against the rest of Major League Baseball.

Through the Angels' first 40 years, they reached the postseason on just three occasions (1979, 1982, 1986 ALCS losses), never playing in a World Series. Two of the team's top players over that span were Chuck Finley (1986–99, 52.1 WAR) and Jim Fregosi (1961–71, 45.9). Despite ranking second and third, behind only Mike Trout (64.3), in WAR for the franchise, they combined for just five Hall of Fame votes (of 807).

Things abruptly turned around for the franchise in 2002, as the team reached, and won, its first World Series, to start a competitive run that, really, has only just recently begun to let up. Prior to their championship season, the Halos had never won more than 93 games in a single year, but over an eight-year stretch, from 2002–09, the team averaged 93 wins per season, reaching the postseason six times—twice as many times as they had in the entire twentieth century. They averaged "just" 86 wins per season from 2010 to 2015, but then failed to reach .500 in the three seasons that followed. Despite having arguably the best player in the game and its best pitcher/hitter hybrid, the Angels are falling.

Two-time MVP Mike Trout, by the age of twenty-seven, accumulated a higher WAR total than 99.105 percent of all players in major league history (64.3), and his teammate, Shohei Ohtani, is the only player besides Babe Ruth with multiple wins and at least 20 home runs in the same season (2018; four wins, 22 HRs).

Still, the Angels won just 80 games in 2018. With Trout hitting free agency after the 2020 season, the Halos' future might be back on shaky ground.

Los Angeles, California

It would be accurate to categorize the twentieth century of Halo baseball as "lean years." To gloss over those four decades, however, would be inappropriate. Sure, the Angels are one of five teams without a player representative in the Hall of Fame, but some all-time greats still put up memorable seasons for the Halos before the turn of the century.

Jim Fregosi *(SS, 1961–71)*: Fregosi is perhaps best remembered for his managerial career that spanned four decades, but, during his playing days, he was one of the game's best shortstops. Fregosi led all shortstop with a 117 OPS+ during the 1960, and was the decade's WAR leader (37.5) at his position.

Various injuries prevented a potential Hall of Fame finale for Fregosi. Following the worst statistical year of his career, in which he batted .233/.317/.326 in 1971, the six-time All-Star was shipped to the New York Mets in an historically lopsided deal that landed California the Strikeout King . . .

Nolan Ryan *(SP, 1972–79)*: The Ryan Express hadn't really picked up steam until joining the Angels in his fifth full season in the big leagues. While Ryan inexplicably dons a Rangers cap on his Hall plaque, he had far more All-Star appearances (five), wins (138), and strikeouts (2,416) with the Angels than with any other team. Among power pitchers, he enjoyed one of the most dominant stretches in baseball history.

In just his first six seasons with California, Ryan led the league in strikeouts five times, fanning over 300 batters each time. Walter Johnson (two), Steve Carlton (one), and Pedro Martinez (two) combined for just five career 300-K campaigns, despite 63 years of MLB service among them.

In 1973, he bested Sandy Koufax's Modern Era strikeout record by one, recording 383 Ks in a single season. He led the league with 23 double-digit strikeout games (the entire LA Dodgers team finished a distant second, as a team, with just 15). Ryan's 15 games with a dozen or more strikeouts in 1973 are the most in baseball history. For perspective, Max Scherzer (who led MLB with 300 strikeouts) only had five such games in 2018.

Just 15 players have recorded a 300-plus strikeout season during the entire Live Ball Era (post-1919). Ryan averaged 302 Ks during his eight years with the Angels.

Rod Carew *(1B, 1979–85)*: Carew is in the Hall as a Minnesota Twin, but he was fantastic in his six seasons with California to close out his career. The five-time Halo All-Star sits second among Angels in career batting average and on-base percentage (.314, .393, respectively), trailing only Vlad Guerrero's .319 batting average and Mike Trout's .416 on-base percentage.

At thirty-seven years old in 1983, Carew was batting .500 as late as May 6, and .400 as late as July 15. He finished up at .339, hitting .402 in his first 268 plate appearances, and just .273 in his final 268.

Nolan Ryan, holding the baseball from his record-breaking 383rd strikeout of the 1973 season. (Jon Rogers Collection, PD)

Despite low home run totals, Carew was feared by the opposition. He had five qualified seasons with the Angels in which he had more intentional walks than home runs. His 12 total—along with his seven with the Twins—are the most since the intentional walk officially became a statistic in 1955.

Jim Abbott *(SP, 1989-92, 1995-96)*: There were a few other players that have come along in major-league history who played while having just one hand (Pete Gray, 1945; Chad Bentz, 2004–05), but Abbott was, by far, the most talented and accomplished.

Being born with no right hand was no insurmountable obstacle for Abbott, who entered pro baseball highly touted, secured by the Angels with the eighth overall pick in the 1988 draft.

In 1991, Abbott finished third in AL Cy Young voting (18–11, 2.89 ERA), putting up the second-best pitching WAR for the Angels since 1977 (7.6). Over a two-year stretch, from 1991–92, Abbott was truly one of the best pitchers in the American League, finishing second to only Roger Clemens in ERA (2.83, minimum 350 IP).

After a trade to New York, Abbott managed to toss no-hitter for the Yankees in 1993, but he was never as dominant as he was his prior two seasons with the Angels. After a return to California, Abbott actually had one of the worst full-season pitching performances ever.

Abbott pitched to a 2–18 record in 1996, with the highest ERA ever recorded in AL history (7.48, minimum 140 IP).

No matter. Abbott's abilities far outshined his apparent disability on the baseball diamond, and he remains one of professional sports' most enduring, and endearing, heroes.

The Resurrection

Given the franchise's bleak history prior to the twenty-first century, the only thing perhaps more impressive than the Angels' seemingly out-of-nowhere World Series run in 2002 has been their ability to maintain that success over time. Some of the best players of this era have played major roles in keeping Anaheim relevant over the past 17 years.

Garret Anderson *(OF, 1994–2008)*: Anderson is one of just two players (Darin Erstad) with the Angels through the team's name change from California to Anaheim to Los Angeles (of Anaheim), but he played his best baseball in 2002 and 2003.

Anderson led the Halos offense in 2002, and the American League in doubles (tied with Nomar Garciaparra with 56). It was only the third 55-plus doubles season in the AL since 1936. His 83 go-ahead home runs rank third most in franchise history, behind the fishy pair of Mike Trout (96) and Tim Salmon (86). And he single-handedly raises the franchise's all-time team batting average a point.

Vladimir Guerrero *(OF, 2004–09)*: Vlad was elected to the Hall of Fame in 2018, becoming the very first player to wear an Angels cap on their HOF plaque.

While Vlad's numbers were marginally more gaudy with the Montreal Expos, he won his only MVP with the Angels in 2004, and led Anaheim to the postseason in five of his six seasons with the club—something he never did once in Montreal.

Vlad had four seasons with at least 200 hits and 30 home runs (2004 and 2006 with Anaheim), trailing only Lou Gehrig, who had seven such seasons in his Hall of Fame career. With tremendous bat control and unparalleled range in the batter's box, Vlad is the only player since Stan Musial in 1963 to finish his career with over 400 home runs and fewer than 1,000 strikeouts.

Albert Pujols *(1B, 2012–)*: Pujols is one of just 12 players in MLB history with at least 400 home runs and fewer than 1,300 strikeouts (633 HR, 1211 K; Guerrero joins him with 449 HR, 985 K).

Pujols was one of the best players to ever put on a uniform while with St. Louis. In his 11 seasons as a Cardinal, he averaged 40 home runs and 121 RBIs. Reggie Jackson never had a single season with 40 home runs and 120 RBI in his entire career.

The Anaheim iteration of Pujols has yielded much different results. In his seven years with the Angels, Pujols has averaged just 27 home runs and 93 RBIs, while seeing his batting average drop from .328 in St. Louis to .260 in Anaheim. His career batting average is now .302 after 18 years. Still, his 40 home runs were good for fifth in the AL in 2015, and, at thirty-five years old, made him the oldest right-handed batter to slug at least 40 home runs in a season since Mark McGwire hit 65 in 1999.

Mike Trout (OF, 2011–)

What Pujols was for St. Louis, **Mike Trout** has been for Anaheim.

Where to start? Trout led the league in runs (129), stolen bases (49), and OPS+ (168) his very first full season in the big leagues (2012), cruising to Rookie of the Year, and finishing runner-up for MVP. He secured the MVP hardware two seasons later, in 2014, leading the league in runs (115), RBIs (111), and total bases (338).

Already, at twenty-seven years of age, Trout is measuring up to the game's all-time best . . .

- Trout is tied with Willie Mays for the most seasons (two) with at least a .320 batting average, 25 home runs, and 30 stolen bases all-time.
- Only Babe Ruth (five) and Barry Bonds (10) have more seasons during the Live Ball Era with at least a 165 OPS+ and 10 stolen bases than Trout's seven.
- In 2014, he became the first player to lead the American League in runs, RBIs, and strikeouts since Babe Ruth in 1923.
- He has more career seasons with at least a .550 SLG and 15 SBs than Mickey Mantle has—three to two.

- He has more career seasons with at least 65 XBHs and 65 BBs than Joe DiMaggio—four to three.
- Trout has five seasons with at least a 9.0 WAR—the same number as Lou Gehrig, one more than Mickey Mantle, two more than Carl Yastrzemski, three more than Henry Aaron, four more than Mike Schmidt, and five more than Derek Jeter.
- He has already passed Mays in career top-two MVP finishes—more than Aaron and Griffey Jr. combined.

Sho Time

Shohei Ohtani, a two-way star of the Japan Pacific League, signed with the Angels on December 9, 2017. With the Nippon Ham Fighters in 2016, his last full season in the JPPL, Ohtani batted .322/.416/.588, with 22 home runs, along with a 1.86 ERA and 0.957 WHIP in 140 innings pitched. Naturally, the Babe Ruth comparisons are warranted for the twenty-four-year-old phenom.

Ohtani started his rookie season as-advertised, finishing with a 3.31 ERA and 1.161 WHIP in ten starts before an elbow injury halted his mound privileges. He still managed 367 plate appearances though, batting .285/.361/.564 with 22 home runs. When he was out there, he was one of the most feared batters in the league—one of just seven players in the AL with at least 350 PA to post a .925 or higher OPS.

Ohtani brought to baseball something the game had not seen in nearly a century—99 years, to be exact—as he became just the second player in history to hit at least 20 home runs during a season in which he won three games. The other? Babe Ruth, who hit 29 home runs and won nine games in 1919.

He also became the first ever player with double-digit home runs (at-bat) and at least 40 strikeouts from the bump.

Los Angeles Angels center fielder Mike Trout has five seasons with at least 9.0 rWAR. That is as many as Lou Gehrig, one more than Mickey Mantle, and five more than Derek Jeter. (Erik Drost, CC BY-SA 2.0 [https://creativecommons.org/licenses/by-sa/2.0], via Flickr)

On September 5, 2018, imaging results from an MRI revealed a damaged UCL in his pitching elbow—Tommy John surgery. Typically, that would end a pitcher's season, but Sho the Hitter was undeterred, going 4-for-4 with a pair of homers on the day he received the bad news! He batted .313/.376/.614 in the 23 games that followed the announcement.

In 2019, Ohtani will serve as designated hitter while his pitching alter ego "sits out" until 2020.

STATS INCREDIBLE!

3: Times Nolan Ryan struck out at least 19 batters in a single game in 1973, an MLB record. Only Randy Johnson (1997) even had two such games in a season.

58: Red Sox batters faced by Ryan on June 14, 1974. He struck out 19 and walked 10 in a 13-inning no-decision. He threw 278 pitches, and struck out leadoff man Cecil Cooper six times. The Angels won, 4–3, in the 15th.

1983: The year Angels representative Fred Lynn hit the first, and only, grand slam in the history of the All-Star Game.

70: The 2000 Angels are the only team in MLB history with three 70+ extra-base hit outfielders (Darin Erstad, Garret Anderson, Tim Salmon).

9.78: Trout's WAR per 162 games, second only to Babe Ruth (10.49). Remarkably, this does NOT factor Ruth's 20.4 WAR as a pitcher.

6: The number of players in the American League's 118-year history to hit a walk-off grand slam while trailing by three runs, with two outs. Angels shortstop Dick Schofield was the fourth to pull the trick, giving the Angels a 13–12 win over the Tigers on August 29, 1986.

32.8: Number of strikeouts per home run allowed by starting pitcher Garrett Richards in 2014, the best ratio by a qualified pitcher since Pedro Martinez in 1999 (34.8 K/HR).

184: Andrelton Simmons's career defensive runs saved to date. This ranks eighth all-time among all players, and just one-half of a run behind Willie Mays, who ranks seventh. Every player above Andrelton has played over 2,000 games—he has yet to play his 1,000th.

54: Nolan Ryan had a career record of 324–292. He had a positive impact on his team's probability of winning in 54 of those 292 losses, sporting a 2.13 ERA with 456 strikeouts in 417⅓ innings pitched, completing 24 of the 54 games.

1913: In 2018, Shohei Ohtani became the first pitcher to have a game with a home run and a stolen base and a also a game with at least a dozen strikeouts in the same season since Walter Johnson (Washington Senators) in 1913.

3: Three players in history have homered in three straight games and had a double-digit strikeout game in the same season: Shohei Ohtani (2018), Ken Brett (Philadelphia Phillies, 1973), and Babe Ruth (Boston Red Sox, 1916).

28: Tony Gwynn (San Diego Padres) struck 40 times in 133 games in 1988, his age-28 season. Andrelton Simmons struck out 44 times in 146 games in 2018, his age-28 season.

OAKLAND ATHLETICS

Est. 1901

In 1981, Rickey Henderson, at the age of twenty-two, stole 56 of 78 bases during his first tour with the Athletics. In 1998, Rickey Henderson, at the age of thirty-nine, stole 66 of 79 bases during his third tour with the Athletics.

Two thousand and twenty-two will be a big year for the Oakland Athletics. That marks the year that their tenure in Oakland will top the franchise's 54-year tenure in the City of Brotherly Love.

All but forgotten, the Athletics had an extremely successful run in Philadelphia, winning five championships over nearly six decades. By city, that total ranks them behind only the New York Yankees (27), St. Louis Cardinals (11), and Boston Red Sox (eight). So, why the move? The A's, among the most successful franchises in professional sports to change locations, were historically up and down.

Established in 1901 as a charter American League franchise, the Athletics of Philadelphia were owned and managed by Connie Mack for its first 50 years. While Mack was known for shrewd moves, like poaching crosstown Phillies players—most notably Nap Lajoie in 1901—he was also quick on the trigger to unload his rosters and tank seasons. From 1910 to 1914, the A's averaged 98 wins, and appeared in four World

Series, winning three. In 1915, they finished last, with 43 wins, and the 14th worst record in the history of baseball's Modern Era. The following season? Thirty-six wins and a .235 winning percentage—the worst record since 1886, at a time when flat-sided bats were fair play and handlebar mustaches were practically a requirement.

Team photo of the Philadelphia A's first World Series appearance, 1905. Featured, most notably, is manager Connie Mack, "The Tall Tactician" (center, suited), and his star pitcher, seated to his right, Rube Waddell. (Boston Public Library, McGreevey Collection)

All in all, the Philadelphia A's finished with five championships, despite an unremarkable .477 win percentage. With the NL Phillies making the World Series in 1950, capturing the city's fans at a critical time, the Athletics were exiled to Kansas City by 1955.

The franchise's 13 years in KC are mostly forgotten because the team never really got close to .500 during any season. By comparison, the Athletics' first 13 seasons in Oakland, starting in 1968, featured a run of three straight World Series titles and an 84-win average—ten more than their best finish in Kansas City. The Athletics had found their home.

Hall of Famers Reggie Jackson, Rollie Fingers, and Catfish Hunter led the A's dynasty of the 1970s, cementing the franchise's standing in California. Since, the A's won their final title in 1989, led by Mark McGwire and Dennis Eckersley, and have averaged better than 85 wins per season since Billy Beane took over the GM position in 1998.

Oakland still has four years and two championships to go to top its Philadelphia past, but a strong 97-win showing in 2018 might foretell the best is yet to come.

The $100,000 Infield

John McInnis (first base), Eddie Collins (second base), Jack Barry (shortstop), and Frank Baker (third base).

That was the Athletics' starting infield from 1911–14 that reached the World Series three times, winning titles in 1911 and 1913. The "$100,000 Infield" moniker was a distinction of the quartet's market value, and Connie Mack's willingness to splurge when the timing was right. Barry was a serviceable shortstop, but the stars were Collins, Baker, and McInnis.

"Cocky" Collins: his .333 batting average is 26th all-time, and .337 average over 13 seasons with the A's is third in franchise history. Notoriously selective at the plate, Collins (1,031) is one of just three players in MLB history with 1,000 more walks than strikeouts (Ted Williams, 1,312; Barry Bonds, 1,019).

Solidly entrenched in the Deadball Era, Collins had 16 seasons in which his WAR was at least double his season home run total, finishing with 124.0 WAR for his career (4.96 WAR per season) to just 47 home runs (less than two per season). Barry Bonds, in all but one of his 22 seasons, had home run totals at least TRIPLE his WAR.

"Home Run" Baker: He was the Babe Ruth of the Deadball Era. Baker led the league in homers his last four years with the Athletics (1911–14), totaling just 42 over that span. In 1921, Baker's first season playing with the Babe, Ruth hit 42 homers just through his first 100 games. Baseball historian Bill James called Baker's time with the $100,000 Infield (.334 BA/31.0 WAR) "by far, the greatest four-year stretch by a third baseman in baseball history."

"Stuffy" McInnis: The lone non-Hall of Famer of the trio, McInnis had a career that seems to beg for enshrinement.

His 20-home run total over 19 years is very low for a first baseman, even in the Deadball Era, when the single-season record stood at just 27. But, aside from leading all first basemen in fielding percentage six times, his *small ball* bat was among the very best in the game during the 1910s.

[Fun fact: Of Ned Williamson's 27 home runs in 1884, 25 came at Chicago's Lakeshore Park, which was 186 feet to left field, 300 feet to center field, and 190 to right field. Prior to 1884, balls over the fence were ground rule doubles. After the 1884 season, Chicago left the friendly confines of Lakeshore for the more spacious West Side Park.]

During the decade, McInnis batted .300 over more seasons (seven) than any other first baseman in baseball. Over the span of his career (1909–27), McInnis recorded 13 seasons with more walks than strikeouts, more than any other player at his position. And he's one of just 16 players during the Modern Era to average 30 or more at-bats per strikeout for his career.

The New Bill James Historical Baseball Abstract ranks each of the 1912 through 1914 $100,000 Infield seasons among the top five infields in the game's history.

Jimmie Foxx

One of the most gifted hitters of all time, Jimmie Foxx spent half of his Hall of Fame career in Philadelphia in the 1930s putting up numbers that had scarcely been matched in the game's history, before or since.

Foxx debuted at the age of seventeen with Philly in 1925, and from his first at-bat to his last, 20 years later, Foxx never at any point had his career batting average dip below .325.

In 1932, Foxx had the most hits of any player in a 50+ home run season (213 hits, 58 HRs). His .364 batting average is the highest for a 50-plus homer season by anyone not named "Babe" in baseball history.

Only four players have ever batted at least .350 with 45 home runs and 140 RBIs in the same season. Foxx *averaged* .350 with 46 home runs and 144 RBIs over a four-year stretch with the A's from 1932–35.

The Bash Brothers

During the late 1980s, the Deadball Era was long-forgotten and the home run was king.

First baseman Mark McGwire and outfielder Jose Canseco played together for seven seasons with the Athletics (1986–92), winning a title in 1989. A spoof on the "Blues Brothers" film, the duo was referred to as the *Bash Brothers* as an homage to their tremendous home run power.

[Note: It's impossible to bring up these two without mentioning their connection to PEDs (performance-enhancing drugs). Along with Barry Bonds, they are the primary poster boys for the Steroid Era drug problem during a span of about two decades in Major League Baseball. We acknowledge it happened, and we don't condone the use of PEDs, aside from the Flintstones Chewables variety. That being said, home runs are awesome, so let's try to have a little fun with this.]

During their time together with the A's, aside from being the best power-hitting duo on one team, they were the top two home run hitters in all of baseball. From 1986 to 1992, no one hit more homers than McGwire (220) and Canseco (230; 4 with Texas in parts of 1992).

Jose Canseco *(OF, 1985–92, 1997)*: From the depths of stat obscurity, it can—and should—be noted that, in 2014, White Sox slugger Jose Abreu broke Canseco's records for home runs by a Cuban-born rookie, and home runs by all rookies named Jose (36 to 33).

In a more conventional statosphere . . .

In 1988, Joey Rats became the first member of the 40–40 club, hitting 42 home runs and stealing 40 bases, but he wasn't classically fleet of foot, averaging just 12 swipes per season over his career, from 1985 to 2001. What he did well, though, he did great—over that span, no one in the American League hit more than Canseco's 462 home runs.

Mark McGwire *(1B, 1986–97)*: Big Mac set the power bar high early on in Oakland, establishing a new rookie record (since broken) for home runs with 49 in 1987. Slugging .618, McGwire was one of just two rookies in American League history with a slugging percentage over .600 (Rudy York, 1937; .651).

Compared to his Bash Brother, or really any other of the game's greatest sluggers, McGwire was a true one-trick pony. While Canseco averaged 12 steals per season, McGwire stole a total of just 12 bases during his *entire 16-year career*. He hit 583 home runs, 11th-most in MLB history, while accumulating just 252 doubles—687th most in MLB history. His six career triples are half the number Babe Ruth had in one season in 1919 . . . while pitching for the Boston Red Sox.

Though McGwire had 583 home runs to just 785 singles for his career, including 354 homers to only 353 singles in his final eight seasons, it is unfair to pile on the nonsensical one-dimensional production. The one-trick Clydesdale slugged and walked himself to the 10th-best OPS of all-time (.982).

Rickey Knows all of Rickey's Stats

The "Man of Steal" played 25 seasons in the big leagues—14 of which came over four different stays in Oakland.

Rickey's 1,406 stolen bases are not only an all-time record, but if you split him into two players, they would have enough swipes to rank both first (939) and 47th (467) all time. He broke Lou Brock's record at just thirty-two years old and did not slow down from there—stealing bases at a more efficient rate after breaking the stolen bases record (79.6 percent) than Brock did in his entire career (75.3). If that is not enough, Rickey was a more efficient base stealer just in his 40s (76.2 percent), too!

Rickey Henderson, taking off to steal one of his MLB-best 103 bases in 1983. Hall of Famers Eddie Murray (1B) and Cal Ripken (SS) man the infield for Baltimore. (Gary Soup)

Rickey's fleet feet were emphasized by his ability to get on base by any means necessary. He had three seasons with at least 100 walks and 100 stolen bases, while every other player combines for just two. He also had sneaky pop and tallied a pair of 20-plus homer, 80-plus stolen base seasons; only Eric Davis (Cincinnati Reds) has even one. Moreover, no other player in history has even a single 20–70 season.

His career is perhaps highlighted best by his 1990 MVP season, during which he batted .329/.345/.506 *after* falling behind 0–2 in the count and became the first player with an OPS of 1.000 or better and 65 or more stolen bases in a season since Ty Cobb in 1911.

STATS INCREDIBLE!

349: Starting pitcher Rube Waddell's strikeout total in 1904 that stood as an American League record for 69 years (383; Nolan Ryan, 1973).

4: The number of times the American League has had a new single-season strikeout record. Waddell set the first three.

16: The American League single-season home run record, set in 1902 by A's outfielder Ralph "Socks" Seybold, that stood until Babe Ruth took the crown with 29 in 1919. A's second baseman Nap Lajoie established the original mark with 14 in 1901.

33: Outfielder Reggie Jackson's home run total through his first 71 games of 1969—a 75-homer pace. He finished with 47.

41: MLB record for consecutive relief appearances without issuing a walk, set by A's bullpen ace Dennis Eckersley from August 17, 1989 to June 10, 1990.

18.33: Eck's K/BB in 1989. Best by a pitcher with at least 50 strikeouts since Candy Cummings in 1875—when nine balls were required for a walk.

23.97: The number of miles covered by Rickey Henderson while stealing his MLB record 1,406 bases.

10/100: Rickey Henderson had 10 home runs and 130 stolen bases with Oakland in 1982. He's baseball's only 10/100 man, and the first 10/90 player since Harry Stovey in 1890.

4: Singles hit by Mark McGwire on September 20, 1987—the only four-single game of his career.

4,000: On July 18, 1927, with the Athletics, Ty Cobb hit a double against his former team, the Detroit Tigers, establishing the 4,000 hit club.

31: Herb Washington's career stolen base total (1974–1975). The world-class sprinter never came to bat.

66: Rickey Henderson had 66 stolen bases through his first 66 games of the 1982 season.

41: Dennis Eckersley made a record 41 consecutive relief appearances without issuing a walk from August 17, 1989 to June 10, 1990.

19: Matt Olson did not hit a single home run in his first 19 career games, but then hit 25 homers over his next 52. In all, his 71 games to 25 homers is third fastest in history.

51: Larry Lintz and Matt Alexander combined for one hit, two walks, and 51 stolen bases in 1976.

110: A's General Manager Billy Beane did not have a single walk in any of his final 110 big-league plate appearances ... Ironic.

9: Nap Lajoie brought in the Modern Era with 48 doubles, 14 triples, and 14 home runs, to go with just nine strikeouts in 1901.

.247: Khris Davis's batting average each of his last four seasons, but that is just about the only thing that has not seen an improvement. Davis has realized an uptick in runs, hits, extra-base hits, home runs, RBI, total bases, and WAR each season during that stretch.

SEATTLE MARINERS

Est. 1977

Only seven players in baseball history have bested each leg of Edgar Martinez's career .312/.418/.515 slash line. It is a roll call of MLB legends: Ted Williams, Jimmie Foxx, Lou Gehrig, Rogers Hornsby, Babe Ruth, "Shoeless" Joe Jackson, and Dan Brouthers. In fact, David Ortiz matched each leg of Edgar's career slash line just ONCE in a season (2007).

Seattleites must be a patient bunch.

The Mariners have been around for 42 years and have finished over .500 just 14 times. Meanwhile, the Yankees haven't finished *under* .500 since 1995, when a twenty-one-year-old Ichiro batted .342/.432/.544, hitting a cross-league career-best 25 home runs, for Orix Blue Wave of the Japan Pacific League. And the Mariners have never won a World Series, or even appeared in one.

After 12 straight losing seasons to start the franchise, the stars aligned for Seattle—literally. In 1989, outfielder Ken Griffey Jr. was called up and future ace Randy Johnson arrived via trade, bringing together two of the greatest players of the next generation of Major League Baseball.

Both players made their All-Star debuts the following season, and by 1991, had helped Seattle finally break .500 (83–79). With

Alex Rodriguez added to the mix full-time, and Edgar Martinez emerging as baseball's premier DH, by 1996, the once-forlorn franchise had a gluttony of riches ... and a window.

During the 10 years Griffey, Johnson, and Martinez played together (1989–98), the Mariners finished over .500 five times and won the division twice (1995, 1997). But, looking back, the Mariners' opportunity to win a championship was mostly confined to just the two-year stretch, with A-Rod, from 1996–97, when the quartet of superstars were at the peak of their Seattle powers.

Of the four, only Rodriguez and Martinez remained by 2000, and the Mariners still won a franchise-best 91 games. The following year, A-Rod left for the Texas Rangers. The team upped the ante and won an AL-record 116 games. Over any four-year stretch during the 2000–10 decade, only the Yankees (100 Ws, 2001–04) averaged more wins than the Mariners (98 Ws, 2000–03).

While, as of the start of the 2019 season, Seattle hasn't reached the playoffs since 2001, Mariners history has proven that turnarounds can be swift and mighty. General Manager Jerry Dipoto is constantly "wheeling and dealing," and reinforcements always seem on the way. The next batch, coupled with 2018 first time All-Star, Mitch "The Shed" Haniger, could make Seattle's long, bumpy road very much worth the wait.

Junior, Griffey
Ken Griffey Jr. was a lauded nineteen-year-old phenom when he started with the Mariners in 1989. The anticipation soon gave way to monstrous expectations, as "The Kid" spent significant time in the 1990s as the face of baseball, and *the chosen one* to take the home run, and all of baseball, to new heights. Of course, this was overblown.

It's easy to look at Griffey's career for what might have been if he was able to stay healthy and take a crack at Henry Aaron's then-home run record (755 career HRs). But then, you're cheating the career that actually *was* . . .

During the 1990s, Griffey led all of his American League contemporaries in home runs (382) and runs scored (1,002), earning an All-Star nod and Gold Glove each season. Judged historically, Griffey was just as special:

- Had five seasons—four of which were consecutive, from 1996–99—with at least 45 home runs and 15 steals, which is just two fewer than those of every other Hall of Famer combined.
- Had two seasons with at least 55 home runs and 15 stolen bases, matching the total of all other major-league players in history. His 56 home runs and 20 stolen bases in 1998 makes him the only 55/20 player ever.
- Hit more home runs in the month of May than any other player (134). Mr. May is also the single-season home run champ among center fielders, hitting 56 in both 1997 and 1998.
- Among outfielders, only Willie Mays had more consecutive seasons as an All-Star and Gold Glove winner (12 to 10).
- From September 19, 1995 to July 14, 1998, Junior batted .305/.389/.653, averaging 60 home runs and 157 RBIs per 162 games played.

Edgar

Historically, designated hitters have had a difficult time gaining enshrinement in baseball's Hall of Fame. Chicago's Frank Thomas is routinely considered the first primary DH to enter the Hall (2014), but he still played 42 percent of his 2,322 career games at

Griffey, looking little, awaits a pitch in 1997. (Flickr Clare_and_Ben, CC BY-SA 2.0 [http://creativecommons.org/licenses/by-sa/2.0])

Like most power hitters of the '90s, Junior had a lot more bulk on him by the end of his career, ca. 2009. (Jeff Corrigan Sports Photography, CC BY-SA 3.0 [http://creativecommons.org/licenses/by-sa/2.0], via Wikimedia Commons)

first base. Edgar Martinez (DH, 1987–2004), meanwhile, played just 29 percent 2,055 MLB games in the field—a sticking point that appeared to be his sole barrier toward enshrinement, before he was finally voted in in 2019 (his final year of ballot eligibility), along with fellow longtime DH Harold Baines.

The designated hitter has been a part of the American League since 1973, and it should not be ignored as a full-time job—just as voters don't ignore closers (Bruce Sutter, Rich Gossage, Rollie Fingers, Dennis Eckersley, Trevor Hoffman, Lee Smith, and Mariano Rivera have all been enshrined). It was a longtime confounding double-standard, as voters are comfortable with enshrining specialists, just not of the hitting variety, even though designated hitters typically have an exponentially greater impact on the game than their pitching counterparts.

Players who contributed only with their glove work—actually hurting the team on offense—have been enshrined among baseball's immortals. Ozzie Smith, Luis Aparicio, and Phil Rizzuto are all examples of players who had negative batting runs for their career, making their Hall of Fame contributions on defense. Worth noting, Edgar had more batting runs than Smith, Aparicio, and Rizzuto had combined fielding runs, 531.5 to 502.8—proving that a longtime injustice, was finally made right with Edgar's 2019 induction.

Martinez was a late bloomer, clubbing 264 home runs with 1,057 RBIs after age thirty (of 309 HRs, and 1,261 RBIs for his career). He reached base safely 2,369 times in his 30s, for a .4360 on-base percentage—just slightly ahead of Ty Cobb in his 30s (2,341 TOB, .4357 OBP). Only 13 players in baseball history have a better career OBP than Martinez (minimum 7,000 plate appearances). One of them is Barry Bonds, and the rest are all Hall of Famers. The next three players ranking below the slugger are also in the Hall.

During a three-year stretch, from 1995–97, Martinez's teammate, Ken Griffey Jr., compiled a stout .385 OBP. Martinez topped it during the same stretch with a .386 . . . with two strikes against him.

Martinez had two seasons with at least 25 home runs, 50 doubles, and 110 walks (1995–96)—the same number of seasons that every other player in MLB history had combined. That is rare company.

Boston legend David Ortiz is often cited as the greatest DH of all-time, and a shoo-in Hall of Famer. It's important to note that, in terms of career WAR, one full season (162 games) played by Edgar Martinez is worth about 235 games played by Ortiz.

The Big Unit

It's hard not to snicker at the notion that a man named *Randy Johnson* could be nicknamed "The Big Unit" and neither is an adult film alias. Actually, the nickname supposedly originated from teammate Tim Raines exclaiming that Johnson was "a big unit" his rookie season in Montreal. Until Jon Rauch (6-foot-11) debuted in 2002, Johnson, at 6-foot-10, was the tallest player in the game's history. Looking back on his Mariners career, he was also one of the most talented.

In 1989, his first season with Seattle, Johnson had a career-worst 18.2 K%, which was still a better rate than Jim Palmer's three Cy Young seasons. For his career, the strikeout artist punched out 28.56 percent of the batters he faced, the most ever by a qualifying pitcher. Nolan Ryan, the all-time strikeout leader (5,714 Ks), would have to un-retire and strike out 1,050 straight batters to pass Johnson in career strikeout percentage.

Johnson led the league in ERA (2.48) and strikeouts (294) during his Cy Young 1995 season, but his 18–2 record was historically unique. It is the best win percentage (.900) in the American League since 1937. Taking his three-season totals from 1995–97, Johnson managed a remarkable 43–6 record, for an .878 win percentage, the highest three-year percentage in modern baseball history (minimum 70 games). Over a single season, only four AL pitchers were able to top the percentage that Johnson maintained over three years.

The Unit reached even higher heights, dominating the regular and postseasons while winning four straight Cy Youngs with the Arizona Diamondbacks, en route to Hall of Fame enshrinement in 2015. His premature departure was something Seattle fans had hoped would not repeat with their current starter, Felix Hernandez.

King Felix

It's not just a nickname—the Seattle pitcher has been a legitimate King of the Hill. In 2015, Hernandez completed his 11th season for the club, surpassing Johnson in M's seasons pitched. As such, he's managed to take Johnson's crown atop a slew of franchise pitching categories.

As of the end of the 2018 season, Hernandez leads the franchise in ERA (3.34), pitching WAR (51.0), strikeouts (2,467), WHIP (1.197; minimum 1,000 innings), and remarkably, wins (168). The wins haven't always come easy for the King.

His 13 wins in 2010 were the lowest total ever for an AL Cy Young–winning season. He led the league with a 2.14 ERA in 2014, but had a remarkable 2.45 ERA and 0–6 record in games he didn't win that season. By the end of 2014, his 4.25 ERA in non-win starts was the lowest of the Live Ball Era (minimum 175 non-win starts). Before his thirtieth birthday, he had made 119 career starts with 0–2 runs in support—more than Pedro Martinez had until his retirement at age thirty-seven (110). The game hasn't been kind to Hernandez *after* his thirtieth birthday, as he's 25–27 with a 4.62

ERA since 2016 and 8–14 with a 5.55 ERA in 2018 alone. Still, over 14 years in the big leagues, his entire body of work has been special.

Hernandez was the first pitcher in baseball history with six straight seasons of 200 or more strikeouts and 75 or fewer walks (2009–14). His 1.170 WHIP through his first 10 seasons (min. 2,000 innings) is the lowest in the American League since Roger Clemens posted a 1.123 from 1984–1993.

STATS INCREDIBLE!

409/398: Alex Rodriguez (409) and Ken Griffey Jr. (398) hit the most home runs in MLB history before their thirtieth birthdays.

4,924: Most hits by a father-son combo in MLB history. Ken Griffey Sr. and Jr. bested Bobby and Barry Bonds by 103.

174: Randy Johnson's ERA+ from 1994 to 2002. Felix Hernandez had a career-best 174 ERA+ in 2010. First-ballot Hall of Famer Tom Glavine had a career-best 168 ERA+ in 1998.

94: Double-digit strikeouts games for Johnson with the M's, a franchise record. The next five closest in club history tallied 91 combined.

21.197: A-Rod was 21 years and 72 days old on the final day of the 1996 season. He batted .358/.415/.631 that season—the highest batting average, on-base percentage, and slugging percentage in a qualified season by a player his age or younger since Cap Anson (.415) in 1872, Al Kaline (.421) in 1955, and Mel Ott (.635) in 1929, respectively.

0: Starter Hisashi Iwakuma became the first ever Tokyo native to toss a no-hitter in Major League Baseball.

2,467: Felix Hernandez is the all-time strikeout leader among Venezuelan-born players.

8: Times Junior homered on Opening Day (all with the Mariners). Frank Robinson and Adam Dunn also share the record.

12: Number of players in baseball history who have at least 830 career extra-base hits and an on-base percentage of at least .430. One is Barry Bonds and eleven are Hall of Famers, including 2019 inductee Edgar Martinez.

39,065: The number of pitches Ichiro has seen during his MLB career, of which, only 25 have come while he did not have a lifetime batting average of .300 or better. He singled to center in his tenth career at-bat, raising his lifetime batting average to .300. His career batting average would never again dip below that mark.

73: From June 23, 1995 to June 20, 1996, Edgar Martinez had 73 doubles over the span of 162 games. He even added two three-baggers!

0.8: Difference between Tony Gwynn's 69.2 career WAR and Martinez's (68.4). Only one was a first-ballot Hall of Famer.

181: Ichiro Suzuki's intentional walk total, ranking him 28th all-time, despite being 724th in homers (117).

2001: The year Ichiro became the first player to win a league batting title, stolen base crown, and Gold Glove Award in the same season. Dee Gordon (2015) is the only player to do it since.

84: Rickey Henderson had a big league record 81 leadoff home runs. The Mariners as a franchise have 84 . . . three of which belong to Rickey.

403: Ken Griffey Jr. played 403 games from September 19, 1995 to July 14, 1998. He averaged 60 home runs and 157 RBI per-162 games during that stretch.

606: Games played by Nelson Cruz through four seasons with the Mariners. He has 671 batted balls of at least 100 mph since coming to Seattle.

32.3: James Paxton had a 32.3 strikeout percentage in 2018, third-best in Mariners history among pitchers with at least 150 innings. Randy Johnson ranks first, second, fourth, fifth, sixth, ninth, and tenth. King Felix fills out the list at seventh and eighth. Justus Sheffield has some "Big Maple" shoes to fill . . . .

8: In 2018, James Paxton became just the eighth pitcher in history to have both a no-hitter and a 16-plus strike-out game in a single season. He and Max Scherzer (Washington Nationals, 2015) are the only pitchers ever to do so in back-to-back starts. He threw just 105 pitches in his 16-strikeout game, the fewest pitches ever recorded by a pitcher to finish a game with at least 16 strikeouts.

Ichiro's iconic batting stance, 2010. (Dave Sizer, CC BY 2.0, [http://creativecommons.org/licenses/by-sa/2.0], via Wikimedia Commons)

TEXAS RANGERS

Est. 1961

Nolan Ryan had more complete game no-hitters (seven) than complete game no-walkers (four) during his Hall of Famer career.

When the Washington Senators (Twins) split for Minnesota after the 1960 season, Major League Baseball moved up expansion and awarded the nation's capital a bright, shiny new team for 1961—the Washington Senators. The players and historical records were off to Minneapolis while just the name and penchant for losing remained. Washington had essentially traded in its old clunker for a brand new lemon.

Over 11 seasons in Washington, the Senators averaged a dismal 67 wins and 94 losses. Ownership and management, save for a very short-but-sweet managerial stint from first-timer Ted Williams, bumbled the operation from the onset and the team was sold and moved to Arlington, Texas, by the 1971 season.

The Rangers, named after Texas's statewide law enforcement agency, finished dead last the first two years in their new AL West digs, and wouldn't finish first in the division until 1994, a strike-shortened season with no World Series. But, it hasn't been all doom and gloom in the Lone Star State.

President Richard Nixon throws out the ceremonial opening pitch of the Senators' 1969 season. Washington manager Ted Williams, left, looks on. (Warren K. Leffler, US News and World Report, LOC)

In the mid-1970s, the Rangers were mixing-and-matching Hall of Famers with All-Star-caliber players in and out of the starting rotation. Gaylord Perry, Ferguson Jenkins, Bert Blyleven, and Dock Ellis never formed their own *super rotation*, but they all played a short-term role in bringing respectability to Texas from 1977–79, featuring a then-best 94–68 finish for the ball club in 1978.

A solid foundation of ownership mixed with a Texas-size level of enthusiasm and patience among the fan base has made the Rangers a team worth watching, and worth the wait. The Rangers broke through to the postseason in the late-1990s, and made serious runs at the World Series in 2010 and 2011. They've finished with 90 or more wins five times this decade, and while they only won 67 in 2018, that's the exact amount they won in 2014 before returning to the playoffs in 2015.

Nolan Ryan and the Two Towers

With the Rangers, **Nolan Ryan** was kind of like Gandalf from *Lord of the Rings*. He was really old (forty-two to forty-six), absurdly powerful (3.43 ERA, 10.1 K/9), and helped lead the way for two aspiring heroes (Ivan Rodriguez and Juan Gonzalez). Of course, it might not be polite to call "Pudge" Rodriguez the mightiest of Hobbits, and, sadly, rings were never part of the journey for the 1990s Rangers.

After helping the Astros reach new heights in the '80s, Ryan seemed to do the same for the Rangers in the '90s, signing in Texas for the 1989 season. He played there for five seasons in his forties, and dominated much of the time. He wasn't just great for his age … he was just great.

As far as quadragenarian power pitching starters go, Ryan is in a class of his own:

- He's the oldest pitcher to lead the league in strikeouts (forty-three years old; 232 Ks).
- In 1990, he became the oldest player in MLB history to lead the league in WHIP (1.034). The following season, at age forty-four, he set a new bar, pitching an MLB-best 1.006 WHIP.
- He's the only qualified starting pitcher in baseball history, over age forty-one, to have a season with at least 10 K/9— and he did it three times, 1989 through 1991, leading the AL each year (11.3, 10.2, 10.6, respectively).
- Of the 49 players over age thirty-nine to pitch a full season, Ryan and Randy Johnson are the only players to lead the league in strikeouts. Johnson, forty, did it once in 2004 (290 Ks). Ryan did it for four straight years from 1987–90.

Ryan pitched in Advil commercials into his fifties, but Major League Baseball is a whole different ballgame. After Ryan's final season in 1993, the torch was passed on to a new, offensive, generation of Rangers baseball.

Geriatric, but historic. Nolan Ryan led the league in strikeouts his first two years with Texas. He was forty-two and forty-three years old. (Chuck Anderson, CC BY 2.0 [http://creativecommons.org/licenses/by-sa/2.0], via Wikimedia Commons)

Juan González: Juan Gone was an immediate hit his first three full seasons in the majors, knocking in 102 runs in 1991, and leading the league in homers the following two seasons (43 and 46, respectively). He missed parts of two seasons with Texas due to injury, but even so, over an eight-year stretch (1992–99) he compiled a per-162-game average of 48 home runs and 146 RBIs. By comparison, career RBI leader Henry Aaron's best eight-year, per-162 stretch was 45 home runs and 116 RBIs from 1966–73.

The shame of González's career is that, taken wholly, it seems unfinished. Steroid-use rumors aside, he was a great player that retired too early. Registering just one plate appearance after his thirty-fifth birthday the two-time MVP finished with a higher home run percentage than Barry Bonds (6.07 to 6.04).

Ivan Rodriguez: the 2017 Hall of Fame inductee like González, was great from the onset. He was an All-Star his first 10 full seasons, winning Gold Gloves each year. His progression as a hitter was profound, as his batting average improved from (*deep breath*) .260 to .273 to .298 to .303 to .313 to .321 to .332 to .347 over that span. Although he was one of the best hitting catchers in the game's history, his defense set him apart.

Pudge tops in career WAR among Rangers (50.1), is also tops in career defensive runs saved (DRS) for the team (128.0) and has the most DRS overall among catchers in baseball history (147.0).

Of course, there were a lot of other players that had key roles in turning the franchise around in the '90s, including Will Clark, Ruben Sierra, and most notably, Rafael Palmeiro, the Rangers' career offensive WAR leader (41.1).

Post-2000

Before the 2001 season, the Rangers made headlines, signing Alex Rodriguez to an historic, 10-year $252 million contract. While the team didn't do well during the three years he served in Texas under the deal, individually A-Rod was a star, achieving the highest OPS+ of any Ranger in history.

He led the league in home runs all three seasons, and he's the only Ranger to eclipse the 50-homer mark, doing it in back-to-back years in 2001–02 (52, 57). Those two totals hold the top-two spots ever in a season by a shortstop. A-Rod encored with 47 more home runs in 2003, which is tied with Ernie Banks (1958) for third most at the position.

The 2010 and 2011 Rangers nearly powered their way to World Series championships, losing to the Giants and Cardinals, respectively, in the final showdown. Outfielder Josh Hamilton, an All-Star each season, was a big part of that success, especially during his 2010 MVP year.

Hamilton is one of just 15 players in the last 60 years to bat at least .350 with 30-plus home runs and 100-plus RBI in a season, going .359/32/100 in 2010. He is also one of just six players this millennium to bat at least .350, slugging .625 or better in a season. In either case, no one has matched Hamilton's 2010 season since.

Third baseman Adrian Beltre joined the team as a free agent in 2011 after leading the league in doubles. Besides helping Texas repeat as AL champions that year, Beltre, who retired after the 2018 season, was one of the most important additions to a Rangers team that has been consistently competitive ever since.

Yo, Adrian

Since joining the team, no other third baseman in baseball has had as many hits (1,277), runs (612), home runs (199), and RBI (699) as Beltre.

Upon his retirement after the 2018 season, Beltre sits 16th all-time in hits (3,166), 14th in extra-base hits (1,151), 11th in doubles (636), 30th in home runs (477), 14th in total bases (5,309), 39th in times on base (4,111), 24th in RBI (1,707), and 26th in position player WAR (95.7). But those juggernaut offensive numbers fail to highlight what is perhaps his greatest asset, his glove. He ranks fourth all-time in defensive runs saved with 237.7, good for second all-time among third basemen, sandwiched between Hall of Famer Brooks Robinson (293.1) and potential future Hall of Famer, Scott Rolen (175.4).

Beltre's one of two players with at least 2,000 hits, 200 home runs, and 200 defensive runs saved, joining Brooks Robinson and Roberto Clemente. If one were to remove the home run qualifier, only Hall of Famer Ozzie Smith joins the short list.

Looking at nothing more than his bat and his mitt, Beltre is the only player in baseball history with at least 2,000 hits, 300 home runs, and 200 defensive runs saved, eclipsing those totals by 1,166 hits, 177 home runs, and 37.7 defensive runs saved.

Beltre played 21 years in the big leagues, only eight of them with Texas. So, though the Rangers will retire Adrian's No. 29 during the 2019 season, it is still entirely possible that he does not don their logo on his eventual Hall of Fame plaque—we hope he wears no cap at all, so we can all touch his head . . . .

STATS INCREDIBLE!

6: Complete games thrown by forty-two-year-old Nolan Ryan in 1989. Twenty-six-year-old Cy Young winner and NL MVP Clayton Kershaw led all of baseball with six complete games in 2014.

203: Batters that Ryan struck out in 1991, while allowing just 183 total baserunners. He was forty-four.

1,283 ⅔: Career innings pitched by ace closer Mariano Rivera, including 1,173 strikeouts and 998 hits allowed. Ryan recorded 1,437 strikeouts and just 933 hits allowed in 1,271⅔ innings pitched *after turning forty.*

2000: The year Rangers utility man Scott Sheldon became the only player in MLB history to play every position (including pitcher and DH) and bat in every spot in the lineup.

11: Intentional walks collected by Rangers first baseman Prince Fielder in 2014, one more than Miguel Cabrera. Fielder played just 42 games that year, while Cabrera played all but three.

3,368: The number of batters faced by Yu Darvish needed to reach 1,000 career strikeouts, fewest all-time. Kershaw is second at 3,919; Nolan Ryan's 1,000th career strikeout came against his 4,036th batter faced.

616: Yu Darvish's strikeout total through 75 career games. He's the first player ever with over 600 through as many games.

200/50: Alex Rodriguez had 201 hits and 52 home runs for the Rangers in 2001. He was the first player with at least 200 hits and 50 homers in a season since Jimmie Foxx in 1932.

Also ...

18: A-Rod's total stolen bases that season, making him the first player with at least 200 hits, 50 home runs, and 15 stolen bases since Babe Ruth in 1921.

2.284: Cliff Lee averaged 2.284 strikeouts per *ball three* in 2010. The MLB average was 2.174 strikeouts-per-*walk* that season. His 10.28 strikeouts-per-walk was the best ratio by a pitcher with at least 200 innings since Candy Cummings in 1875, when nine balls were required for a walk and the mound was but 55 ½ feet from home.

198: Nolan Ryan had 198 career non-win quality starts. He was 0–107 with a 2.27 ERA, 1.166 WHIP, and 9.77 K/9 in those starts.

4,358: The San Diego Padres drafted shortstop Matt Bush on June 7, 2004. He made his big league debut with Texas 4,358 days later, after being released from prison, on May 13, 2016, but as a pitcher (3.35 ERA in 136 games to date).

1902: J. P. Arencibia and Chris Gimenez both caught and pitched in games for the Rangers in 2014, making them the first pair of teammates to both pitch and catch in a season since 1902. Jeff Mathis and Alex Avila did so for the Dbacks in 2018.

17: The 2017 Rangers had nine different players each with at least 17 home runs, most all time.

88: Home runs through 2018 season by Joey Gallo, to just 82 singles. It is the most home runs ever by a player with more big flies than singles.

II. NATIONAL LEAGUE

NATIONAL LEAGUE EAST

ATLANTA BRAVES

Est. 1871

Henry Aaron homered at a rate of once every 13.08 plate appearances during his age thirty-seven to thirty-nine seasons. Barry Bonds homered at a rate of once every 13.08 plate appearances during his age thirty-seven to thirty-nine seasons.

The Braves are the oldest continuously operating team in baseball, founded in 1871—just seven short years before Edison's bright idea for the incandescent lightbulb.

They started out in Boston as part of the National Association before becoming a charter member of the National League in 1876. In the 25 seasons leading up to American League expansion of Major League Baseball (1901), the Red Stockings/Beaneaters held their own, finishing in first place eight times. But, that success would be short-lived.

In a situation similar to what happened in Philadelphia, between the Phillies and Athletics, the Beaneaters had some of their best players poached by the incumbent AL Boston Americans (Red Sox). Three of the Beaneaters' top five players, in terms of WAR, jumped to the Americans to start the 1901 season. The Americans' new tenancy would prove to have far-reaching consequences for their NL counterpart, but in the short-term, it just made the Beaneaters lousy.

They finished over .500 just once over the next 13 seasons, shifting team names between the Doves, Rustlers, and Braves in the process, proving superstition always had an illogical stranglehold on America's pastime.

Their 1914 season is probably the sole reason why we call them the "Braves" today. That year, in one of professional sports' most dramatic turnarounds of all time, the Braves won the World Series over the Philadelphia Athletics despite being in last place, at 26–40, in early July. They finished out going 68–19, blowing away the NL competition, and in turn, the A's for the championship. The success was sudden, and contained, but the effects were memorable. Over the next 33 years, the Braves would finish better than fourth place just three times. But hey—at least the name stuck. The city? Not so much.

The Braves actually had a short spurt of success in the mid-1940s, culminating in a losing effort to the Cleveland Indians in the 1948 World Series (4–2). The pull of greener pastures was too much, however, and by 1953, the Braves were Milwaukee-bound. And it was probably the greatest relocation in sports history.

In Milwaukee, the Braves set new National League attendance records in 1953, 1954, and 1957. The play on the field dramatically improved, as Hall of Famers Eddie Mathews (1953) and Henry Aaron (1955) each played their first (of 30 total) All-Star seasons for Milwaukee. The rest of baseball took notice, and the Braves' success would serve as the catalytic thrust behind the Athletics', Dodgers', and Giants' move out west, all within the same decade.

It's not a stretch to call the Braves "The Team that Aaron Built," considering the Braves had their first really great run while Henry Aaron was at the top of his game. During the 14 straight seasons he led the team in WAR (1956–69), the Braves had just one sub-.500 season, with three first-place finishes, plus a World Series title in 1957.

The move to Atlanta wasn't performance-based—the Milwaukee Braves are still the only multi-year franchise to never have a losing record. It was entirely about money, and Atlanta was a much bigger market. The city fought hard to keep the team, but, by 1966, the Braves had a new permanent home.

The Braves fell back into a long stretch of mediocrity in Atlanta, reaching the playoffs just twice over a 25-year stretch. Then, they went out and won the division every year from 1991 to 2005. Ho-hum. They made it look easy, dominating with a trio of Hall of Fame aces—Greg Maddux, Tom Glavine, and John Smoltz—and becoming a fixture in the MLB playoffs every single year for an entire generation.

[Consider: During their run, the Braves won their first division crown the same year the first web page was developed. One billion or so websites later, the Braves would finally relinquish the crown.]

It was an exciting era for the franchise, and it was loud about it, considering, at the time, Braves games were televised nationally on Turner Broadcasting networks. They've reached the playoffs just four times in thirteen seasons since, but the sweet smell—*Mets fans read: stench*—of prosperity still wafts about Atlanta, like the residual fumes of a speeding race car, lingering long after the race is through.

Surely, the Braves have found a permanent home in Atlanta. In 2017, they moved into the brand new, state-of-the-art, Sun-Trust Park—"The House that Success Built."

Spahn & Sain

The Braves' brief mid-1940s spurt and 1948 Series run is often credited to the pitching arms of Warren Spahn and Johnny Sain. If the duo sounds familiar, it's most likely because of the poem that bears their name, nicknamed, "Spahn and Sain and Pray for Rain."

Reality, as is usually the case, tells a much different tale (see: *Tinker to Evers to Chance*).

Hall of Famer Spahn, a 14-time All-Star who led the league in wins eight times during his 21-year career, was inarguably amazing. He was, however, just breaking into the big leagues at this time, and the extent of his eventual 363-win greatness was far less defined.

1950 Braves rotation, featuring Warren Spahn (far right), and Johnny Sain (center) . . . Oh, yeah, and Vern Bickford, who led the league in complete games that season (27) and more than doubled Sain in pitching WAR (5.0 to 2.4). (Author unknown; Baseball Digest, March 1951)

In Sain's case, he had his three best seasons for the Braves during the team's only three winning seasons of the decade, from 1946–48. He averaged a 22–14 record over that span, with a 2.77 ERA, which is stellar. However, there was certainly no dramatic drop-off from there, and the Braves rotated in a slew of talented arms.

- In 1946, Mort Cooper had the third-best ERA on the team (3.12), and actually led the entire league in WHIP (1.106).

- In 1947, Red Barrett had somewhat of a statistically-identical season to Sain, with a 3.55 ERA, 111 ERA+, and 1.201 WHIP (Sain: 3.52/112/1.293).
- In 1948, the year attributed to the poem, Spahn actually finished LAST in the four-man rotation in ERA (3.71) and ERA+ (105).

No disrespect to Spahn, or Sain—they helped the Braves finish better than the league average in ERA, ERA+, and WHIP all three seasons, with Boston leading each category in 1948. But it was much more of a well-rounded, team effort.

Not aesthetically pleasing, but, maybe try:

Spahn, Cooper, Barrett, Sain—heck—just pray for rain.

Hammerin' Hank

Because of Henry Aaron's tremendous accomplishments, Eddie Mathews doesn't get his proper due—not even in the title of this section.

Aaron (755 HRs) would go on to break Babe Ruth's home run record (714 HRs), but during the 14 years the two sluggers played together, he only hit 47 more homers than Mathews (468 to 421). And actually, Mathews hit more before his thirtieth birthday than the champ (370 to 342).

Mathews was one of baseball's quickest studies, hitting the most home runs in MLB history before his age-twenty-four season (153; tied with Mel Ott). All-time, among primary third basemen, he sits behind just Mike Schmidt in homers (512), WAR (96.6), and OPS+ (143). Fitting that, no matter how you frame it, Mathews always ends up behind someone else in the end.

The aforementioned Aaron is, of course, the prime example.

Aaron had a stellar, 23-year MLB career, and ranks first all time in RBIs (2,297) and total bases (6,856). Barry Bonds may be the current Home Run King (762 to Aaron's 755), but Aaron still owns a few less-extravagant home run records of his own:

> *"Bad Henry" is the all-time home run champ for the months of June (150) and July (152), and he hit more at home than any other player (385). He had the most games with at least one home run (692) and the most games in which he homered without striking out in MLB history (485). He hit the most home runs ever by a player before his 40th birthday (713).*

Of course, it's not all about home runs with Aaron. He had more career RBIs than Hall of Famers Ralph Kiner (1,015), Rod Carew (1,015), and Wade Boggs (1,014) *JUST IN GAMES IN WHICH HE DIDN'T HOMER* (1,060). He's seventh in career WAR (143.0), and had an MLB-best 15 seasons with at least 300 total bases—more than Eddie Mathews (six), Mickey Mantle (five), and Tony Gwynn (three) *combined*.

Three Aces (One Chip)

It's a pretty good hand in poker, and, as it turns out, it's unbeatable in the National League East.

The Hall of Fame pitching trio of Tom Glavine, John Smoltz, and Greg Maddux played together for ten seasons, from 1993–2002, helping the Braves win every division crown during that span. They are credited most for Atlanta's success at the time, but, let's not forget 2018 Hall of Fame inductee, Chipper Jones.

Jones, a career Brave (1993–2012; .303 BA, 468 HRs), was one of the best third basemen in history, and the only one at the hot corner with at least 2,500 hits and 1,500 walks. He's also the only player

*Tom Glavine, pitching in spring training prior to his 1998 Cy
Young season. Future Hall of Fame third baseman Chipper Jones
in the background.* (2 on a Whim Creations, CC BY 2.0 [http://
creativecommons.org/licenses/by-sa/2.0], via Wikimedia Commons)

at the position with a career slashline of at least .300/.400/.500. His
.930 OPS and .529 slugging percentage are tops among primary
third basemen. Taking a look at where he ranks among switch-
hitters, he is the only one with at least a .400 on-base percentage
and 1,000 extra-base hits, as well as the only one with, again, that
aforementioned career slash line. His .470 on-base percentage in
2008 is a Braves record, regardless of position—and no one in
baseball has matched it since.

In addition to Jones, All-Stars such as Fred McGriff, who
averaged nearly 35 home runs per 162 games played from 1988–
97, despite missing 66 games due to the 1994–95 strike (costing
him 500 home runs and likely the Hall of Fame), and David
Justice were actually quite formidable at the plate during their
tenure in Atlanta . . . but why bury the lede? That era for Braves
baseball was all about the bump.

Tom Glavine *(1987–2002, '08; 244 Ws, 3.41 ERA)*: It's a tired analogy, but, like Scottie Pippen to Michael Jordan, Tom Glavine, though great, played very much in the shadow of the incomparable Greg Maddux. But, it still doesn't diminish the fact that Glavine was among the game's best lefties of his generation.

Glavine led all qualified left-handed National League pitchers in ERA in the 1990s (3.21). Sure, Maddux, a right-hander, bested him with a 2.54, but they were still the only two NL pitchers that decade with ERAs below 3.30 (minimum 200 games).

And he was one of the best two-way players of his era, hitting .245 over a four-year stretch, from 1995–98, while his opponents batted just .240 against him.

Glavine knew how to turn it up when necessary—in 1997, opponents batted .239 against him with the bases empty. That number shrunk to .204 with men on base, and then just .184 with runners in scoring position.

John Smoltz *(1988–2008; 210 Ws, 154 SVs, 3.26 ERA)*: Like his placement in this chapter, Smoltz, in both style and substance, fell somewhere in between Glavine and Maddux.

He was a power pitcher, twice leading the league in strikeouts, and still holding the career postseason strikeout record (199). But, midway through his career, he developed impeccable control, topping Glavine's best-ever strikeout-to-walk ratio (2.78) each of his final seven full seasons as a starter.

Smoltz underwent Tommy John elbow ligament surgery prior to the 2000 season, and, as a result, found himself relegated to bullpen work for a while—where he thrived. He led the league in saves his first full season as the Braves closer in 2002 (55 SVs) and ended up the all-time saves leader among pitchers with at least 200 wins (154 SVs). Smoltz is also the all-time Tommy John surgery strikeout leader, with 3,084 Ks. Tommy John himself is fourth, with 2,245.

Greg Maddux *(1993–2003; 194 Ws, 2.63 ERA)*: Maddux made 363 career starts for the Braves and never once had consecutive starts in which he failed to throw at least five innings. He had an MLB-record 244 career starts without surrendering a single walk. In short—he was in control.

During a completely dominant stretch in which he won four consecutive Cy Youngs (1992–95), Maddux averaged a 1.98 ERA, a 202 ERA+, and a 0.953 WHIP. Only eight other pitchers in the last 100 years have even recorded a *single* season with a 202 or better ERA+ and a WHIP of 0.953 or less. Amazingly, half of the pitchers to do so have accomplished this feat since 2015—Jake Arrieta (2015; 215 ERA+, 0.865 WHIP), Zack Greinke (2015; 222 ERA+, 0.844 WHIP), Corey Kluber (2017; 202 ERA+, 0.869 WHIP), and Jacob deGrom (2018; 216 ERA+, 0.912 WHIP).

Maddux is the only pitcher in National League history with a 260 ERA+ season—and he did it TWICE, *in consecutive seasons*, from 1994–95 (271, 260, respectively). All-Century Team member Nolan Ryan had a career-best 195 ERA+ in 1981, while Maddux averaged a 195 ERA+ over six seasons, from 1993–98. He's tied with Curt Schilling for the most seasons with a 6.00 or better strikeout-to-walk ratio (four), and in 1995, he became the first pitcher in baseball history to have at least 180 strikeouts and 25 or fewer walks in a season (181 Ks, 23 BBs)—since joined by Cliff Lee (2010; 185 Ks, 18 BBs) and Phil Hughes (2014; 186 Ks, 16 BBs).

[Balls & Strikes- Maddux walked just 121 batters on four pitches during his eleven seasons with the Braves; 63.6 percent (77) of them were intentional walks. He averaged 1.65 strikeouts per BALL THREE during his Braves career, and he issued just 499 bases on balls over the final 501 starts of his career.]

Atlanta also frequently surrounded their trio of aces with capable arms to help carry the load. The 1998 Braves are the only team in baseball history with five pitchers with at least 150 strikeouts in a single-season (Maddux, 204; Smoltz, 173; Denny Neagle, 165; Kevin Millwood, 163; Glavine, 157).

Ahead of Schedule

The Braves captured the National Leagues East by surprise in 2018, besting the heavily favorited Nationals by 8.0 games. Star first baseman Freddie Freeman performed as expected, but it was breakout performances from young studs Ronald Acuña Jr., Mike Foltynewicz, and Ozzie Albies that put them over the top.

Freeman has seemingly taken a page out of Joey Votto's book and flown under the radar over his last three seasons, making just one All-Star team (2018) with no top-five MVP finishes; this despite the fact that he batted .306/.396/.549 (150 OPS+) averaging 6.34 WAR-per-162 games played with a .394 wOBA and 146 wRC+.

Acuña Jr., twenty years old, hit 26 home runs through his first 100 games in the big leagues. No player under the age of twenty-one has ever hit more home runs through their first 100 career games. He also became the youngest player in baseball history to hit a grand slam in the postseason, doing so in Game 3 of the NLDS off Walker Buehler.

Foltynewicz, now a five-year veteran, despite being just twenty-six years old in 2018, averaged 9.93 strikeouts-per-nine, becoming the youngest pitcher in Braves franchise history to average at least a strikeout-per-inning over a qualified season. He's just the third ever to do so overall, joining Javier Vazquez and John Smoltz, who did it three times.

Albies, twenty-one—who on May 10, 2018, became the youngest player to hit a grand slam out of the leadoff slot since Bobby Doerr on August 1, 1939—became the youngest player with at least 40 doubles, 20 home runs, and 10 stolen bases since Alex Rodriguez in 1996.

Atlanta Braves outfielder and 2018 National League Rookie of the Year Ronald Acuña Jr. slashed .293/.366/.552 in his first season, with 26 doubles, 26 home runs, and 64 RBI spanning 111 games. (Ian D'Andrea [CC BY-SA 2.0 (https://creativecommons.org/licenses/by-sa/2.0)], via Wikimedia Commons)

Stats Incredible!

9: The number of players that struck out five times in a single game in 2018 (twice by Giancarlo Stanton in a six-day span). Henry Aaron never once in his 23-year career ever struck out more than three times in a game.

37: Greg Maddux won four straight Cy Young Awards from 1992–95. He had 37 CGs to just 33 HRs allowed during that span.

.248: The Braves' win percentage in 1935 (38–115)—the second-worst finish since 1900. Incidentally, also Babe Ruth's last team in the big leagues.

10: Major-league record number of seasons in which Maddux stole at least one base without being caught.

30/30: In 1991, Braves outfielder Ron Gant became just the fourth player in MLB history with multiple 30+ home run/30+ stolen base seasons (Willie Mays, Bobby Bonds, Howard Johnson). Since then, nine others have joined the club: Bobby Abreu, Jeff Bagwell, Barry Bonds, Ryan Braun, Vlad Guerrero, Ian Kinsler, Raul Mondesi, Alfonso Soriano, and Sammy Sosa.

.198: Melvin (previously and now again called B. J.) Upton Jr.'s batting average during his Braves career (267 games). Pitcher Tom Glavine batted .226 for the Braves from 1991–98 (267 games).

266: Complete games pitched by Warren Spahn in which he allowed two or fewer runs. No other pitcher during the Live Ball Era (post-1919) even has 200.

107: Career games in which Greg Maddux pitched 7+ innings, surrendered two or fewer runs, and did not win—a Live Ball record.

294: Phil Niekro's record for games started after turning forty.

237: Hugh Duffy's former single-season hits record (now T-21st) for the Beaneaters in 1894, after playing in just 125 games. His 162-game pace would have netted him 307 hits. It's the second-highest hits total for a player under five-foot-eight.

58: Total pitches thrown by Red Barrett in a nine-inning complete-game shutout on August 10, 1944. It's the lowest pitch total for a complete-game shutout in MLB history.

25/25: Center fielder Andruw Jones, winner of ten straight Gold Gloves (1998–2007), had at least 25 home runs and 25 defensive runs saved in four straight seasons, from 1998–2001. No other outfielder in history has more than one such 25/25 season.

19: Andruw Jones's age in 1996, making him the youngest player to homer in a postseason game (Game 7, NLCS; 19 years, 177 days), and youngest player to homer in a World Series game (Game 1; 19 years, 180 days).

174: From May 1, 1942 to June 22, 1947, pitcher Johnny Sain had 174 straight plate appearances, as a batter, without a strikeout.

2.21: Johnny Sain returned to baseball in 1946 after serving three years in the United States Navy. He had a 2.21 ERA and no strikeouts in 104 plate appearances at bat.

1.60: ERA of Greg Maddux from 1994 to 1995. The last qualified pitcher with an ERA that low in a *single* season was . . . Greg Maddux.

47: Henry Aaron's career-high home run total in 1971, at age thirty-seven. He played in just 139 games that season.

42.8: Pitcher Johnny Sain had just 20 strikeouts in 856 plate appearances, averaging 42.8 plate appearances per strikeout. By comparison, Tony Gwynn averaged a strikeout per every 23.6 plate appearances during his career.

13: In 2018, Nick Markakis made his first All-Star Team, doing so in his 13th big league season. He had 185 hits to just 129 swings and misses on the year.

5: From August 11–14, 2018, Ronald Acuna Jr. became the first player to homer in his first official at-bat in five straight games since Willie Mays from June 21–25, 1954. Acuna became the first leadoff man in baseball history ever to do so.

1: Henry Aaron and Babe Ruth each had one career three-homer game for the Braves. Bad Henry did so in 3,076 games; the Babe did it in just 28.

3: Warren Spahn missed three full seasons serving in the United States Army during World War II. He was the most decorated ballplayer in WWII; his awards included a Bronze Star and two Purple Hearts.

363: Warren Spahn had 363 career wins and 363 career hits.

352: If all of Mark McGwire's 1,626 career hits were home runs, he would still have 352 fewer total bases than Henry Aaron.

MIAMI MARLINS

Est. 1993

The late, great Jose Fernandez of the Marlins struck out 31.2 percent of batters he faced. No starting pitcher in history recorded strikeouts at a greater rate. Had Nolan Ryan struck out batters as efficiently as Fernandez did, he would have had 7,043 strikeouts.

As a franchise, the Marlins are not too dissimilar to the Philadelphia Athletics. Both teams had success in between periods of complete futility. Surely, the Marlins wouldn't mind matching the A's championship tally in Philly (five), but they'd probably prefer to keep their operation on the east coast.

Miami, then known as the *Florida* Marlins, was an expansion franchise in 1993. To their credit, they were the fastest expansion team in history, at the time, to win the World Series (1997), and are still the fastest expansion team to two championships (2003). The Marlins, however, have never won a division, have only qualified for the postseason twice, have, at times, alienated the fan base with controversial roster overhauls, and have finished either last or second-to-last in NL attendance for 18 of the last 20 years. If all this adversity seems like a mountain overlooking a mole hill of positives, consider—the Phillies waited 97 years to get their first championship . . . and another 28 years to get their second.

Obviously, World Series rings are important. The Marlins have two while the Rays, Rangers, Brewers, Padres, Mariners, Rockies, and Nationals are all still seeking their first. It's hard not to consider the team a success. And there has always seemed to be a method to their madness.

Miami has been a master at building contenders from the ground up. Three key homegrown players—Charles Johnson (C), Edgar Renteria (SS), and Luis Castillo (2B)—all got their start in baseball with the Marlins in 1992. Renteria had the game-winning hit in the 1997 World Series over the Cleveland Indians, and starter Livan Hernandez would take home the Series MVP with help from his Gold Glove batterymate, Johnson. Castillo, while not much of a factor that season, played more games in a Marlins uniform than any other player (1,128), and is in the top 10 in most franchise offensive categories. The team has built around young, core players like this at several turns in its history.

Miguel Cabrera (2003), Hanley Ramirez (2006), and Giancarlo Stanton (2010) all spent their rookie seasons with the Marlins, and are three of the best baseball products of the twenty-first century. But, the team's best never seem to stick around.

As the Marlins build, the trend seems to be that they trade their best veteran talent for young players . . . that eventually become their best veteran talent that is baited down the line for new, fresh fish. It's a volatile business model, and regardless of how the team's successes and failures are measured, Miami's biggest challenge may be resisting the temptation to sell off not just their best players, but their franchise in its entirety.

1997

Renteria and Hernandez were the young World Series heroes, but the championship club in 1997 consisted of mostly thirty-plus-year-old veteran talent.

Kevin Brown (SP, age thirty-two), Moises Alou (OF, thirty), Gary Sheffield (OF, twenty-eight), and Bobby Bonilla (3B, thirty-four) all finished in the top five in WAR for the team that season, playing significant roles. By the end of the following season, all four would be just a memory with the Marlins. But a good one.

Brown had the best two-year stretch of his career with the Marlins in 1996–97, going 33–19 overall with a 2.30 ERA. Brown only spent those two seasons with the Fish, but still ranks third in total pitching WAR in team history (14.9). He was *that* good.

Leading the league with a 1.89 ERA in 1996, Brown became one of just 11 National League players in 30 years (1967–96) to record an ERA below 2.00. He was effective, though sometimes erratic, hitting a league-leading 16 batters that year (number of intentional unknown). Brown's 1.89 ERA coupled with his 16 hit batsmen mark the lowest ERA and most batter plunked since Walter Johnson in 1915, when he had a 1.55 ERA, beaning 19 batters.

The 1996 season was also a special year for Sheffield. The 500 home run club member had a career-high 1.090 OPS that season, batting .314/.465/.624. Sheff (142 BBs) and Barry Bonds (151 BBs) became the first NL players since Jim Wynn in 1969 (and fourth and fifth NL players overall) to have 140 or more walks in a season season. Sheffield is one of just seven players in history (also Bonds, Jeff Bagwell, Mark McGwire, Harmon Killebrew, Ted Williams, and Babe Ruth) with at least 40 home runs, 120 RBI, and 140 walks in a single season. Only Sheffield and Williams (1949) did so with 70 or fewer strikeouts.

The Marlins had a lot of star power on that 1997 squad, but, in terms of WAR, their best position player was catcher Charles Johnson (4.4)—a defensive prodigy, operating in anonymity. The four-time Gold Glove winner had the highest defensive WAR in the league in 1997 (2.6)—the year he allowed just one passed ball while never committing a single error. He didn't see any significant playing time until 1995, but Johnson still ranks third in the league in total defensive WAR during the 1990s (9.6).

2003

What a story.

The Marlins were 15–21 to start 2003. From there, they hired a new manager (Jack McKeon), called up a couple young studs (Dontrelle Willis and Miguel Cabrera) and, you know, went on to win the World Series. Ho-hum.

The Marlins were in last place in the division as late as June 18th (34–39), but went 58–32 the rest of the way, to capture the NL Wild Card and make their second improbable run for glory.

Small-ball was a key component of the '03 team. They had the best 1–2 hole hitters in baseball, with Juan Pierre (204 hits and 65 stolen bases) and Luis Castillo (187 Hs, 21 SBs) leading things off. No other 1–2 combination in the game had as many hits or stolen bases that year.

Dontrelle Willis caught the league by storm that year, going 14–6 with a 3.30 ERA, and one of the wackiest deliveries in baseball history.

Willis's pitching motion was a combination of Nolan Ryan's high-leg kick and Nuke LaLoosh's skyward mid-delivery stare. It worked great for a time, as Willis won the franchise's first Rookie of the Year award at season's end, and finished runner-up for the Cy Young two years later. Though he lost his magic touch prematurely, pitching his final full season by 2007, Willis still made an indelible mark on the franchise.

After his final year with Miami, Willis was the franchise leader in pitching WAR (17.2), and is currently second behind Josh Johnson (25.9). Over a three-year stretch, from 2003–05, Willis (46–27, 3.27 ERA) was one of only three pitchers in the National League with at least 45 wins and a sub-4.00 ERA.

Miguel Cabrera, finishing fifth for Rookie of the Year in '03, had a hot start and kept on going. With an eleven-year (and counting) career in Detroit that has seen Miggy win a Triple Crown, two MVPs, and four batting titles, it may be easy to forget how great he was with the Marlins.

Look no further than how the Marlins performed with Miggy on the field versus when he was off it. They were 35–40 (.467) without him in 2003, but 56–31 (.644) with him. He led them to a 11–6 (.647) record in the postseason en route to capturing their second World Series crown.

In Marlins history, no position player, over any qualifying amount of plate appearances, has touched Cabrera's .313/.388/.542 slash line with the team, and he still ranks first in team history batting average, second in OPS (.929), and fifth in total position player WAR (18.3).

JDF

Tragically, the Marlins, and all of baseball, lost a phenom in Jose Fernandez on September 25, 2016. More than just a great ballplayer, Fernandez lit up the field with his smile and personality. The final outing of his career featured eight innings of shutout baseball during which he struck out a dozen Nationals without allowing a walk. It was the fourth game of his career in which he struck out at least a dozen batters without allowing a free pass—and while we lost him just after his twenty-fourth birthday, that is good for 12th all-time, tied with Max Scherzer and Nolan Ryan. It's one more than Justin Verlander and two more than Tom Seaver.

In his short career, Fernandez had 66 more strikeouts than baserunners allowed, sandwiching him between Chris Sale (+142) and Clayton Kershaw (+61) for second all-time among starting pitchers. He averaged 11.25 strikeouts-per-nine and had a 31.2 strikeout percentage, both tops in history among starting pitchers.

His 1.49 ERA at Marlins Park is the best home ERA of all time among starters.

For some perspective, Nolan Ryan would have to return to baseball and strike out 1,932 straight batters to pass Jose Fernandez in career strikeout percentage.

Back to the Future

The Marlins, as they've been known to do throughout their short team history, cleaned house after the 2017 season, this time under new ownership. With a 4 percent stake in the franchise, but 100 percent visibility at the helm, Yankee legend Derek Jeter took over as CEO. Jeter was Cap'n Consistent during his 20-year career, playing 136 more postseason games than the entire Marlins franchise to date (158 to 22).

The 2017 team was the first since the 1999 Orioles (and the first NL team since the 1935 Giants) to have three outfielders reach base safely at least 250 times each. But by 2018, all three of those outfielders were dealt—Giancarlo Stanton (New York Yankees), Christian Yelich (Milwaukee Brewers), and Marcell Ozuna (St. Louis Cardinals).

Stanton played 986 games during his tenure with the Marlins, clubbing 267 home runs, fourth most all-time through as many games. He capped off his stay in Miami by capturing the MVP crown in 2017, tallying 7.6 WAR, while hitting 59 home runs—a season that was emphasized by a stretch of 75 games from July 5 to September 28, during which he hit 38 home runs and knocked in 79 runs.

Miami sits at six-and-a-half feet above sea level—Giancarlo Stanton's height—but it certainly feels like Jeter & Co. are underwater on their investment, having bought in for $1.2 billion for a club that's perennially last in attendance and currently devoid of any top-100 prospects.

In 2018, the ever-rebuilding Marlins' José Ureña improved his first-half performance (2–9, 4.39 ERA) by going 7–3 with a 3.31 ERA over his final 12 starts. Ureña has hit the most batters in the National League in two straight seasons (2017, 2018). Shown is Ureña at Triple-A New Orleans in 2016. (Minda Haas on Flickr (Original version) UCinternational (Crop) [CC BY 2.0 (https://creativecommons.org/licenses/by/2.0)], via Wikimedia Commons)

STATS INCREDIBLE!

183: Hall of Famers batted just .201/.276/.317 in 183 plate appearances against Dontrelle Willis . . . and if that is not enough, Barry Bonds had just a .511 OPS in 15 plate appearances against him.

130: Juan Pierre's career plate appearances with the bases loaded. He batted .381/.408/.487 and struck out just twice.

2.19: Jose Fernandez had a 2.19 ERA in 2016; it was the lowest by a first-year pitcher in 103 years, when Reb Russell had a 1.90 ERA in 1913.

94.5: Mat Latos's ERA after his first start of 2015, AND *The Kingdom: Miami's Spiritual Easy Listening Station.*

188: Career stolen bases of Dee Gordon, through five seasons—more than his father, Tom Gordon, allowed during his 21-year career (167).

0.4: Juan Pierre's WAR in 2005, playing in all 162 games. Barry Bonds had a 0.6, playing in just 14 games.

9.02%: 200 of Pierre's 2,217 (or 9.02 percent) career hits were bunt-hits.

41: Times Pierre faced Hall of Famer Greg Maddux in his career. He batted .342 and never struck out. Only Tony Gwynn faced Maddux more times without a K. He faced *future* Hall of Famer Curt Schilling 40 times, batting .385 and striking out just once.

5,136: Days between Suzuki's first home runs for both the Mariners (2001) and Marlins (2015). He's the first Japanese-born player to homer for each franchise.

25.1: Stanton's cumulative WAR from his age twenty to twenty-five seasons, with 181 home runs in 708 games. Miguel Cabrera, had 4.1 fewer WAR, and six fewer home runs, despite 172 *more* games during his age twenty to twenty-five seasons.

1: On August 15, 2018, José Ureña became the first pitcher to be ejected after hitting a batter with the first pitch of the game during (at least) the Live Ball Era.

35: In 2017, Giancarlo Stanton and Marcell Ozuna became the first Marlins teammates ever to each hit at least 35 home runs in a season . . . *so they traded them.*

42: In 2015, Dee Gordon became the first player to lead the National League in batting average and stolen bases since Jackie Robinson in 1949.

NEW YORK METS

Est. 1962

Michael Conforto is the only player in baseball history with an RBI in the Little League World Series, College World Series, and MLB World Series.

The New York Mets, founded in 1962, are not one of baseball's oldest franchises—not even close. In their relatively brief existence, however, they have proven to be one of its most popular, and compelling teams.

Their first four seasons were historically dreadful, debuting with the third-worst record in modern baseball history in 1962 (40–120) and playing just .300 ball through 1965 (194–452). Naturally, they were dubbed the "Miracle Mets" after a 100-win, World Series championship season in 1969, considering the team had never previously eclipsed 73 wins in a single season.

[Did you know?: The Mets' color scheme is a combination of the Brooklyn Dodgers' blue, and the New York Giants' orange—both teams that split the Big Apple for the West Coast, opening up a spot for the expansion Metropolitans.]

Ace Tom Seaver played a big role in the turnaround. He won the Rookie of the Year in 1967, and the Cy Young in 1969, going 25–7, accounting for 25 percent of his team's wins and just 11 percent of its losses. History may not grant Seaver proper credit, but he was as singularly responsible for the Mets' amazing turnaround as was any one player for any one team, ever.

Adding Seaver paid big dividends for New York, even though, during the phenom's first ten big league seasons, the team finished just a shade under .500 (804–809; .498). In the 1980s, the Mets doubled up, drafting *two* wunderkinds, setting up the longest sustained stretch of contention in franchise history.

Outfielder Darryl Strawberry and ace righty Dwight Gooden are remembered as the faces of the Mets in the 1980s, but their 1986 club was historically well-balanced, winning the franchise's second World Series after a 108-win regular season—the fourth-highest win total in National League history. The team had everything:

✔ *Power-hitting superstar (Strawberry)*
✔ *Unhittable ace (Gooden)*
✔ *Unhittable backup aces (Ron Darling, Bob Ojeda)*
✔ *Hall of Fame catcher (Gary Carter)*
✔ *Sweet-swinging mustachioed first baseman (Keith Hernandez)*
✔ *Prototype leadoff man (Lenny Dykstra)*

The Mets averaged an impressive 95 wins per season from Gooden's rookie year (1984) until 1990. That's an amazing run, for sure, but the team seemed capable of more.

By 1991, not a single starting position player remained from the '86 club. By 1993, they finished with their worst record since 1966 (59–103; .364). They rebounded at the turn of the century, reaching the World Series in 2000, but, in total, the Mets have only reached the postseason five times since 1988. It's been a struggle regaining that magic from over 30 years ago.

The Mets played sub-.500 ball the last two seasons, after reaching the World Series in 2015, and losing in the wild-card round in 2016. Still, ace starter Jacob deGrom might be the best

Doc Gooden warming up at Candlestick Park in 1991. (Brad Hunter)

pitcher in baseball, taking home 2018 NL Cy Young honors after posting a microscopic 1.70 ERA, the second-lowest qualified ERA since 1996.

New York needs to work on surrounding deGrom with a talented core, but it's a good start. Another amazin' Mets run would not be the least bit surprisin'.

Summer of '69

If you were to look back at a 1969 Mets lineup card, it might be difficult to pin 100 wins on them and a World Series title. They finished below the league average in every discernible offensive category—you'd have to invent a new stat, like EAR (Effort Above Replacement) to shine a positive light on their offensive output. The nine players on the team with at least 300 at-bats combined for just five All-Star appearances for their entire careers. Mets third baseman David Wright had seven, all by himself. The Mets' pitching staff had to be stellar, and it was.

They finished second in the league in ERA in 1969 (2.99) and first in WHIP (1.181). Starters Tom Seaver and Jerry Koosman carried the load.

Koosman—who shares a 1968 Topps rookie card with the '69 team's relief hurler and spot starter, Nolan Ryan—was phenomenal that year (17–9, 2.28 ERA), but Seaver finished with the Cy Young, at 25–7 with a 2.21 ERA. Only two other pitchers (Steve Carlton and Ron Guidry) have recorded a season with at least 25 wins and a sub-2.25 ERA since. And it may not have been his best statistical season.

Seaver won three ERA titles during his first seven years in baseball (1970, 1971, 1973) maintaining a 2.38 overall—the lowest ERA in the game during that span. Hall of Famer Randy Johnson never pitched a single season with an ERA of 2.25 or better, but Seaver averaged a 2.25 mark over a *four-season stretch*, from 1968–71.

He was probably the '70s' best, earning top marks in the National League during the decade in ERA (2.61) and wins (tied–178; Carlton). Hall of Famer Tom Glavine's best single-season WHIP was a 1.095 in 1991—Seaver maintained 1.073 for the *entire decade*.

The Great '80s

The Dodgers won one more title than the Mets during the 1980s (two to one), but New York probably had the most talent all the way through. They were stacked.

Darryl Strawberry *(OF, 1983–90)*: The Mets' all-time home run leader (252) took Rookie of the Year honors in his debut season, and was a force throughout his Mets career, averaging 32 home runs per season. He never clubbed fewer than 26 home runs with New York and was the first player in baseball history with at least 15 home runs and 15 stolen bases in each of his first six seasons. The only player to do it since? Barry Bonds.

He is one of just five players all time with at least 250 home runs and 200 stolen bases before their age-thirty season. After turning thirty, Strawberry hit just 55 home runs over his final eight years in baseball. Still, he is one of just four players in history to be drafted first overall and also lead their draft class in career WAR (1980; Ken Griffey, Jr., 1987; Chipper Jones, 1990; Alex Rodriguez, 1993).

Dwight Gooden *(SP, 1984–94)*: Doc followed up his 1984 Rookie of the Year campaign by winning pitching's Triple Crown in 1985 (NL-leading 24 Ws, 1.53 ERA, 268 Ks). At just twenty years old, he became the youngest to take the Crown, and the youngest Cy Young winner in history. Gooden certainly peaked early, recording the highest single-season strikeout total for a teenager in 1984 (276; age nineteen), and the lowest ERA in a sophomore season (1.53) since Dutch Leonard's Deadball Era 0.96 in 1914.

Gooden never had an ERA above 3.83 during his nine full seasons with the Mets, but, like Strawberry, his career is lopsided, marred by unfulfilled potential. His 157-win total before age thirty is the best in baseball since Catfish Hunter's 1975 season (184 Ws). He would win just 37 games in five seasons then after.

Keith Hernandez *(1B, 1984–89)* and **Gary Carter** *(C, 1985–89)*: Hernandez and Carter were two very accomplished players before joining the Mets, and lucky for New York, they enjoyed some of their best seasons *after* age thirty.

Hernandez wasn't a big home run hitter with the Mets (80 dingers in seven seasons), but he was the franchise's most complete player at the position. He leads all Mets first basemen in batting average (.297; minimum 500 games), and the "Pretty Boy" owns 25 percent of all Gold Gloves in franchise history (five, 1984–88)— and yet, Jerry still wouldn't help him move!

Carter had at least 100 RBIs his first two seasons with New York. His three seasons with 100 or more RBIs after his thirtieth birthday are the most among thirty-plus-year-old catchers in baseball history. Sure, former Mets backstop Mike Piazza had six seasons with at least 100 RBIs, but Carter remains the all-time leader in seasons with at least 25 home runs and 140 games caught, with five. Of note, only Yogi Berra (four), Mike Piazza (three), Johnny Bench (two), and Roy Campanella (two)—all Hall of Famers—also have multiples.

2015 and Beyond

The 2015 Mets took the division and NLCS in much of the same way the 1969 club did it—with great pitching.

Noah Syndergaard, Matt Harvey, and Jacob deGrom all played pivotal roles in a rotation with a "Big Sexy" anchor in Bartolo Colon. Sydergaard, Harvey, and deGrom combined for a 2.80 ERA with 559 strikeouts in 530.1 innings pitched over 83 starts and became the first trio of Mets starters each with at least 165 strikeouts in a season since David Cone, Sid Fernandez, Dwight Gooden, and Frank Viola all did so in 1990, two years before Syndergaard was even born.

But the success was short-lived, and after losing the 2016 NL wild-card game, the team from Flushing floundered, finishing fourth in each of the last two seasons.

Harvey, who posted a 2.53 ERA over 65 starts in his first three seasons with New York, compiled a 6.23 ERA over his next two and a half seasons before being dealt to Cincinnati.

Syndergaard has been dominant when on the bump for New York, but trips to the disabled list for various ailments ranging from a torn lat muscle, to a strained index finger, to even hand, foot, and mouth disease have limited him to just 32 starts over the past two seasons.

Jacob deGrom has only gotten better, but he's had a difficult time doing it on his own. After going 45–32 with a 2.98 ERA, (130 ERA+) with 731 strikeouts in 680⅔ innings in his first four

Jacob deGrom, the 2018 National League Cy Young Award winner, led all of baseball in ERA (1.70), FIP (1.98), and HR9 (0.4), along with posting a National League-best ERA+ (216). That year, deGrom recorded a MLB single-season record 24 straight quality starts. (slgckgc, CC BY-SA 2.0 [https://creativecommons.org/licenses/by-sa/2.0], via Flickr)

seasons, deGrom elevated his game to another level. Despite an historical 2018 season in which he led the league in WAR (10.0), ERA (1.70), and FIP (1.98), he had just a 10–9 record over 32 starts to show for it. He closed out the season with 29 consecutive starts in which he allowed three or fewer runs—tying Jake Arrieta's MLB record—and was rewarded with just an 8–9 record during that stretch (Arrieta was 24–1 during his streak!). The Mets won just 11 of those 29 games. If that isn't enough, he had a 2.09 ERA just in the games he did not win on the year, which on its own would have stood as the league-leading mark by over a quarter of a run. It is not all bad, though; his streak is still alive, so perhaps in 2019, the Mets can salvage a .500 record, for him, in what would be the best such streak in baseball history.

STATS INCREDIBLE!

9: Matt Harvey's win total in 2013. The first sub-2.50 ERA pitcher in history with at least 175 innings pitched and 175 strikeouts to not reach double-digit wins. He was joined by Cole Hamels of the Philadelphia Phillies . . . baseball is funny like that sometimes.

20/20: The 1988 Mets were the first team in baseball history to have three players with 20 home runs and 20 stolen bases (Darryl Strawberry, Kevin McReynolds, Howard Johnson).

.911: Mike Piazza batted .300/.351/.560 with 25 home runs in 370 plate appearances against Hall of Fame pitchers. If that is not enough, he also hit .364/.440/.955 with four home runs in 25 career plate appearances against Roger Clemens.

411: Tom Seaver's MLB record for consecutive starts with at least one strikeout.

3: World Series record for blown saves, "accomplished" by closer Jeurys Familia in 2015.

42: Bartolo Colon's age during the 2015 postseason, making him the oldest player to pitch in extra innings of a World Series game since Dolf Luque (age forty-four) in 1933.

6: Consecutive postseason games in which second baseman Daniel Murphy homered, an MLB record. No Met has even homered in six straight *regular* season games.

40: Rickey Henderson had seven stolen bases in ten postseason games in 1999. He had three steals just in Game 2 of the 1999 NLDS. He was forty years old.

7.6: John Olerud had a 7.6 WAR in 1998, besting both Mark McGwire (7.5) and Sammy Sosa (6.5) as they chased Roger Maris.

16: Dwight Gooden struck out 16 batters in consecutive games on September 12 and 17, 1984. He is the only pitcher in history to strike out 16 or more in back-to-back games.

5: David Wright had five career seasons with at least 40 doubles, 20 home runs, and 15 stolen bases. He's tied with Bobby Abreu for most in baseball history. Barry Bonds, Willie Mays, Henry Aaron, Ken Griffey Jr., and Derek Jeter combined for five (one each).

166: Mike Piazza had a 166 OPS+ in 1996, the highest ever by a player to catch at least 140 games in a season, besting the 159 posted by fellow Hall of Famer Roy Campanella in 1951.

43: In 2016, Bartolo Colon, who turned forty-three that May, became the oldest player with at least 15 wins and one home run at-bat in a season since Phil Niekro in 1982. He also led the team in innings pitched, victories, age, and weight that season.

15: Mike Piazza had an RBI in 15 straight games from June 14 to July 2, 2000—the longest streak since Ray Grimes had a record 17 straight in 1922.

3: Curtis Granderson became the first player with three go-ahead home runs in a World Series for the losing team since Babe Ruth in 1926.

[It was the ninth inning with two outs and the Yankees down a run; Lou Gehrig was on deck and Bob Meusel at bat. Babe Ruth was caught stealing second to lose the World Series for the Yankees.]

19: Strikeouts by Tom Seaver in a single game on April 22, 1970. He pitched a two-hit complete game over the Padres, and struck out the last 10 batters he faced, still a major league record.

449: Matt Harvey's strikeout total, against just 94 walks, through his first 65 career games. No pitcher in history has more Ks with fewer BBs through their first 65.

3: Go-ahead home runs by Curtis Granderson in the 2015 World Series. Derek Jeter had just two in his long postseason career. Granderson is the first leadoff man with multiple go-ahead homers in one Series.

PHILADELPHIA PHILLIES

Est. 1883

On May 29, 2010, Roy Halladay tossed the 20th perfect game in MLB history. Just 130 days later, on October 6, 2010, he no-hit the Reds in Game 1 of the NLDS. He is just one of six pitchers to throw two no-hitters in one season and the only pitcher to throw a no-hitter in both the regular season and postseason.

For generations, the Cubs were known as baseball's cuddly, lovable losers. The Phillies think that's cute. They need only take a snapshot of their dismal franchise record, with the caption, "hold my beer."

In 2007, Philadelphia was the first pro franchise to reach 10,000 losses, and to this day, it ranks atop the all-time list (10,919). In terms of winning percentage, it's the worst franchise established prior to 1969 (.472), and the only nineteenth century-born team under .500.

It hasn't always been sunny in Philadelphia. But, like the Cubs, there is a lot to love about this team.

While things started off dreadfully for Philly (17–81; 1883), the club actually played well overall in its 20 seasons prior to the World Series era (1903–present), finishing .500 or better 13 times from 1883–1902. Things took a turn for the Phils at the start of the twentieth century, but they're not entirely to blame for their own misfortune.

The Athletics set up shop in Philadelphia as part of American League expansion of Major League Baseball in 1901, and things got hostile in the City of Brotherly Love. Connie Mack, shrewd owner and manager of the upstart A's, poached the Phils' roster, most notably stealing away Nap Lajoie, one of the greatest batsmen in the game's history.

Lajoie batted .426 that year with the A's, establishing the single-season Modern Era record, and royally pissing off the Phillies. In a desperate attempt to win back the star second baseman, the Phils had Lajoie's crosstown jump deemed illegal, and, starting in 1902, the only Pennsylvania team that could justly claim him was the Phillies.

Naturally, Mack then traded his rights to Cleveland, where Lajoie played so well, they named the team after him. Fortune did not favor the Phillies for quite some time then after.

The Phils made an unsuccessful World Series run in 1915, but, over a 31-year stretch from 1918–48, the Phillies had just one winning season. 31 *years!*

No wonder Phillies fans are so fond of their near-misses—especially the NL Champion "Whiz Kids" in 1950 and the "Macho Row" club in 1993—because actual championship glory was so rare. Moreover, on September 20, 1964, with just a dozen games remaining in the season, the Phillies had a commanding 6½-game lead in the National League, all but assuring a trip to World Series. However, as Yogi Berra once said, "It ain't over till it's over," and Gene Mauch's Phillies would prove that—dropping ten of the final twelve games, surrendering the National League title to the would-be world champion Cardinals. But after a 97-year drought, the Phillies won their first championship in 1980, and then, after a 20-year all-sports citywide drought, they won their second in 2008.

Baker Bowl (1920), baseball's first "bandbox," featured a right field wall just 280 feet from home plate, but roughly 24 feet higher than Boston's Green Monster. (Anonymous)

Citizens Bank Park, 2007. High walls and an inward-angled left-centerfield wall are prominent features of each. While Baker Bowl's right field fence stood 60 feet high, CBP's is a comparatively-short 13.3 feet. (en.Wikipedia Phillyfan0419, PD)

Any other team, in any other city, might not have survived the lulls that so often plagued Philadelphia's Phillies. But, the City of Brotherly Love—and often Love-Hate—has always had its arms firmly wrapped around its hometown Fightin' Phils.

Old Pete & Chucky

The 1915 Phillies captured the National League Pennant, due in large part to **Grover Cleveland Alexander** *(SP, 1911–17)*, one of the team's, and league's, all-time best pitchers. Dead ball or not, Old Pete dominated that season, winning his first of three pitching Triple Crowns (31 Ws, 1.22 ERA, 241 Ks) and accounting for 34 percent of Philadelphia's total wins on the year (90).

That year, Alexander was the first NL pitcher with at least 195 strikeouts, a 195 or better ERA+, and sub-1.95 FIP, only two pitchers in league history have since joined the club—Bob Gibson (1968) and Clayton Kershaw (2014). Jacob deGrom was very close in 2018—1.99 FIP, 269 K, 216 ERA+.

The 1915 season was just the beginning for Alexander. In 1916, he won his second consecutive Triple Crown (33 Ws, 1.55 ERA, 167 Ks), setting a new franchise record for wins in a single season that still stands. And 1917 was his third straight season with at least 30 wins (30 Ws, 1.83 ERA, 200 Ks), but it would be his last in Philadelphia.

The Phillies reportedly dealt him in anticipation of the thirty-year old being drafted in World War I, and they were correct in their assumption. Alexander returned from combat a changed man—he won another Triple Crown with Chicago in 1920, but injuries, illness, and alcoholism stymied his potential and quality of life.

Chuck Klein *(OF, 1928–33, 1936–44)* didn't exactly reign over a successful term in Phillies history. He was, however, the club's best player (and league MVP) during that aforementioned single winning season (1932) in more than three decades (1918–48). He was one of the game's greatest talents, on one of its poorest teams.

At the time, Klein was the fastest player to reach 100 career home runs (390 games) and is still the fastest to 1,000 career hits (683 games).

He's the only player in baseball history with at least 50 doubles, 10 triples, 30 home runs, and 20 stolen bases, doing so in 1932. That season also made Klein the first player in history with multiple 50-plus 2B, 30-plus HR seasons (1930, 1932)—a feat unmatched for nearly 70 years, before Todd Helton (2000–01) and Albert Pujols (2003–04, 2012) finally joined the club.

Klein and Rogers Hornsby are the only members of baseball's 40/140 club (home runs/singles). No other player has joined their ranks since Klein slugged 40 homers with 143 singles in 1930.

The shallow right-field wall at Klein's home field Baker Bowl is credited for boosting his offensive performance, but it often allowed outfielders to play in and turn would-be singles into outs. To be fair, Klein, as a right fielder, also turned this to his advantage, recording 44 outfield assists in 1930—yet another MLB record that still stands.

Schmitty and Lefty

Mike "Schmitty" Schmidt *(3B, 1972–89)* and Steve "Lefty" Carlton *(SP, 1972–86)* were two of the best players of their generation, and are most commonly described as the two best players in team history. It's no surprise, then, that the Phillies were finally able to win their first World Series, after 78 years trying, while their two best players dominated the competition.

Schmidt (.286 BA, 48 HRs, 121 RBIs) and Carlton (24 Ws, 2.34 ERA, 286 Ks) won the National League MVP and Cy Young Award, respectively, carrying the Phils to 91 regular season wins, an NL East division crown, and eventual World Series victory over the Kansas City Royals in 1980. It was a tremendous team victory—the only franchise championship until 2008—but both players were among Philadelphia's most consistent and dominant individual champions.

Schmitty is the franchise's best player, all-time. His total Phillies career WAR alone (106.8) is just 1.4 wins shy of Jimmy Rollins and Chase Utley . . . combined (46.4, 61.8, respectively). He also leads the team in defensive WAR (18.4), Gold Gloves (10), home runs (548), RBIs (1,595), runs scored (1,506), total bases (4,404), walks (1,507), extra-base hits (1,015), times on base (3,820), and times mentioned as the game's greatest third baseman (a gazillion).

He's the only player in history to amass 500 home runs from the hot corner (509). No one hit more out in the 1980s (313), and only the Babe led the league in homers more times than Schmitty (11 to 6). With all that power, it's sometimes forgotten that the converted shortstop was also fleet of foot.

Schmidt had as many seasons with 35-plus home runs and at least a dozen stolen bases (six) as Barry Bonds had in his career.

Mike Schmidt at Philadelphia's Veterans Stadium, hitting a home run off the Reds in 1987—his 21st home run of the season and 516th of his career. (Squelle, CC BY-SA 3.0 [http://creativecommons.org/licenses/by-sa/3.0], via Wikimedia Commons)

On the pitching side, **Lefty** was every bit as dominant for the Phillies as Schmidt was with his bat and glove. The 329-game winner (a franchise-best 241 with Philadelphia) retired with a then-record four Cy Young Awards, all with Philadelphia. In the 11 seasons that spanned his first Cy Young season to his last (1972–82), Carlton averaged 19 wins and 226 strikeouts, with a 2.96 ERA.

In 1972, his first season with the team, Lefty won the NL Triple Crown (27 Ws, 1.97 ERA, 310 Ks) and accounted for 45.8 percent of the team's victories (59). He had six complete games, with a 3.79 ERA in his 10 losses.

His 10 losses that season were made possible by the Phillies' futile offense, which scored no more than one run in five of them and no more than two runs in seven. His 27 wins were almost impossible. Since 1953, only Denny McLain (31 Ws; 1968) has won more games in a single season—and Lefty won his with the "support" of the second-worst offensive team in the National League (3.22 runs per game). Carlton and Sandy Koufax are the only pitchers of the Live Ball Era (post-1920) with a season with at least 25 wins, 300 strikeouts, and a sub-2.00 ERA.

Unfortunately for the Phillies, the rest of the team went just 32–87 in 1972, with a collective 4.22 ERA.

In stark contrast, Philadelphia's 2011 rotation was stacked, top to bottom.

The Core Four

The Phillies entered the twenty-first century having finished over .500 just once in the previous 16 seasons. As a franchise, they turned their focus toward building up a long-neglected farm system through the MLB draft, and the results were a great success. Homegrown products Jimmy Rollins, Chase Utley, Ryan Howard, and Cole Hamels were the franchise cornerstones for a decade, and some of the greatest talents to ever wear the uniform.

Rollins *(SS, 2000–14)* was arguably the greatest shortstop in team history. He's the franchise leader in hits (2,306), doubles (479), and second in extra-base hits (806). He accomplished a lot in his 15 years with Philadelphia, but one season sticks out in particular.

In 2007, Rollins won league MVP honors, totaling 20 triples, 30 home runs, and 41 stolen bases. He's the only player in history with a 20/30/40 season. Rollins is the only Phillie since Nap Lajoie in 1897 to have a 20-triple year, and he's one of just seven MLB players ever with at least 20 triples and 20 home runs in the same

Part of the best double-play combination in team history, Utley (26) and Rollins (11), together from 2003–14, sealed the bond with a handshake before each game. (Kevin Durso)

season—the first NL player to pull the feat since George Brett in 1979.

In his career, Rollins has totaled 115 triples, 231 homers, and 470 stolen bases. No single player in history has ever had more of each. His ten career seasons with 20+ doubles, 10+ home runs, and 30+ stolen bases are also unmatched in MLB history. His four seasons with at least 20 doubles, 10 home runs, and 30 stolen bases are the most by a shortstop since Honus Wagner had his fifth in 1909.

Utley *(2B, 2003–15)*, in his prime, was one of the best players in baseball, though he never won a league MVP like Howard and Rollins did (2006, 2007, respectively), or a World Series MVP, as did Hamels in 2008. Historically, he should be recognized as one of the most valuable second basemen in team—and baseball—history.

His 65.4 career WAR is just 0.1 fewer than Craig Biggio, 1.7 fewer than Roberto Alomar, and 2.6 fewer than Ryne Sandberg—all Hall of Famers. His peak WAR seasons are in very rare company. He had a 17.3 WAR combined in 2008 and 2009, the highest total by a second baseman in consecutive seasons since Hall of Famer Joe Morgan's back-to-back MVP years of 1975 and 1976. From 2005 to 2009, Utley had five straight seasons with at least a 7.0 WAR. Every other eligible second baseman in history with at least four total 7.0 WAR seasons is in the Hall of Fame, including Jackie Robinson (four), Sandberg (four), Charlie Gehringer (five), Morgan (five), Nap Lajoie (seven), Eddie Collins (eight), and Rogers Hornsby (eight). He is one of just four second basemen in history with at least 250 home runs and 150 stolen bases. The other three are, again, Hall of Famers Morgan, Sandberg, and Biggio. It is worth noting that Chase also had 141 career defensive runs saved, while the other three combined for -88.4 defensive runs saved (yes, negative).

Utley batted .301/.388/.535 during that five-year peak from 2005 to 2009. Only six other second basemen have slashed that in a *single* season since Robinson broke the color barrier in 1947, and none of them did it twice. Only four other second basemen in history (Biggio, Gehringer, Hornsby, Lajoie) have equaled in a single season the .388 on-base percentage, 73 extra-base hits, and 15 stolen bases Utley averaged over that five-year stretch. Utley's peak also yielded a great deal of World Series success.

He has seven career World Series home runs. Duke Snider is the only National League player with more (11). In 2009, he tied "Mr. October," Reggie Jackson, for most home runs in a single World Series, with five, a record that has since been tied by Astros slugger George Springer in 2017. His career 689 slugging percentage during World Series play ranks sixth best all-time among players with at least 50 plate appearances, behind David Ortiz, Jackson, Babe Ruth, Lou Gehrig, and Lenny Dykstra.

[Fun fact: Dykstra's career 1.094 postseason OPS ranks third all time among players with at least 100 plate appearances, behind only Lou Gehrig (1.214) and Babe Ruth (1.214). Dude was Nails.]

Howard *(1B, 2004–2016)* came out strong, reaching 100 career home runs in just 325 games, an MLB record. It was 51 games quicker than runner-up Ralph Kiner. He was also the fastest to 200 (658 games) and the second-fastest to 300 (1,093, six more than Kiner). In 2006, he bested Mike Schmidt's previous single-season franchise home run record by 10, clubbing 58 home runs; in 1945, *the entire Phils team hit 56.* He's the only member of the team's 50+ home run club, and only three other Phillies since the 1920s have even hit 40-plus (Schmidt, Jim Thome, Dick Allen).

[From 1871 to 1995, 23 players collected at least five qualified seasons batting .300/.375/.550 or better. Among them are 22 Hall of Famers and Dick Allen.]

From September 6, 2005 to September 9, 2006, "The Big Piece" batted .312/.405/.689 with 65 home runs and 162 RBIs over a 162-game span.

Ryan Howard in 2012, becoming the second-fastest batter to 300 career home runs in baseball history. (Michael Kirk Photography)

Hamels (2006–15) was one of the franchise's greatest starting pitchers, providing Philadelphia with a bona fide ace at the top of its rotation for about a decade. He sits fourth in team history in pitching WAR (42.4), but, overall, the support he received from his offense was historically uneven.

During his Phillies career, the team's bullpen blew 29 wins for him. Of his 90 losses with the team, 36 (40 percent) were in quality starts, sporting a 2.58 ERA in those losses. In fact, he went at least seven innings and allowed no more than two earned runs in 21 (23.3 percent) of the games *he* lost. In all, Hamels had 57 starts in which he went at least seven innings and allowed two or fewer runs, and did not *earn* a win; in 12 of these he did not allow a single earned run. He was 0–21 with a 1.63 ERA in those starts.

Hamels was 9–9 with a 2.46 ERA in 2014. This was the best season in terms of ERA by a pitcher with at least 30 starts and fewer than 10 wins since Tricky Nichols went 4–29 with a 2.38 ERA in 1875. Tricky had a 7.66 RA (ERA, but including unearned runs) that season. Hamels was 0–9, with a 3.04 ERA in the games he didn't win that season.

Final 70 starts with Phillies – 2.95 ERA, 21–21
Final 81 starts with Phillies – 3.04 ERA, 23–28
Final 100 starts with Phillies – 3.14 ERA, 30–33

Five Aces

The Phillies won a franchise-record 102 games in 2011, before exiting in the opening-round NLDS. Early playoff exits tend to mute regular-season accomplishments, so it might be difficult to remember, or consider, that the Phillies may have fielded the greatest starting rotation of all time. Well, at least among five-man rotations. Maybe.

The five-man has roots that date back to the early part of last century, but it didn't become a staple of the game until the 1970s. In terms of ERA, the best rotation during the Live Ball Era (post-1919) was the 1981 Houston Astros' unit (2.43 ERA), but they're penalized by playing just 110 games during a strike-shortened season. The Phillies' 2011 quintet, featuring predominantly Roy Halladay (19–6, 2.35 ERA), Cliff Lee (17–8, 2.40 ERA), Cole Hamels (14–9, 2.79 ERA), Vance Worley (11–3, 3.01 ERA), and Roy Oswalt (9–10, 3.69 ERA), ranks third during the five-man era (40th during Live Ball), and is the best in baseball since 1985.

That year, the Mets qualified as having the best five-man ERA (2.84), but they were top heavy, with Doc Gooden at his peak of complete domination (24–4, 1.53 ERA). The Phillies rank a tad behind at 2.86, but were deep and dangerous, top to bottom.

During the Live Ball Era, regardless of rotation size, the Phillies' Five ranks eighth in WHIP (1.110), and fifth in K/9 (7.9; NL record

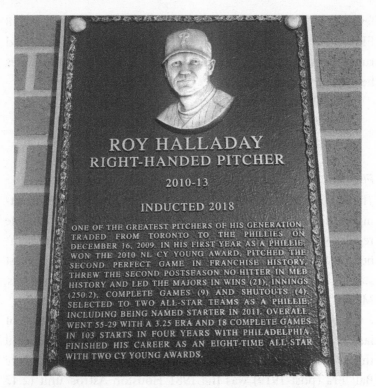

Roy Halladay was inducted to the Phillies' Wall of Fame on August 4, 2018, at Citizens Bank Park, nearly seven months after the plane crash that cost Doc his life (Matt Rappa).

until 2014), with the very best strikeout-to-walk ratio (4.22). Of course, it's hard to quantify "best" and no one ever seems to agree on a team, or even method.

[*What's In a Win? The 1971 Baltimore Orioles have often gotten the "best rotation" moniker, because they were just the second team since 1920 with four 20-game winners, but the 1972 O's actually had a better ERA (2.58 to 2.91), with the fourth-best WHIP of the Live Ball Era (1.094).*]

For simplicity's sake, let's assume the Phillies fielded the best five-man rotation. And five is better than four. So . . . the 2011 Phillies had the greatest rotation of all time. Maybe.

Moving Phorward

The Phillies have not finished above .500 since their magical 2011 season that ended too soon, but the 2018 squad showed a great deal of promise. They sat at 15 games above .500 as late as August 7, before stumbling to the finish line with a 16–33 record over the final 49 games of the season to end up 80–82.

Aaron Nola had 10.5 pitching WAR, the highest by a Phillies pitcher since Steve Carton in 1972—when he won 27 of the team's lowly 59 victories—and became the first starting pitcher in Phillies history with a WHIP below 1.000 while averaging at least a strike-out per inning. Sophomore Rhys Hoskins amassed 52 home runs

Through his first 109 career games at Citizens Bank Park, Philadelphia Phillies first baseman Rhys Hoskins has slugged 25 doubles, 30 home runs, and 91 RBIs. (Ian D'Andrea, CC BY-SA 2.0 [https:// creativecommons.org/licenses/by-sa/2.0)], via Wikimedia Commons)

through his first 203 games—eighth most all time by a player through as many games. Among Phillies players with at least 600 plate appearances through 203 career games, his .889 OPS ranks fourth, behind only Chuck Klein (1.025), Dick Allen (.952), and Ryan Howard (.932).

Phillies fans wait with high hopes for the team's return to glory. With money to spend, they may not be waiting long . . .

STATS INCREDIBLE!

20: Consecutive games in which Pete Rose reached base safely multiple times, from September 3 to September 22, 1979. He batted .500/.589/.603 during that span.

19: Consecutive games in which Rose recorded a hit and did not strike out, from June 9 to June 27, 1982. No player has had a longer streak since.

70: In 1984, Juan Samuel had 70 extra-base hits and 72 stolen bases. He and Ty Cobb (1911) are the only players in baseball history with at least 70 extra-base hits and 70 stolen bases in a season.

2: Home runs hit by starting pitcher Rick Wise during a June 23, 1971 blanking of the Reds, 4–0. Amazingly, Wise no-hit the Big Red Machine, turning in, arguably, the single most dominant performance by a player in baseball history.

7: Number of players in MLB history with at least 900 extra-base hits and 400 stolen bases. Among them are five Hall of Famers, Barry Bonds, and Phillies great Bobby Abreu.

5: Number of players with at least 2,400 hits, 1,400 walks, and 400 stolen bases—Bonds, Rickey Henderson, Joe Morgan, Eddie Collins, and Abreu.

9: Number of seasons in which Abreu had 60+ extra base hits and 20+ stolen bases—the most in baseball history.

4: Record number of players on one team with at least 60 extra-base hits and 20 stolen bases (Rollins, Utley, Shane Victorino, and Jayson Werth; 2009).

16: Home runs hit by Pat Burrell on three-ball counts in 2002, most in recorded history. His 12 full-count home runs that season are also a record.

238: Number of strikeouts by Cliff Lee in 2011, and he did not throw a single wild pitch that year. Lee collected the most strikeouts in a season in baseball history without a wild pitch. The following season he became the first pitcher with at least 200 strikeouts and fewer than 30 walks since Cy Young in 1904. The season after that, he faced 876 batters—walking just one on four pitches.

147: On October 21, 1993, with the Phillies facing elimination, Curt Schilling shut out the Blue Jays on 147 pitches in Game 5 of the World Series. Schilling would go on to be one of the most clutch pitchers in postseason history, winning five of five starts with his teams facing elimination.

2,234: Career hits for Michael Jack Schmidt, of which 548 were home runs. His final hit, though, was a bunt single.

.400: Outfielders Ed Delahanty, Billy Hamilton, and Sam Thompson batted .401 from 1894 to 1895. They combined to go 1,218-for-3,039 over the two-season span. In 1894, the Phillies had four outfielders bat above .400—the afore-mentioned trio, in addition to the team's leading hitter that season, Tuck Turner.

66: Number of wins by which Robin Roberts fell shy of 300 career victories, it's also the number of complete game losses he had in his career. Roberts also had 37 career starts in which he went at least eight innings, allowed no more than two runs (earned or unearned), and *lost*. This is the most during the Live Ball Era.

6: Seranthony Dominguez did not allow a hit or a walk in any of his first six career appearances, the longest such streak to begin a career.

5: There have been five players in baseball history that have at least a .350 on-base percentage, 250 home runs, 150 stolen bases, and 100 defensive runs saved. Among them, two Phillies, in Chase Utley and Mike Schmidt (along with Willie Mays, Carl Yastrzemski, and Barry Bonds).

18: Home runs clubbed by Rhys Hoskins through his first 40 games, an MLB record. It was the most in the NL since Wally Berger hit 15 through his first 40 in 1930.

WASHINGTON NATIONALS

Est. 1969

EXPOS—*Vlad Guerrero (4.48) and Tim Raines (4.49) both averaged more WAR-per-162 games played during their careers than Reggie Jackson (4.25) and Derek Jeter (4.27).*

NATIONALS—*In 2018, Max Scherzer joined Lefty Grove, Sandy Koufax, Nolan Ryan, and Randy Johnson as the only pitchers in baseball history with multiple Immaculate Innings (nine pitches, three strikeouts). Scherzer stands alone as the only pitcher with multiple no-hit, no-walk performances, both coming in 2015.*

The Nationals have only been around for 14 years, so they still have that new-franchise smell. But baseball in the nation's capital is not a novel concept.

Professional baseball in DC dates back as far as 1872, with several short-lived iterations, such as the Olympics, Blue Legs, and even a few unaffiliated Nationals squads taking the field. Of course, the one with the most staying power was the Washington Senators, a charter American League franchise that played in D.C. for 60 years before shipping off and becoming the Twins of Minnesota in 1961. In its place, the franchise now known as the Texas Rangers tried its hand for a decade in DC (1961–71), also as the Washington Senators. It didn't work out.

The first Senators team slogan:

"First in war, first in peace, and last in the American League."

The second Senators team slogan:

"First in war, first in peace, and STILL last in the American League."

There's your reason why "Senators" maybe wasn't given much serious consideration when it came time to name the new one. If luck plays any role at all, it is probably a good omen that, instead of moving *out*, this was the first existing MLB franchise moving *in* to Washington.

The franchise began as the expansion Montreal Expos in 1969, the first MLB team located outside of the United States. From the onset, they were dreadful.

The Expos failed to reach .500 in any of their first ten seasons. In the 35 years they played in Montreal, their only successful campaigns of note came during the strike-shortened seasons of 1981 and 1994.

The 1981 season is the only year the Expos made the playoffs*—with an asterisk, however, because of a bizarre one-time rule that allowed them to advance with a second-place record.

In 1994, they finally had their first (and only) first-place finish—but, this time the strike lasted and there would be no playoffs to make.

Tragic.

The 1994 strike, famously, struck a damaging shot to the popularity of baseball everywhere. To the Montreal Expos specifically, it was a death blow.

By 2001, stadium attendance dropped to just 7,935 per game. The Seattle Mariners' attendance the same season was over five times higher (43,302 per game). The Florida Marlins, the next-to-worst draw in baseball, doubled Montreal's average (15,765). *Heck, even the Milwaukee Brewers' Triple-A affiliate Indianapolis Indians drew 578 more fans per game in 2001.* Yikes.

Major League Baseball took control of the club and eventually moved it to Washington in 2005. And after an Expos-esque rocky start, the Nationals have actually found a way to win with regularity—a novel concept for both the franchise and city.

One fan's plea for the Expos' return, at an exhibition game between the Cincinnati Reds and Toronto Blue Jays, at Montreal's Olympic Stadium on April 3, 2015. (Resolute)

'Spos with the Most

Not coincidentally, three of the Expos' best players—Gary Carter, Andre Dawson, and Tim Raines—all played together during one of the franchise's best five-year stretches, from 1979–83.

Gary Carter *(C, 1974–84)*: Carter was the Expos' first Hall of Fame representative, and one of the best catchers of his generation. During the 11 years he was an Expo (1974–84), no catcher in the National League had more hits (1,365), doubles (256), triples (23), home runs (215), RBIs (794), runs scored (683), walks (549), or high-fives (many) than Carter. He was also a tremendous defensive player, leading the league in defensive WAR over the same span (20.9) while collecting three straight Gold Gloves, from 1980–82. In overall WAR per 162 games, Carter is tops among Expos with a 6.01 average.

Andre Dawson *(OF, 1976–86)*: Seven years after Gary Carter's induction, Dawson became the franchise's second Hall of Famer. He was a true double threat, averaging 20 home runs and 23 stolen bases during his 11 seasons in Montreal. During that stretch, from 1976–86, Dawson led the National League with five 20/20 seasons. No one else even had four. Dawson was the only player during the 1980s to collect at least 250 homers and 150 steals (250 HRs, 199 SBs).

Forget double threat; Dawson was a triple threat, winning six straight Gold Gloves with Montreal (1980–85) and eight overall. Among National League outfielders in the 1980s, Dawson was second to only Barry Bonds in defensive runs saved (73.1 to 77.1).

Tim Raines *(OF, 1979–90)*: "Rock" Raines, the franchise offensive WAR leader (48.2), finally earned election to the Hall of Fame in 2017, his tenth and final year on the ballot. What took so long?

The speedster's calling card was the stolen base, and no one—not even the Man of Steal Rickey Henderson—*did it more consistently or more efficiently.* He is the only player in baseball history to steal at least 70 bases in six consecutive seasons, doing so from 1981–86.

And his 84.7 percent success rate on stolen base attempts for his career is the best in baseball history (minimum 400 attempts). Rickey, who of course topped Rock in sheer stolen base numbers, was not quite as selective as Raines—the "Greatest of All Time" would have to return to baseball and steal 448 consecutive bases without being caught to pass Raines in stolen bases efficiency.

[*Rickey, if you are reading this . . . Challenge accepted?*]

From 1982–86, Raines had at least 30 doubles and 70 stolen bases each season. Prior to 1982, the last *single* 30/70 season was Ty Cobb's way back in 1915. In 1987, Raines failed to replicate his past five 30/70 seasons. But no matter, as Raines batted a mighty .330/.429/.526 with 50 stolen bases, making him the first player to bat at least .325/.425/.525 with 50 stolen bases since 1922 MVP George Sisler accomplished the feat. The only player with such a season since? The 1990 AL MVP Rickey Henderson.

The .294 career hitter was also a whiz from the batter's box, reaching base safely 3,977 times in his career—more than 3,000 hit club Hall of Famers Tony Gwynn, Nap Lajoie, Lou Brock, and Roberto Clemente. His career .385 on-base percentage bests 62.4 percent of all Hall of Fame position players, including Willie Mays at .384. His .425 slugging percentage bests Rickey Henderson at .419. His 123 OPS+ bests 500 home run club member Ernie Banks. And his 69.4 WAR tops a man whom many call the "greatest hitter of a generation"—Tony Gwynn, at 69.2.

Still part of the 14.0 percent of BBWAA writers who did not vote Rock for induction in 2017? Of the 19,429 players (through 2018) to ever play major-league baseball, Tim Raines is the only one to amass at least 100 triples, 150 homers, and 600 stolen bases. He did so handily, with 113 three-baggers, 170 big flies, and 808 thieveries.

According to Baseball-Reference.com, Lou Brock is the most similar player to Raines. Here's how the two measure up against each other in a few key offensive categories:

Raines vs. Brock

BA: Rock

OBP: Rock

SLG: Rock

OPS: Rock

TOB: Rock

HR: Rock

SB%: Rock

OPS+: Rock

WAR: Rock

Additionally, Lou Brock had a career-high .385 on-base percentage in 1971. That was Rock's career on-base percentage. Brock had a career-best 83.8 stolen base percentage in 1968, which falls short of Rock's career stolen base percentage of 84.7. In fact, Brock would have to return to baseball and steal 762 consecutive bases without being caught to pass Tim Raines in career stolen base efficiency. Now, this is in no way a knock of the Hall of Fame career of Lou Brock, who did, at the time, exactly what was expected of a leadoff hitter, by hitting for average and stealing bags; however, we just feel as though Rock's Hall of Fame career was just that much better.

Rock's induction in 2017 was a long-overdue reward for a very worthy career. Analytics and "new stats" don't just allow us to apply accurate value for today's players; they give us a chance to revisit and celebrate the stars of baseball's past.

The Impaler

Vladimir Guerrero *(OF, 1996–2003)* came a bit later with Montreal, but may have been the franchise's most talented player.

He batted .325/.391/.602 with a 151 OPS+, .411 wOBA, 146 wRC+, 105 runs, 39 home runs, 116 RBI, and 22 stolen bases during his five-year peak with Montreal . . . and he didn't win an MVP Award until two years later when he was with the Angels. Throughout his 16-year MLB career, Guerrero was famous for his ability to hit *any* pitch *very* hard. If he could reach the ball, he could hit it out of the park. Despite routinely lunging for pitches way out of the zone, he made great contact, finishing second to only Albert Pujols in 30-plus homer, sub-75 strikeout seasons over the past 20 years (Pujols, 10; Vlad, 6).

The 173 home runs and .927 OPS he had in six seasons with the Angels was a remarkable tally. That stint helped propel him toward Hall enshrinement in 2018, garnering 92.9 percent of the vote, after debuting just 3.9 percent short of the 75 percent cutoff in 2017. He went in as an Angel. Still . . . his start in Montreal was better. His 144 OPS+ through his first six Expos seasons is better than the starts of Manny Ramirez (141), Mike Schmidt (141), Miguel Cabrera (140), and Barry Bonds (138).

In 2002, Guerrero batted .336/.417/.593 with 39 homers, 364 total bases, and 40 stolen bases—making him just one of nine players in history to have at least 360 total bases and 40 stolen bases in a season; add 70 walks to that criteria, and he stands alone (84) as the only player with such a season in history. Vlad, Willie Mays (1957), and Larry Walker (1997) are the only players ever with a .333+ BA/ 33 HR/ 33 SB season.

Overall, Guerrero had four seasons with at least 200 hits and 30 home runs. Only Lou Gehrig had more, with seven.

Nats' Bats . . . and Arms

The Nationals are enjoying some sustained success in Washington these days, finishing over .500 the last seven seasons, averaging 91 wins per. The postseason has been a different story, as they've failed to win a single postseason series in four tries during that span.

Former No. 1 overall draft pick Stephen Strasburg (94–52, 3.14 ERA) has had difficulty staying on the field, but when healthy, he's been one of the most dynamic pitchers in baseball. Strasburg has reached double-digit strikeouts without allowing multiple walks in 26 of his first 206 career games, second all-time only to Corey Kluber (33) through as many career games and already one more than Nolan Ryan had during his entire career. Moreover, the thirty-year-old has seven career seasons with 150-plus strikeouts and a strikeout percentage of at least 25 percent. Only Randy Johnson (12), Nolan Ryan (12), Clayton Kershaw (nine), and Pedro Martinez (eight) have more.

Max Scherzer has been brilliant during his first four seasons with the Nationals, winning two Cy Young Awards and capturing

Washington Nationals RHP Max Scherzer has five seasons with at least 240 strikeouts and a sub-1.000 WHIP. No other pitcher in history has more than three, and every pitcher with exactly three—Tim Keefe, Walter Johnson, Sandy Koufax, and Pedro Martinez—is in the National Baseball Hall of Fame. (Keith Allison, CC BY-SA 2.0 [https://creativecommons.org/licenses/by-sa/2.0], via Flickr)]

In 2015, Bryce Harper (twenty-two; .330, 42 HRs) became the youngest player to bat at least .330 in a season with 40 homers since Joe DiMaggio in 1937 (twenty-two; .346, 46 HRs). DiMaggio was about five weeks younger than Harper. (Kevin Durso)

two more top-five finishes. Overall, he has finished in the top five in six straight seasons. He already has had five seasons with at least 240 strikeouts and a WHIP under 1.000. No other player in history has more than three and all of those with exactly three—Tim Keefe, Walter Johnson, Sandy Koufax, and Pedro Martinez—are in the Hall of Fame. Mad Max has 82 career games with double-digit strikeouts, already eighth most all time, and his 21 games with ten or more strikeouts and no walks are tied with Roger Clemens for fourth most all time, behind only Clayton Kershaw (22), Curt Schilling (27), and Randy Johnson (36).

On the offensive side, Bryce Harper—who is 173 days younger than 2017 AL Rookie of the Year Aaron Judge—was the face of the franchise for the last seven seasons.

At just twenty-two years old, he had one of the best offensive seasons in history, batting .330/.460/.649 in 2015—the youngest to slash at least that in a qualified season since Levi Meyerle in 1871. Harper is one of only three players in league history to lead the NL in home runs before turning twenty-three (Eddie Mathews, twenty-one; Johnny Bench, twenty-two). He also became the youngest player in baseball history with at least 40 homers and 120 walks in a season. The previous youngest was Babe Ruth in 1920, the year that birthed the Live Ball Era.

Harper already has a better WAR season (10.0, 2015) than the career highs of both Henry Aaron (9.4, 1961) and Ken Griffey Jr. (9.7, 1996). Harper's historic 2015 made him the youngest player to lead the majors in both on-base percentage and slugging percentage since Stan Musial in 1943. Stan repeated the feat in 1944, then enlisted in the United States Navy in 1945.

The Man's impossible feat proved a tough act to follow, as Harper has struggled to maintain, as he has tallied 2.5 fewer WAR over his last three seasons combined than he did just during his MVP campaign of 2015.

Overall, Harper's place in Nationals history is secure, cemented by his performance during the 2018 Home Run Derby, when he stood victorious in front of his hometown crowd, joining Ryne Sandberg (Chicago Cubs, 1990) and Todd Frazier (Cincinnati Reds, 2015) as the only players ever to do so.

Harper's likely departure from DC via free agency would leave a certain void; one difficult to fill by anyone, other than perhaps another very young superstar.

Enter Juan Soto

Juan Soto's entire rookie season came as a teenager, during which he mashed 22 home runs. His 22 home runs as a teen are tied for second most all time with Bryce Harper—who had 103 more plate appearances as a teenager. He became the first teen in baseball history to amass three multi-homer games, and his .923 OPS is the highest mark ever by a player with fewer than 20 years on earth.

Soto's first 116 games, during which he batted .292/.406/.517 could perhaps be more aptly compared to Mike Trout, who slashed .316/.374/.539 during the first 116 games of his career. He became the sixth player in history with at least a .400 on-base percentage and a .500 slugging percentage during a season with at least 400 plate appearances prior to his age-twenty-one season. The others? Alex Rodriguez (1996), Al Kaline (1955), Ted Williams (1939), Mel Ott (1929), and Jimmie Foxx (1928), all of whom—aside from Soto—did so in their age-twenty season.

STATS INCREDIBLE!

158: The Montreal, Canada record for career wins, by Expos pitcher Steve Rogers (which, ironically, is the civilian name of Captain *America*.)

3: The number of players in baseball history with multiple seasons of at least 50 XBHs and 70 SBs. Ty Cobb had two, Rickey Henderson had two, and Tim Raines had four . . . consecutively.

7: The number of players in baseball history with at least 600 XBHs and 700 SBs. Among them, Tim Raines was the final player to receive his "Call to the Hall."

3: The number of seasons with at least 50 XBHs and 90 SBs in baseball history, two of which occurred during the 1800s: Pete Browning in 1887, Tom Brown in 1891, and Tim Raines in 1983.

91: Team-record total go-ahead home runs Vladimir Guerrero had with Montreal, 13 more than Andre Dawson and 23 more than Gary Carter.

0: The number of pitchers Bryce Harper faced that were younger than him, through four minor-league levels and his first three MLB seasons.

1.109: Harper's OPS for the 2015 season. He is the youngest player with a season OPS of 1.100+ since Joe Kelley in 1894. He is the youngest player to lead the league in OBP (.460) and homers (42) since Ty Cobb in 1909 (.431 OBP, 9 HRs).

.649: Harper's slugging percentage in 2015. He's the youngest player with a SLG% that high since Joe DiMaggio in 1937.

506: The number of players selected before the Expos took Tom Brady in the 1995 MLB Draft. The New England Patriots selected him 199th overall in the 2000 NFL Draft.

8.2: In the 2014 18-inning NLDS Game 2 Giants win over the Nats (2–1), Jordan Zimmermann became the first pitcher ever to leave a postseason game with a shutout intact with two outs in the ninth inning.

1894: In 2016, Trea Turner became the first rookie with at least 10 home runs, 20 stolen bases, and a .330 batting average since Jimmy Bannon in 1894.

6: Hits by Max Scherzer with two outs and runners in scoring position in 2018, just one fewer than Mike Trout on the season.

41: Nationals closer Sean Doolittle was drafted 41st overall by the Oakland Athletics in 2007 . . . as a first baseman! He batted .312/.423/.482 in college and was a California League All-Star as a first baseman in 2008.

1911: In 2016, Trea Turner became the first rookie to slug at least .565 with 30 or more stolen bases since "Shoeless" Joe Jackson (Cleveland Naps) in 1911.

LIII: Super Bowl LIII featured a battle of starting quarterbacks, Tom Brady, who as aforementioned, was drafted as a catcher for the Expos, and Jared Goff, whose father was a catcher for the Expos and who played his final major league season the year after Montreal selected Brady. (Cameo fact from NBC Sports Chicago's Christopher Kamka).

NATIONAL LEAGUE CENTRAL

CHICAGO CUBS

Est. 1871

Claude Passeau tossed a complete game shutout against the Dodgers on June 7, 1946. The game was tied 0–0 in the bottom of the 9th inning when Passeau secured his own shutout, hitting a walkoff, two-run home run.

"Fly The W!"

"The Cubs have done it! The longest drought in the history of American sports is over!"—Pat Hughes, 670 WCSR Chicago

Prior to 2016, the Chicago Cubs had not won the World Series since 1908, which is a really long time. Just think—every 100 years, there is, essentially, a whole new batch of humans. For over a century, the names changed, but the story remained the same—the Cubs were losers. North Side Chicago fans leaned into it, though, and became the Lovable Losers of Major League Baseball, if not all of professional sports.

Beyond taking it in stride, Cubs fans seemed to take their fate as a point of cultural pride, clinging to their moribund destiny as they would a slice of Lou Malnati's sausage and pepperoni deep dish. They didn't root for failure; success just never became a prerequisite for love and appreciation. But maybe that's changed. The Cubbies couldn't pull off the big "W" again in 2017 or 2018, but they've maintained a consistent, championship level of success that might shift the fabric of the fans' cultural identity as swiftly as the franchise flipped the script in 2016.

After finishing in a virtual tie with the Milwaukee Brewers for the division in 2018, faltering in game No. 163, the Cubs captured a Wild Card spot and reached the postseason for the fourth consecutive time, a first for the 143-year old club, and this team has some serious winning roots.

Not to be confused with the crosstown White Sox, the Chicago White Stockings (they wouldn't be the "Cubs" until 1903) were there at the very beginning of organized baseball. They came together in 1871, and were charter members of the original National Association that eventually became the National League in 1876. The White Stockings, perhaps the most talented early franchise, added two very influential players in team, and baseball, history that first year—Al Spalding and Cap Anson.

Spalding was 252–65 over the course of his seven-year career (yep, that's 36 wins per year), but don't get too excited. He played in the age of underhand pitching, when called strikes were sometimes a mere suggestion, and the batters could announce where they wished the incoming pitch to be located. It's a natural evolutionary path for such a nuanced game, but it's important to remember, by modern standards, they were playing something like middle-school gym class softball. Still, Spalding was the best, and his .795 career winning percentage, in some circles, counts and is still a major-league record. But, his playing career doesn't even begin to explain his influence on the game.

He is still relevant today because of the sporting goods company he founded in Chicago that bears his name. He was one of the first players to use a glove in the field, and became one of the most influential visionaries in supplying what would quickly become a booming sporting goods market. To be fair, he's also the alleged architect of the unsubstantiated claim that Abner Doubleday invented the game, and that its birth was in Cooperstown, New York. Great stories sell product, and that was perhaps his motive. Great players, though, can also do the trick.

Cap Anson, Spalding's teammate and fellow Hall of Famer, was certainly one of the game's greatest, and most influential, players. His 27 seasons in Major League Baseball are still a record (tied with Nolan Ryan), and he was the very first member of the 3,000 hit club—even considering the fact that a variety of wild factors (in 1887, walks counted as hits) have Major League Baseball (3,081), MLB.com (3,011), and Baseball-Reference (3,435) all in disagreement over his actual hits total. His 20-year run as player/manager with Chicago saw the club win five pennants and reach two pre-Modern Era World Series. There was a tradition of success with Chicago baseball, and that continued into the 1900s.

No team was more successful during the first decade of the World Series era (1903) than the Cubs. From 1903–12, the team averaged 98 wins and 53 losses, for a .648 total winning percentage, which is higher than the Philadelphia Phillies have ever had for any one single season in their 133-year history. The Cubs appeared in half of the first eight World Series (1906–08, 1910), and were the first team with multiple wins (1907–08).

From there, things took a turn for the worse—for 108 years. And somehow, a goat was to blame.

You can take your pick of goats—traditional (fan, Steve Bartman, *maybe* interfering on a play that would have helped get the Cubs to the World Series in 2003), or literal (the "Curse of the Billy Goat" story about a man damning the Cubs after being forced to leave the game ... with his goat). Either way, it's hard to win a World Series, and when it doesn't happen for a lifetime—multiple lifetimes, even—peripheral factors tend to shoulder an illogical portion of the blame.

Over the years, iconic names have passed through Chicago's North Side, coming and going without a ring. From Grover Cleveland Alexander (named after President Cleveland, and later portrayed in a movie by would-be President Reagan) and Hack Wilson, to Ernie Banks, Ryne Sandberg, and Sammy Sosa. Fans still packed Wrigley Field regardless of the team's fate. The Cubs have only once finished in the bottom half of NL attendance rankings since 1983, and haven't finished among the bottom two since 1966. The field probably has something to do with it.

Considered among baseball's few *cathedrals*, Wrigley is a spectacle, and a throwback to an age that represents not only baseball's infancy, but the dawn of American sports culture overall. It opened in 1914 (originally, Weeghman Park) and, with a few exceptions, has managed to keep its traditions intact, even if its most iconic feature—the outfield ivy—wasn't added until a renovation in 1937. Fans love it, within city limits and beyond, as Wrigley is one of

The ChiFeds of the Federal League, playing during the inaugural season of Weeghman Park, famously known later as Wrigley Field. (Author unknown. 1914 US postcard.)

2014 Wrigley Field, Cubs vs. Reds, 100 years later. (Daniel Betts)

the nation's must-sees for any eager baseball fan. In consideration of total entertainment value, perhaps the experience trumps the team's performance.

Regardless, it would be a mistake to downplay the Cubs' commitment to win again. The franchise returned to the playoffs for the first time in seven years in 2015, and then finally won their elusive World Series in 2016. The Cubs look eager to give their fans something else to love about their Cubbies—a new, winning tradition.

"Baseball's Sad Lexicon"

The famed "Tinker to Evers to Chance" double-play infield highlighted those successful Cubs squads of the early 1900s, made famous by the poem, "Baseball's Sad Lexicon," by Franklin Pierce Adams (when poetry was still a thing). (Joe) Tinker, (Johnny) Evers, and (Frank) Chance were all career sub-.790

OPS players, but Hall of Famers, still—the Cubbies were that infamous.

Shortstop Tinker still ranks tops in franchise history in defensive WAR (29.7), more than the second and third-ranked Cubs combined (Billy Jurges, 15.1; Ryne Sandberg, 13.6). He batted just .266/.307/.391 in 1908, but still registered a higher WAR that season (7.8) than Sammy Sosa did during his famous 66-homer MVP campaign in 1998 (6.5).

Evers ranks fifth all-time in franchise history for defensive WAR (12.8), and was a decent, if unspectacular, .270/.356/.334 career hitter. Chance, however, picked up the offensive slack, batting .297/.394/.395, and, in franchise WAR, ranks as the Cubs' top first baseman of the Modern Era (45.5).

Mr. Cub

Ernie Banks was no borderline Hall of Famer. Arguably the franchise's greatest player, Banks redefined the shortstop position. With apologies to Joe Tinker, Banks was a beast.

The 19-year lifetime Cub (1953–71) ranks first in franchise history in extra-base hits (1,009) and second in home runs (512) and RBIs (1,636). Banks was the Cubs' first black player to appear in a game, and was one of baseball's first shortstops to break the mold at his position (even though he played more career games at first base . . . never matter).

Banks was the first member of the 500 home run club to spend significant time at shortstop, and was actually the very first shortstop to hit even 250. He had four straight seasons with at least 40 home runs from 1957–60, while former National League home run champs Henry Aaron and Willie Mays never had more than two straight. Four times he led the league in extra-base hits, again besting Mays (two) and current home run king, Barry Bonds (three).

At the time of his retirement in 1971, Banks ranked tops all-time in home runs as a shortstop (277), which was just 54.1 percent of his career 512 homers.

Slammin' Sammy

Sammy Sosa's nickname is a fun homonym that works both as an ode to his tremendous home run production, and as a bashing, or slam, of his character.

Alleged steroid use aside, the controversial Cubs outfielder had one of the greatest offensive runs in baseball history. Through Major League Baseball's first 122 years (1876–1997), only one player hit as many as 61 home runs in a single season (Roger Maris; 61, 1961). Then, over a four-year stretch, from 1998–2001, Sosa *averaged* 61 homers. His 1.058 OPS during that period is higher than any one single-season OPS from Hall of Fame outfielders Willie Stargell, Rickey Henderson, or Reggie Jackson.

He's the top home run hitter in franchise history (545), and is third in RBIs (1,414). His 609 bombs overall are good for ninth in MLB history. And he owes it all to a sudden, tremendous uptick in production during the second half of his career.

Through his first nine seasons, Sosa averaged a per-162 game average of 31 home runs and 96 RBIs. His final nine seasons, the slugger bumped those per-162 averages to 52 home runs and 132 RBIs.

He owns 37.5 percent of all 60-home run seasons in baseball history (three of eight), and that figure is unlikely to change anytime soon, as the game has since shifted into a decidedly pitching-friendly age.

2016

Everything came together perfectly for the Cubs in 2016.

After an extraordinary Cy Young season in 2015 (22–6, 1.77 ERA), Jake Arrieta was probably the third-best pitcher on the 2016 Cubs, behind Jon Lester (19–5, 2.44) and Kyle Hendricks (16–8, 2.13). The trio headlined a truly historical rotation.

In terms of starting pitching, the Cubs had the lowest WHIP of the Modern Era (1.067), 14th-lowest ERA (2.96), third-lowest OBP against (.279), and fifth-best win percentage (.675). Twelve pitchers had a WHIP below 1.100 in 2016, and one-third of them pitched for the Cubs (Hendricks, Lester, Arrieta, John Lackey). While starting pitching was probably their most valuable asset, third baseman Kris Bryant was their most valuable player.

Bryant backed up a Rookie of the Year award in 2015 by winning MVP honors in 2016, leading the league in runs scored (121) and finishing third in home runs (39). He posted Major League Baseball's highest ever WAR through two seasons (13.5; Frank Robinson, 13.4; Ted Williams, 13.0). He also became the first player in baseball history to start his career with back-to-back 25-homer/75-walk seasons.

On June 27 of that year, Bryant pulled a rare feat when he became just the ninth player of the Live Ball Era with five extra-base hits in a single game.

Infielder Javier Baez, who finished second in MVP voting in 2018, had only 450 plate appearances in 2016, his first full season in the bigs. Still, his potential and versatility was on display, becoming the first player with at least 10 homers and 10 stolen bases while playing at least 25 games at second, third, and shortstop since Frankie Frisch in 1925.

Bryant and Baez, both under Cubs control through 2021, should be the National League's most formidable pair over the next few seasons. Baez has turned the corner and Bryant, despite multiple DL trips in 2018, still has the highest ever WAR for a Cubs position player through his first four seasons (21.6).

Chicago, outfielder Ian Happ hit the very first pitch of the 2018 season for a home run. The Cubs defeated the Marlins, 8–4. (Mary Chastain)

STATS INCREDIBLE!

2: In 2015, Kris Bryant became the first Cubs rookie with multiple walk-off home runs in a season since Gabby Hartnett in 1923 (two, each).

2.26: Jake Arrieta's FIP (fielding independent pitching) in 2014—the best by a Cubs pitcher with at least 150 innings since Grover Cleveland Alexander in 1919.

151: Sammy Sosa's OPS+ in 1999, and Wade Boggs's OPS+ with Boston in 1985. Sosa hit 63 home runs, while Boggs hit just eight.

163: Average games played per season by Cubs Hall of Famer Billy Williams over a five-year stretch from 1965–69. In fact, he averaged 162.25 games played from 1963–70.

4: The number of seasons Ernie Banks had a 7.5+ WAR—more than Sosa (one) and Derek Jeter (two), combined.

120: Cap Anson's RBI total as a member of the Colts/Cubs in 1891. At thirty-nine years old, he's the oldest player in baseball history to lead the league.

.339: Hall of Fame catcher Gabby Hartnett batted at least this high for three separate seasons during his 19-year Cubs career (1922–40). No other catcher during the Modern Era had more than two such seasons.

1896: On July 29, 2014, backup catcher John Baker took the mound for the Cubs in the 16th inning, making him the first Cub to pitch and catch in the same season since Malachi Kittridge in 1896.

9: Earned runs surrendered by Jake Arrieta in the second half of 2015 (107.1 IP). His 0.75 ERA was the lowest for any half in baseball history. Former teammate Jeff Samardzija had three starts with at least nine earned runs surrendered that year.

Blackjack: In 2018, Javy Baez became the first player in baseball history to hit at least 21 home runs and steal 21-plus bases during a season in which he played 21 or more games at second base, third base, and shortstop.

13+: Javy Baez is just one of two players in baseball history to homer in the 13th, 14th, and 15th innings. The other:

Willie Mays. Baez and Mays each have 12th-inning home runs, too, for good measure.

1930: In 2018, Anthony Rizzo became the first left-handed throwing player to appear at second base, third base, and pitcher during his career since George Sisler, who last played in 1930.

99: Kris Bryant's RBI total in 2015, the most by a Cubs rookie since Charles Irwin had a franchise rookie record 100 RBIs in 1894.

3: Career seasons by Anthony Rizzo with at least 25 home runs and 20 times hit by pitch, most in baseball history.

61: From 2014 to 2016, Jon Lester had 61 strikeouts to 55 walks . . . after falling behind 2–0 in the count.

6: In 2018, Cole Hamels became the first in-season acquisition in baseball history to allow one run or fewer in each of his first six starts with his new team.

31: Jake Arrieta had 31-start stretch from June 21, 2015 to May 31, 2017 during which he had more no-hitters (two) than games lost (one). He was 25–1 during that span with a 1.09 ERA.

M. BROWN. J. PFEISTER A. HOFMAN C.G. WILLIAMS O. OVERALL. E. REULBACH. J. KLING.
H. GESSLER. J. TAYLOR. H. STEINFELDT. J. McCORMICK. F. CHANCE. J. SHECKARD. P. MORAN. F. SCHULTE.
C. LUNDGREN. T. WALSH. J. EVERS. J. SLAGLE. J. TINKER.

CHICAGO NATIONAL LEAGUE BALL CLUB 1906

The 1906 Cubs, featuring the famed double-play unit of Tinker, Evers, and Chance. (George Lawrence Company)

CINCINNATI REDS

Est. 1881

The 1975 world champion Reds are the only Live Ball Era (post-1919) team on which every pitcher had a winning record.

Funny story: The franchise, known early on as the Red Stockings, got its start because of a weird exile of the former National League Cincinnati Reds—a totally unaffiliated franchise. Why did the NL Reds get booted? They were selling beer during games, and playing on Sundays. *SACRILEGE!*

Crazy, but rules are rules, right?

Well . . .

The Reds hadn't actually broken any at the time of their ousting. While the drinking and sabbath rules would eventually go into effect soon after, the Reds, at the time, had merely broken a gentlemen's agreement. Either way, it was enough to get the franchise voted out prior to the 1881 season.

By 1882, the Red Stockings of Cincinnati surfaced in the new American Association, eventually joining the National League in 1890 as the Reds—shiny and new.

The Reds had a rough go of it early on, never finishing higher than third place in any of the club's first 29 years in the NL (1890–1918)—and they only finished that high on four separate occasions.

Hall of Famer Edd Roush led the Reds in 1919 to their first championship—but even that was dubious. The Reds were good, but their opponent, the Chicago White Sox, were a *great* club, which just amplified the evidence that certain Chicago players conspired to throw the Series (see *Black Sox Scandal*; Chicago White Sox). It's one of those rare World Series championships in that it just *kinda-sorta* counts—which made 1940 so important.

That season, Cincinnati won its first controversy-free championship, with a solid, if unspectacular, squad led by the league's best player, Bucky Walters.

Walters isn't exactly a household name, but he's in good company with all-time greats like Cy Young, Walter Johnson, and Sandy Koufax, as Walters won pitching's Triple Crown in 1939, with an NL-best 27 wins, 2.29 ERA, and 137 strikeouts. In 1940 (22 Ws, 2.48 ERA, 115 Ks), Walters finished just 12 strikeouts short of a second straight Crown, but the World Series ring was probably a suitable substitute.

The Reds fell back to mediocrity soon after, winning just one pennant, with a fifth-place average finish, over the following 29 years. They weren't bad—Hall of Famer Frank Robinson had some of his best years during his decade with the team (1956–65), but the Reds struggled to build around him. As it turned out, they ended up building a juggernaut *without* him.

Cincinnati's farm system produced Hall of Famers Pete Rose (1963), Tony Perez (1964), and Johnny Bench (1967) in the 1960s, bolstering the Reds' offense, even with the departure of Robinson in 1965. By 1970, with new skipper Sparky Anderson at the helm, the new-look Reds generation was starting to take shape. Cincinnati was suddenly bigger, redder, and . . . *machinier.*

The Big Red Machine

The Reds made it back to the World Series in 1970, a losing effort to the Baltimore Orioles (4–1). Over the next six years, however, the Reds would play in three more, winning two, while cementing a legacy as one of the greatest collections of talent in baseball history: *The Big Red Machine.*

Sure, **Frank Robinson** was a huge loss. To date, only four Reds (just once apiece) have had a season with at least a .300 batting average, 30 home runs, and 100 RBI, season since Robinson *averaged* a .303 batting average with 32 home runs and 101 RBIs for his entire 10-year Reds career. The team might not have ever replaced him, man-for-man, but they certainly overcompensated, peppering nearly every position with Hall of Fame-caliber talent.

Pete Rose, a.k.a. "Charlie Hustle," a.k.a. "Hit King," a.k.a. "That Guy Banned from Baseball" (never mind that), was the key cog of the Machine. He was already well-established by 1970, coming off two straight batting titles, and averaging 204 hits the previous five years. Barry Bonds never had more than 181 hits in any single season.

There were times during Rose's 24-year career when he was the best—three-time batting champion, seven-time league leader in hits, 17-time All-Star, and 1973 NL MVP—but Rose's legacy was in his ability to outplay, outlast, and out-hustle pretty much every other player to ever step onto the field. He never batted .400 (or even .350), or swatted 50 homers (or even 20), but he was consistent. *Every. Single. Day.*

He reached base safely in 2,993 games in his career, and only seven other players in history have even played that many—Willie Mays, with 2,992, is not one of them.

The all time hit king finished with 4,256 for his career—more than the top 17 single-season hits totals in MLB history combined.

Rose was the kind of player every team likes to build around—a "Moneyball" guy that, even when sporting a poor batting average, could still produce. He batted just .272 in his forties, but with it, a better on-base percentage (.355) than Dave Winfield had during his entire career (.353).

Rose had three seasons with at least 150 singles, 50 extra-base hits, and 75 walks. Wade Boggs is the only player ever with more (four). No other player had even two. Rose's six seasons with at least 150 singles and 50 extra-base hits are the most all-time.

Tony Perez and **Johnny Bench** were the other holdovers from the '60s to make up the offensive machine. Perez's career numbers aren't astounding for his position (.279 BA, 379 HRs in 23 years), but he led all National League first basemen in homers in the 1970s (226) with almost 200 more RBIs (954) than any other first bagger. He wasn't an all-timer, but he was best for his time. Bench, on the other hand, was just a flat-out rock star.

While Mike Piazza has the most home runs by primary catchers (427), Bench (389), with a 75.2 career WAR, blows away Piazza (59.6) and every other catcher in history, in the WAR category. He's one of only five catchers ever with a 40-homer season, and he did it twice, setting the all-time single-season record for his position in the process (45; 1970).

Across all positions, Bench was second to only Willie Stargell in NL home runs during the 1970s, and was the only player in the game to accumulate 1,000 RBIs during the decade (1,013).

Second baseman **Joe Morgan** was the final major cog in the Big Red Machine—with due respect to nine-time All-Star, and five-time Gold Glove shortstop Dave Concepción; 1977 NL MVP George Foster, whose 52 home runs and 149 RBIs that season were both MLB highs for the decade; or Ken Griffey Sr. who, in 1976, became just the second player in Reds history to bat at least .330 with 30 stolen bases (.336 BA, 34 SBs) ... Too much talent, not enough pages.

Morgan turned out to be the difference maker, landing in Cincinnati via trade in November 1972, taking the Reds' production, and his own career, to new levels.

Until that point, Morgan was just a .263/.375/.396 hitter in nine years with Houston. The next eight years with Cincy, Morgan won five Gold Gloves, and MVPs in back-to-back seasons (1975–76), doing things that 5-foot-7, 160-lb. middle infielders aren't supposed to do.

Morgan (1976) and Hack Wilson (1929–30) are the only two players under 68 inches tall to record a 1.000 OPS season. And Morgan is the lightest player to ever do it. Since 1903, only two players under 5 foot 8—Morgan and Paul Waner—have had a .435+ on-base percentage season. *And Morgan averaged .438 over a four-year span, from 1974–77.*

Taking size out of it, Morgan was still a very unique player. In his career, he had four seasons with at least 50 extra-base hits, 50 stolen bases, and 100 bases on balls. Every other player in baseball history combined have . . . ZERO. Over five seasons, from 1972–76, Little Joe averaged a mammoth 10.44 WAR per 162 games played. Hammerin' Hank Aaron had a heck of a career, but he never had a WAR that high in any single one of his 23 seasons.

The Big Red Machine averaged 98 wins per season from 1970–76, winning titles in back-to-back seasons—the last NL squad to do so—in 1975 and 1976, Morgan's MVP seasons.

By 1980, the Machine was effectively dismantled. Only Bench, Concepción, Foster, and Griffey remained of the "Great Eight," and the franchise wouldn't win another title until a ragtag group of new kids took home the hardware in 1990.

The Nasty Boys

It's both correct and incorrect to call the 1990 squad the first Reds team since 1979 to finish in first place. In 1981, Cincy finished with the best record in baseball, but a midseason strike shortened play, and split the season into two independent halves. The leaders of each half moved on to the playoffs. Even though the Reds had the best record in baseball, they didn't lead after either half, and thus didn't participate in the playoffs. Dumb? Yep. Moving on . . .

The 1990 Reds were a club that was probably greater than the sum of its parts. Aside from Silver Slugger-winning shortstop Barry Larkin, the team was rather benign on offense. José Rijo (14–8, 2.70 ERA) and Jack Armstrong (12–9, 3.42 ERA) led a decent rotation, but the real difference maker was the bullpen—heck, even the NLCS MVPs were Reds penmates, Rob Dibble and Randy Myers, who surrendered zero runs and just two hits to the Pirates in 10⅔ innings.

The bullpen, specifically Dibble (1.74 ERA), Myers (2.08), and Norm Charlton (3.02 in relief), referred to themselves as the *Nasty Boys*, and their offerings certainly reflected the moniker.

Dibble (136) and Myers (98) finished 1–2 in baseball in relief strikeouts. In the National League, no bullpen duo had a better combined ERA (1.90). Unfortunately, it proved unsustainable.

Dibble had more 100-plus strikeout, sub-100 inning seasons (four) than anyone in baseball history, and had a phenomenal 1.82 ERA and .185 batting average against over his first 200 games. But injuries would limit his MLB career to just seven seasons. While Myers pitched a full career, his ERA was a pedestrian 3.56 in eight seasons after 1990.

The '90 squad may have been a flash in the pan, but Larkin sure wasn't.

Larkin to Votto

Barry Larkin (1986–2004), a lifetime Red, played during the heart of the steroid era. While he won nine Silver Sluggers and an MVP, while making 12 All-Star teams, the last quarter of his career seemed to be a showcase of shortstops flexing their muscles.

Larkin's career numbers were dwarfed by power-hitting shortstops like Alex Rodriguez and Miguel Tejada early in the 2000s. Larkin, a seemingly clean player, maybe because of this, was not a first-ballot Hall of Famer. But he could have been.

Barry Larkin's display at the National Baseball Hall of Fame. At the center, his 1995 NL MVP Award. (Kevin Durso)

Among players that just played shortstop, Larkin has the third-highest career WAR in baseball history (70.4). During a four-year stretch from 1995–98, Larkin maintained a .921 OPS. Up to that point in the National League, Woody English, Arky Vaughan, Ernie Banks, and Honus Wagner were the only shortstops to put up an OPS that high in a single season. That's good company.

In Larkin's 19-year career, he only twice played in the postseason. First baseman Joey Votto, currently a twelve-year Red entering the 2019 season, has three trips so far, but no rings. It hasn't been his fault.

Votto is one of the best batsmen in the game today, but it's what he does keeping the bat on his shoulder that puts him in the all-time categories.

Through 12 years in the majors, he's led the league in on-base percentage seven times. Only Rogers Hornsby (nine), Babe Ruth (10), Barry Bonds (10), and Ted Williams (12) did so more, and his

.427 career OBP ranks 12th best all time. Each leg of his overall slash line of .311/.427/.530 is topped only by Hall of Famers Williams, Jimmie Foxx, Lou Gehrig, Hornsby, and Ruth.

The wildly underappreciated Votto has rarely gotten the help he needs. Despite batting .340/.503/.601 in 1,355 plate appearances with RISP since 2010, he's averaged just 79 RBIs per season during that stretch. The numbers on the back of his baseball card don't accurately reflect his value on the field.

Perhaps the most impressive thing about Joey Votto is his control over the lumber: he has seen 27,668 pitches over 6,764 plate appearances in his career and he has never popped out to the catcher, pitcher, or first baseman.

STATS INCREDIBLE!

189: The career strikeout total of former NL MVP and eight-time All-Star McCormick. Cubs rookie Kris Bryant had 199 during 2015 alone.

100.3: Average speed (MPH) of an Aroldis Chapman fastball in 2014.

105.1: MPH of a Chapman fastball on September 24, 2010, against the San Diego Padres. It's the fastest verified pitch in history *and* Cincinnati's Country Music Station, B-105.1.

106: Batters struck out by Chapman over 54 innings in 2014. It's the best season K% (52.5) and K/9 (17.67) in history among pitchers with at least 50 innings.

100/100: The Pete Rose–managed 1987 Reds are the only team in history with 100 home runs and 100 stolen bases from outfielders (102 HRs, 120 SBs).

115: Runs scored by Rose in 1973. He was not thrown out at home once.

490: Career hits by Rose off of would-be Hall of Fame pitchers. He batted .303 against them.

224: Rose had 224 more multi-hit games (1,225) than no-hit games (1,001) in his career. Among those 1,001 games in which he failed to hit safely, he reached base safely in 432 of them.

2: Number of seasons Joey Votto has accumulated at least 20 home runs and 135 walks. Only Barry Bonds (six), Ted Williams (seven), and Babe Ruth (eight) have done it more.

16: Sam Crawford's MLB-leading home run total in 1901. A dozen of them were inside-the-park.

50/100: In 697 plate appearances, from May 27, 1986, to July 10, 1987, Eric Davis had 50 home runs and 100 stolen bases. Perspective: Derek Jeter averaged 697 plate appearances from 1996–2012.

.440: Joey Votto led the league in on-base percentage in 2010, 2011, 2012, 2013, 2016, 2017, and 2018. He had a .440 on-base percentage from 2014–2015, the two-year stretch during which he failed to capture the on-base crown.

1: On June 6, 2017, Scooter Gennett became the only player in baseball history with at least five hits, including four homers, and 10 or more RBIs in a game.

105: Homer Bailey has gone 18–32 over 69 starts with a 5.27 ERA and -1.2 WAR since signing his $105MM contract in February 2014. Opponents have batted .291/.353/.468 against him during the duration of his contract.

5: Number of seasons in which Joey Votto has led the league in times safely on base, tied with Barry Bonds for eighth most all-time. Pete Rose leads the way with nine.

7: Joey Votto has had seven seasons in which he batted at least .305/.410/.525 over 400-plus plate appearances. Every other player in Reds franchise history has seven combined.

Cincinnati Reds first baseman Joey Votto has led the National League in on-base percentage in 2010, 2011, 2012, 2013, 2016, 2017, and 2018. He had a .440 on-base percentage from 2014–15, the two-year gap missing during this incredible stretch. (Ian D'Andrea, CC BY-SA 2.0 [https://creativecommons.org/licenses/by-sa/2.0], via Flickr)]

MILWAUKEE BREWERS

Est. 1969

Christian Yelich knocked in 75 runs over his final 74 games of the 2018 season. He batted .367/.444/.727 with a .486 wOBA and 209 wRC+ during that stretch and became the first player in franchise history to win a batting title.

Milwaukee lost the Braves in 1966, and seemed like a good candidate for an expansion team in 1969. Instead, Seattle was awarded the designation, where the Pilots spent just one single season. But, Milwaukee and an ownership group headed by Bud Selig were persistent.

Financial woes killed the Pilots after just one season, and Milwaukee pounced in the eleventh hour, officially obtaining the franchise with just six days to go until Opening Day. To their credit, the Brewers group was prepared, but it's hard to imagine a team could pull this off today. Imagine selling the public on a new baseball team, a week before the start of the season, that doesn't yet exist. Uniforms were the only real concession, as the Brewers basically had to go with a simple variant of the Pilots jersey, with a color scheme that remained essentially unchanged for years.

The Brewers have been a success in Milwaukee, in the sense that the team is still there. From a competitiveness standpoint, it has been a struggle.

Aside from several respectable spurts of competitiveness, the Brewers have only made the postseason five times, with just one league championship in their history. On the bright side, Miller Park looks to be one of the true success stories in new stadium construction, and a real asset for Milwaukee.

In Milwaukee's 18 seasons at Miller Park, it has finished at least in the top half, or better, in league attendance when finishing over .500. That wasn't always the case at County Stadium. In the 10 seasons in which the Brewers finished over .500 in their old digs, they only finished in the top half in league attendance rankings five times. Surely, when the Brewers have been able to put talent on the field, the public has responded favorably.

The Brewers' best run came during a six-year stretch from 1978–83 as they made two postseason appearances, including one trip to the World Series (1982; L – St. Louis Cardinals), while compiling a .564 win percentage (91–71 per 162 games). Hall of Famers and 3,000 hit club members **Robin Yount** *(SS, OF, 1974–93)* and **Paul Molitor** *(3B, 1978–92)* highlighted those Brewers squads, but they never sealed the deal.

Currently, the Brewers have much different uniforms, a new venue, and even a new league (NL, since 1998), but they've enjoyed recent runs that hearken back to the "glory" days. In 2011, they won a franchise-best 96 games and tied that mark in 2018, reaching the NLCS in both seasons.

AL Brew Crew

Robin Yount (shortstop/center field) and Paul Molitor (third base) are the only two Brewers representatives in the Hall of Fame, and spent a combined 35 years with the organization, 15 of which they shared, playing together from 1978–92.

Yount finished his 20-year career, start-to-finish in Milwaukee, in rare company. He is one of just five players in history with at least 3,000 hits, 250 home runs, and 250 stolen bases, along with Craig Biggio, Derek Jeter, Rickey Henderson, and Willie Mays.

The two-time MVP is one of just four players (Hank Greenberg, Stan Musial, Alex Rodriguez) to win the award at multiple positions (shortstop, outfield). Yount (583) and Baltimore's Cal Ripken Jr. (603) are the only primary shortstops in baseball history with over 550 career doubles.

Where Yount stands very much alone is in franchise history, as he ranks first in games played (2,856), runs scored (1,632), hits (3,142), total bases (4,730), doubles (583), and triples (126)—all categories in which Molitor ranks second.

It wasn't that Molitor was necessarily a lesser player than Yount—certainly, the case could be made both ways—but he simply didn't play as long in Milwaukee. Molitor's career overall was pretty special.

Only Barry Bonds, Ty Cobb, and Honus Wagner (heard of 'em?) join Molitor in the 900 extra-base hit, 500 stolen base club. He was not much of a power guy, slugging just 160 home runs during his 15-year Milwaukee career, but he didn't need to be. Instead, Molitor built a Hall of Fame career as a doubles hitter.

No one hit more doubles than Molitor over a 10-year stretch from 1987–96 (344) and, in 1987 particularly, Molitor led the league with 41 doubles, despite playing just 118 games due to injury.

The versatile infielder/DH hit 114 triples and 234 home runs, while stealing 504 bases in his career. No other player in history has more of each.

NL Brew Crew

Milwaukee, which was home to the NL Braves for 13 seasons (1953–65), opted to switch its Brewers to the National League in 1998, after the expansion Tampa Bay Devil Rays and Arizona Diamondbacks created an odd number of teams in each league. While this is not a problem today, Major League Baseball, at the time, was still protecting intraleague play.

The NL version of the Brewers didn't finish over .500 until 2008, but once over the hump, they've had decent runs with some of the game's best players.

The 2011 squad had been the most successful in team history, with 96 victories, winning its first playoff series. However, the team's prosperity proved short-lived, as the team would average just 76 wins per season over the next five years.

Ryan Braun captured the NL MVP in 2011, with teammate Prince Fielder finishing third for the award, but it would be Fielder's final season in Milwaukee, as he would leave for a $214 million payday in Detroit.

Regardless, Fielder had some brilliant seasons in Milwaukee, posting an OPS+ that was 51 percent above league average from 2007 to 2011, averaging 40 home runs per season, including a franchise record 50 in 2007. He is also the franchise's all-time leader in on-base percentage (.390) and slugging percentage (.540).

Ryan Braun, after another brilliant season in 2012, has seen his production diminish—along with his reputation—in the wake of his PED suspension. He is Milwaukee's all-time leader in home runs (322), but is now more of a role player than the superstar he once was.

Their 2017 season had some positive steps forward, as Domingo Santana, Travis Shaw, and Eric Thames became the first Brewers trio each with 30 homers in a season since Cecil Cooper, Ben Oglivie, and Gorman Thomas in 1982. They improved to 86 wins, but they were still missing a few pieces.

Enter newcomers Christian Yelich and Lorenzo Cain, who in 2018 finished 1–2 in position player WAR (7.6 and 6.9,

Ryan Braun was the 2007 Rookie of the Year. (Steve Paluch, CC BY 2.0 [http://creativecommons.org/licenses/by-sa/2.0], via Wikimedia Commons)

respectively). They are the first Brewers teammates in history to finish a season with as many WAR. They improved to a club-record 96 wins (T- 2011), reaching the NLCS and falling just one game shy of the World Series.

The Brewers should be able to make this last. Yelich and Cain are under contract through at least 2021, while Milwaukee still has several years of control remaining on key players such as Jesus Aguilar and Travis Shaw. And on the bump, they boasted one of the best bullpens in the NL a year ago, finishing tops in K/9 (10.4) and second in ERA (3.47). The average age of their top five pitchers in relief innings last year is just 27.

This is a franchise on the rise.

Stats Incredible!

11: Total Milwaukee Brewers to reach double-digit steal totals in 1992, a single-season Modern Era record.

8: Consecutive games, from August 20, 2012 to August 28, 2012, in which the Brewers struck out double-digit batters, the longest streak in MLB history.

565: The combined weight, in pounds, of teammates Prince Fielder and CC Sabathia (2008). Per official weight records, the two are the heaviest hitter-pitcher combo in major-league history.

2: The amount of four-hit games by Robin Yount during the 1982 World Series. He's the only player with multiple four-hit World Series games for a *career*.

.095: Jim Abbott, in his offensive career (24 PAs in 1999), had three sac bunts, two hits, and three RBIs, batting .095/.095/.095. All of his hits and RBIs came off of Jon Lieber. He also pitched a no-hitter for the Yankees in 1993, despite the challenge of having been born with no right hand.

2: Number of career inside-the-park home runs for Prince Fielder (275 or more lbs.), exactly twice as many as stolen base king Rickey Henderson had.

430: Batters faced by Ben Sheets in 2006. He fell behind just nine of them, 3–0. He came back to strike out four while walking just one.

46.6: Strikeout percentage by Josh Hader in 2018. It's the highest ever by a pitcher who faced at least 300 batters.

0: Lorenzo Cain has 114.0 defensive runs saved and a 63.2 ultimate zone rating during his career. Somehow, he has never been awarded a Gold Glove.

5: Christian Yelich became one of just five players in history with multiple cycles in a season in 2018, joining Aaron Hill (2012, D-backs), Babe Herman (1931, Robins), Tip O'Neill (1887, Brown Stockings), and John Reilly (1883, Red Stockings).

1894: In 2013, Carlos Gomez and Jean Segura became the first teammates with at least 20 doubles, 10 triples, 10 home runs, and 40 stolen bases each since Jimmy Bannon and Hugh Duffy in 1894.

8: On April 30, 2018, Josh Hader became the first pitcher in baseball history with at least eight strikeouts during a game in which every out he recorded was a strikeout.

PITTSBURGH PIRATES

Est. 1882

Roberto Clemente batted .328/.369/.488 with 104 runs, 201 hits, 35 doubles, nine triples, 15 home runs, 102 runs batted in, one stolen base, 11 outfield assists, and just one error during the final 162 games of his career.

Baseball's Modern Era (beginning 1900) is such an important distinction in baseball history. Before this time, the critical rules of the game were still being defined.

For much of Pittsburgh's early years, it mired in mediocrity, never finishing in first place in any pre-Modern Era season. History gives the team a pass, however, as its failures occurred during a time when walks required as many as nine balls, and bats could be flat on one side (shocking, literally). Whatever happened pre-1900 isn't particularly lauded or condemned today. It just . . . happened.

Very few people know much about Pud Galvin, Hall of Famer and known PED user (monkey testosterone), Pittsburgh's best player of the era (1885–89, 1891–92), but the Hall of Famer turned out to be baseball's first 300-game winner (365 Ws). To be fair, probably very few know about baseball's first 300-game *loser* back then, either . . . Oh. Wait. Yeah, that's Pud Galvin, too (310 Ls). It was a wacky period.

To the franchise's credit, when the modern game *did* finally start to take shape, and the American League formed in 1901, launching the framework for the Major League Baseball we now know and love ... Pittsburgh immediately stepped up as the game's best.

Pittsburgh won its first two league titles in 1901–02, and played in the first World Series in 1903, falling to the Boston Americans in a best-of-nine (5–3). Hall of Fame shortstop Honus Wagner, unlike Galvin, propelled the Pirates at a time that history would remember fondly.

Wagner joined the club in 1900 and proceeded to lead the team in WAR every season until 1910 (8.3 average). He led the Buccos to their first World Series championship in 1909, and laid the foundation for success that would stretch over several decades. The Pirates, while not regular champions, were seemingly always in the hunt.

In the Modern Era, the Pirates didn't have their 10th sub-.500 season until 1946. Meanwhile, their NL foe, Boston Braves, had reached their 10th sub-.500 campaign by 1911. Things always seemed to turn out well for Pittsburgh.

In 1960, bookended by two sub-80-win seasons, the Pirates came from nowhere to win the pennant (95–59), defeating the Yankees by way of Bill Mazeroski's famous Game 7-ending home run—the only walk-off in Game 7 history. Outfielder Roberto Clemente had his first All-Star season that year, and, much like Wagner a half-century prior, had ignited the charge for another long, successful, Buccos run.

The Pirates thrice won 90 games in the decade following the 1960 title, carrying momentum into the 1970s, when the Pirates excelled. From 1970–79, Pittsburgh played in the NLCS six times, winning the World Series twice (1971, 1979).

[Musical note: The Pirates' theme song that 1979 championship season was "We Are Family" by Sister Sledge, a Philadelphia group. By 1979, the Phillies were mired in a 96-year championship drought. Just thinking maybe Pittsburgh should have let Philly have that one.]

Since Pittsburgh's glorious '70s, things have been mostly rough for the club. They had Barry Bonds, but lost him before he became *BARRY BONDS*. Then they opened the beautiful PNC Park in 2001, but wasted its new-stadium smell, as the franchise was smack dab in the middle of a 20-year sub-.500 stretch of complete futility (1993–2012).

The 2013 NL MVP Andrew McCutchen led the Buccos to three straight postseason appearances from 2013–2015, but Pittsburgh never made it as far as the NLCS. With a 2018 offseason trade of McCutchen to the Giants, the Pirates essentially shelved the Jolly Roger and raised the white flag.

The Flying Dutchman

The New Bill James Historical Baseball Abstract, a book by rock star baseball historian Bill James, covers pretty much everything that ever happened in baseball history in incredible detail. And, in certain spots, it reads like a desperate plea to anoint Honus Wagner as one of the very best players to step into a batter's box.

Willie Mays, Ty Cobb, Ted Williams—all great players. But, according to James, when it comes to Wagner, only Babe Ruth was better. Who knew? Wagner is perhaps penalized for playing during baseball's unsexy Deadball Era, however.

Popularity aside, the Dutchman's stats back the claim:

- In National League history, ranks first in triples (252), and fourth in hits (3,420), doubles (643), and stolen bases (723).
- Won eight batting titles, tied with Tony Gwynn for the most in NL history.
- Was the only NL player during baseball's Modern Era to bat at least .325 with 500 or more stolen bases (.328, 629 SBs).
- Had twice as many seasons with at least 35 doubles and 35 stolen bases than any other player in baseball history (eight)—as many as Ty Cobb (four), "Shoeless" Joe Jackson (two), and Vlad Guerrero (two), combined.

Wagner played before Babe Ruth broke all the rules and home run records. While it doesn't show in his career home run total (101), he was one of the game's elite power hitters when sluggers were primarily keeping balls inside the park.

The mug, and infamous schnoz, of Honus Wagner; 1914. (Charles M. Conlon)

The Flying Dutchman led the league in slugging percentage eight times in his career, and was third in the National League in home runs during his Pirates career (82 HRs; 1900–17). Spanning baseball's Modern Era, Wagner is the only NL player with a .460+ slugging (.468) while hitting fewer than 100 home runs (minimum 4,000 plate appearances). And all this from a predominantly defensive position.

In baseball history, only two shortstops have led the league in every slash-line category (batting average/on-base percentage/

slugging percentage)—both Pirates. Arky Vaughan was the last to do it in 1935 (.385/.491/.607), while Wagner did it THREE TIMES, in 1904 (.349/.423./.520), 1907 (.350/.408/.513), and 1908 (.354/.415/.542).

The Family

The Pirates won the NL East six times in the 1970s, culminating in a 1979 championship behind a galvanizing theme.

"The Family" was etched in the dugout roof, and first baseman Willie Stargell selected the popular disco hit "We Are Family" as the team's theme. The idea was mutually beneficial to the team, and song—national exposure of the single during the Pirates' playoff run helped Sister Sledge sell over a million copies of their album that year. For the Pirates, at least, the family was a long time in the making.

Roberto Clemente *(OF, 1955–72)*: There are plenty of icons in baseball history, and Clemente is one of the most revered. The 12-time Gold Glove outfielder, four-time batting champ, 3,000 hit club member, and 1966 MVP is, to this day, a hero in the Latin community. Sadly, he died in a plane crash in 1972 off the coast of Puerto Rico, on his way to Nicaragua, to help aid earthquake victims. He had finished his previous season with exactly 3,000 hits, but his legacy was about more than numbers.

The vocal black-Latino often said he felt doubly discriminated against, but the burden never showed. Baseball and life were two games Clemente had mastered. He played relentlessly, like his life depended on it, and died helping people whose lives were dependent on his charitable endeavors. The Hall of Fame honored him with enshrinement in 1973, making him one of just three players in baseball history to break the five-year waiting period (Babe Ruth, Lou Gehrig). His No. 21 jersey might some day join Jackie Robinson's No. 42 in universal MLB retirement.

But, about those numbers . . .

Clemente (94.5) is behind just Honus Wagner (120.2) in franchise career WAR. Oddly enough, the two each played exactly 2,433 games with Pittsburgh, with Clemente totaling just nine fewer plate appearances.

He had good speed, leading all of baseball in triples during his 18-year stretch in the bigs (166). Willie Mays was second, but 48 triples behind. Despite all those triples, Clemente only stole 83 career bases. Rickey Henderson had five *seasons* with more stolen bases than that, but had just 66 career triples. Clemente hit 85 triples just after his thirtieth birthday.

The 1973 season was a sudden passing of the torch, as newcomer Dave Parker was tasked with replacing a legend in right field, and Willie Stargell had to step up as the team's main attraction.

Dave Parker *(OF, 1973–83):* "Cobra" started with a bang, batting .318 through his first six years in the big leagues. After his first four full seasons, he had two batting titles under his belt (1977–78), hitting .324 with a per 162-game average of 25 home runs and 109 RBIs.

From 1975–79, his best five-year stretch in a Pirates uniform, Parker led the league in batting average (.321) and triples (47), and was second in doubles (184) and extra-base hits (345).

Willie Stargell *(1B-OF, 1962–82):* A Hall of Fame slugger for 21 years with the Pirates, "Pops" had the respect and admiration of his peers and rivals. One of his notably epic homers at Philadelphia's Vet Stadium in 1971 hit the previously untouchable 600-level, and would be commemorated with a yellow star at its landing spot for over 30 years—and this was at the home of a cross-state rival! But, it was worthy. Teammate Richie Hebner, after venturing up to the landing spot, remarked, "It looked like a twenty-dollar cab ride from there to home plate."

Stargell's 475 home runs are the most in franchise history—296 of which led the majors during the 1970s. He's the only player in baseball history to win the MVP (1979), Roberto Clemente Award (Community; 1974), Babe Ruth Award (Postseason MVP; 1979), Lou Gehrig Memorial Award (Character; 1974), and the Hutch Award (Perseverance; 1978).

Turning the Ship Around

In 2013, the Pirates ended a 20-year losing streak with an improbable 94-win season utilizing *Big Data Baseball* (Travis Sawchik's book; check it out for the whole story). Pittsburgh flipped the script by applying data concepts in order to "steal wins" —they heavily employed shifts, implemented strong pitch framing, and stressed the two-seam fastball, to utilize its movement over the straighter four-seamer.

In 2014 and 2015, the Pirates would have some more of the same success, but failed to make it out of the wild-card game— though they did win 98 games in 2015, their most in a season since the 1909 World Champion Pittsburg* Pirates had a franchise-best record of 110–42.

[From 1891 to 1911, the spelling of the city's name was officially sans 'h']

Now, it is Groundhog Day all over again. After consecutive sub-.500 seasons in 2016 and 2017, the Buccos managed to scrape together an 82–79 record in 2018. It's not exactly the jump they saw five years prior, but it's a positive sign that they're progressing without some of their previously most-heralded stars.

In January of 2018, Pittsburgh traded arguably their best hitter, Andrew McCutchen, and undoubtedly best pitcher, Gerrit Cole, and still made a seven-win improvement on the season prior. Trevor Williams played a big part in the turnaround, putting up a 1.29 ERA through his final 13 starts of the season, surrendering just 11 total earned runs over that span. In support, rotation mate Jameson Taillon finally cashed in on the hype that made him

In 2018, Pittsburgh Pirates RHP Trevor Williams surrendered just 11 runs spanning 12 second-half starts, after allowing 53 runs (48 earned) through 19 first-half starts. (D. Benjamin Miller [Public domain or CC0], from Wikimedia Commons)

the second overall pick in the 2010 draft, finishing 2018 with the ninth-best ERA in the NL (3.21; 32 starts), and tying for tops in baseball in complete games (two) and *shutouts* (one).

Now, the Pirates just need help from some of their prospects—the bounty from aforementioned trades and early draft picks—who lately, and historically, haven't always panned out. It's always a crap shoot. In the end, the Buccos' woes will likely continue unless they can couple *Big Data Baseball* with *Big Money Baseball*.

STATS INCREDIBLE!

1902: The 103–36 Pirates club, which never had a single losing streak longer than two games all season. Only team to accomplish this in the Modern Era.

6: Times Ralph Kiner led the majors in home runs. Only Babe Ruth did it more times (11).

38: The number of games Barry Bonds had both a home run and a stolen base—a Pirates record. Barry also had 64 such games with the Giants, good for their franchise record. His 102 total are the most in baseball history.

14: Career stolen bases by shortstop Dick Groat (1952–67). Rickey Henderson had 1,392 more swipes than Groat. But Groat had one more career triple than Henderson (67 to 66).

10/30: Starling Marte (2013–14) became the first Pirate with 10+ home runs and 30+ stolen bases in consecutive seasons since Barry Bonds (1989–92).

26.9: Percentage of all Pirates hits from 1927–29, from the bats of brothers Paul and Lloyd Waner.

134: In 2015, Gerrit Cole and Francisco Liriano became the first Pirates duo with at least 200 strikeouts each in the franchise's 134-year history.

5: On August 22–23, 1970, Roberto Clemente had consecutive five-hit games.

1958: After the 1958 season, Roberto Clemente opted not to play winter ball in Puerto Rico; instead, he enlisted in the United States Marine Corps Reserves. He served a six-month active duty commitment and was a part of the Marine Corps Reserves until September 1964.

7: Andrew McCutchen and Barry Bonds are the only players with at least 40 extra-base hits, 50 walks, and 10 stolen bases in each of their first seven seasons.

42: Andrew McCutchen and Jackie Robinson are the only players with at least 200 total bases, 50 walks, and 10 stolen bases in each of their first seven seasons.

2: On September 28, 2016, John Jaso hit for the cycle, joining Ray Schalk as the only players in baseball history to hit for a cycle and catch a perfect game.

12: Harvey Haddix threw 12 perfect innings on May 26, 1959. He would lose the game on a walk-off home run that would be ruled a double as batsman Joe Adcock passed Henry Aaron on the basepaths in the 13th.

1: On August 23, 2017, Josh Harrison avenged Harvey Haddix, becoming the only player in baseball history to officially break up a no-hitter with a walk-off home run, doing so against the Dodgers' Rich Hill.

3: For three straight years, from 2012 to 2014, Andrew McCutchen slashed at least .300/.400/.500 with 15-plus stolen bases. Willie Mays had three such seasons in his entire career. Cutch was the first Pirates player to pull off the consecutive feat since Honus Wagner from 1903 to 1905.

ST. LOUIS CARDINALS

Est. 1882

Stan Musial is the only player in baseball history who ranks among the top 60 in singles (19th), doubles (third), triples (19th), and home runs (30th). Note that Musial not only ranks among the top 60 for each, but the top 30 as well. He also ranks 13th all-time in bases on balls. He was able to do this despite giving up 15 months of his career to serve in the United States Navy during World War II. He was . . . The Man.

St. Louis has been called "Baseball Heaven," but let's get scientific . . . Two facts about the St. Louis Cardinals: They are the most successful team in National League history, and their fans are among the most respected and passionate in the game. What's tricky is determining which way to apply the cause and effect—the chicken (Cardinals) or the egg (fans)? Or maybe, correlation does not imply causation, and the success and support that the franchise has had are just two independently dynamite properties, like barley and hops, that have come together to create one truly special brew . . .

Meh. Who cares?

The mid-market Cardinals—fourth in all-time wins (10,827)

Looking like the set of an Old Spice commercial, the team photo of the 1876 St. Louis Brown Stockings—the charter NL club which was the forerunner to today's St. Louis Cardinals franchise. (Author unknown; PD)

with an NL-best 11 championships—are a true American success story any way you look at it.

The Cards (then the Browns), had good genes from the start. They began their run of success in the 1880s, as part of the American Association, winning four straight league titles (1885–88) behind the tutelage of young skipper Charles Comiskey, a natural-born winner.

Comiskey's successful stint with the Browns (1883–89, 1891) was his first in a series of pivotally fortuitous ventures that would eventually lead him to establishing both the Chicago White Sox, and the American League as a whole, in the twentieth century. Just a footnote in the Cards' long, storied history, but Comiskey and the team's early triumphs were tremendously important. The one-and-done Seattle Pilots (Brewers), the original Baltimore Orioles (Yankees), and the Kansas City version of the Athletics could attest to the importance of early success on franchise staying power.

After the Cards/Browns joined the National League in 1892, they hit a bump in the road, finishing over .500 just four times over a 24-year span. A long time, for sure, but since infielder Rogers Hornsby arrived in 1915, the Cardinals, to date, have not had a single sub-.500 stretch that's lasted longer than three seasons.

Hornsby was an all-time great in the game's history, leading the Cardinals in WAR for 10 straight seasons, before guiding the club to its first championship in 1926—interestingly, his last year with St. Louis and first year as player-manager. He was the first in a long string of superstars to pass through the Gateway to the West.

Hall of Famers Grover Cleveland Alexander, Jim Bottomley, Dizzy Dean, Johnny Mize, and Stan Musial all played pivotal roles in helping St. Louis reach nine World Series in 21 years from 1926–46, winning six (1926, 1931, 1934, 1942, 1944, 1946). Then, two literal game-changers in Bob Gibson and Curt Flood highlighted two more championship squads in 1964 and 1967.

Since, the Cardinals have just kept on winning, with a variety of styles. They won three NL titles and one ring with the game's best all-time defender (Ozzie Smith), and they won two World Series in three tries with one of the game's most dominant batsmen (Albert Pujols). Throughout the team's history, it's probably had the greatest collection of hitters, and has been incredibly consistent with rebuilding talent, year after year.

St. Louis always finds players to deliver, and the fans do their part, helping the Cards finish in the top-four in NL attendance 19 of the past 20 seasons.

It's a match made in heaven.

The Bats
Rogers Hornsby *(2B, 1915–26)*: Not much is known about his childhood, but his mom named him "Rogers" after her maiden

name, so we're pretty sure it was a weird situation. He developed into a notoriously difficult personality in baseball, especially during his 15 years managing. Jimmy Dugan, of Penny Marshall's Rockford Peaches, once said, "Rogers Hornsby was my manager, and he called me a talking pile of pigsh-t. And that was when my parents drove all the way down from Michigan to see me play the game. And did I cry?" No. He didn't. Because there's no crying in baseball. But opposing pitchers might have wanted to, after seeing Hornsby step into the batter's box.

Hornsby owns the top five seasons in Cardinals Modern Era history (post-1900) in terms of batting average, and thrice batted over .400 with the team in the 1920s. Consider—there have been just 13 seasons in which a ballplayer batted at least .400 in modern baseball history, and Hornsby hit .402 *OVER A FIVE-YEAR STRETCH*, from 1921–25. During a ridiculous 762-game stretch, from September 9, 1920 to May 30, 1926, he maintained an even .400.

Hornsby ranks first all-time in on-base percentage by a right-handed batter (.434), and is 20 points ahead of any other primary second baseman in career batting average (.358). In the 1,106 wins Hornsby was a part of during his 23-year career, he batted .406/.484/.672. Hornsby even batted .312/.383/.484 in losses, comparable to Hall of Famer Billy Dickey's overall career slash line of .313/.384/.486.

In what is surely a feather in his cap, Hornsby's methods served as inspiration to the great Ted Williams, the only player during the Live Ball Era to top Hornsby's single-season batting average above MLB average (.1433 to .1371; 1941, 1924, respectively).

Stan Musial *(OF, 1941–44, 1946–63)*: A contemporary of Ted Williams, Musial is one of the most comparable to the Splendid Splinter. A quick look at Musial's 22-year Cards career—three-time NL MVP, 20-time All-Star, .331 career hitter—and it's easy to see why he was "The Man" in St. Louis.

Musial was productive from start to finish. He went 2-for-4 in his big-league debut and from that game until his very last, his lifetime batting average never dipped below .319. He won two MVPs, three World Series, and a World War (serving in the US Navy in 1945) before the age of twenty-six. In his final full season, in 1962, at the age of forty-one, Musial hit .330, a league record for quadragenarians.

When he retired in 1963, Musial held National League records for hits (3,630), extra-base hits (1,377), and RBIs (1,951). He was baseball's first 400-homer, 3,000-hit player, and the NL's only 200-homer, 3,000-hit, .400-plus on-base percentage player.

Musial was an extra-base hit king of the Modern Era (third all-time), and distributed them evenly, mashing 475 home runs, but also finishing in the top-10 in career doubles (third, 725) and triples (10th, 177). Since 1920, there have been just nine seasons in which a player hit 40+ doubles and 20+ triples. Musial is the only one to do it twice (1943, 1946).

Over a six-year stretch, from 1943–49, Musial batted .350, averaging 211 hits and 44 doubles per season. Hall of Famer Willie Mays never had a *single season* with either a batting average, hits total, or doubles total that high.

Mark McGwire *(1B, 1997–2001)*: A poster boy for the steroid era, McGwire will have a very difficult time making it into the Hall of Fame. However, because it's impossible to know exactly who else may have been using performance-enhancing drugs at the time, it's hard to penalize the guy too much. After all, when (supposedly) clean, this was the same guy who clobbered the rookie home run record with 49 bombs for Oakland in 1987. His freakish power came naturally, even if his freakish numbers with St. Louis may have been aided.

McGwire's time in St. Louis was all about breaking Roger Maris's single-season home run record (61 HRs), and Mac reached that goal, clobbering the 37-year-old record with 70 homers in 1998. Actually, during his five seasons in St. Louis overall, he averaged 65 home runs per 162 games. While the 1998 home run race with Sammy Sosa (66 HRs) was thrilling, McGwire breaking it was inevitable, and only a matter of whether he'd be able to play a full season.

McGwire struggled to stay healthy throughout his career, and his home run total reflects this. Despite being tops in baseball history in home run percentage (7.61) and at-bats per home run (1 per every 10.6 at-bats), his 583 jacks are just 11th on the all-time list. If Barry Bonds had went deep at the same rate as McGwire, he would have finished his career with a mind-boggling 959 home runs.

Still, McGwire's 135 two-year home run total while with the Cards in 1998–99 is still tops in baseball history. He broke down and was unable to play 100 games in either of his final two seasons (2000–01), but he was still valuable. Over the final 162 games played in his career, McGwire had 49 home runs and 103 walks.

Albert Pujols *(1B, 2001–11)*: Pronounced *POO-holes*, Prince Albert has a name that'll make you snicker, with a game more powerful than a Dick Butkus open-field tackle ... Bat speed quicker than Dick Trickle's No. 84 Buick on a straightaway ... You get the idea.

While his seven seasons in Los Angeles (2012–18) have been rather pedestrian (.260/.315/.453, 27 HRs per year), his first 11 while with St. Louis were historic, yet familiar.

Pujols's .328/.420/.617 slash line with St. Louis is very similar to the .331/.417/.559 posted by Stan Musial over twice as many seasons. However, the baseball card numbers favor Pujols, as he was well ahead of Musial, averaging 28 more runs scored per season (117 to 89) with 32 more RBIs (121 to 89). Of course, it's unfair to compare the two, not just because of generational differences, but because this was Pujols's best stretch of his entire career—not his career as a whole.

But, even if we compare, apples to apples, just their first 11

Albert Pujols homering at Petco Park in 2008—the last season anyone hit .357/.462/.653 or better. (Dirk Hansen, CC BY-SA 3.0 [http://creativecommons.org/licenses/by-sa/3.0], via Wikimedia Commons)

full seasons, Pujols still leads in nearly every offensive category, though Musial (.345/.432/.582) draws to about as close to Pujols as possible.

That's how good he was. But was he better than *The Man*?

Perhaps not, but it is damn close. From a sabermetric standpoint, their WAR through their first 11 full seasons is impossibly close, favoring Musial 89.0 to 86.6, and adjusted OPS offers another slight nod to Musial over Pujols, at 172 to 170.

Pujols was also better than everyone in the 2000s, collecting a rare decade-Triple Crown, leading the National League in batting average (.334), home runs (366), and RBIs (1,112) from 2000–09.

The Arms

No offense to Cardinals pitchers, but, historically, this franchise has been defined by its offense. That being said, two pitchers surely stand out amongst the rest.

Dizzy Dean *(1930, 1932–37)*: It's generally thought that Jay Dean's nickname was a playful knock on his colorful, dimwitted demeanor. On the mound, however, the right-hander was serious, and one of the most talented pitchers in the game's history.

Injuries cut Dean's career to just six full seasons (1932–37), but the Hall of Famer made a major impact in that time, winning an MVP in 1934, finishing runner-up the next two seasons, and ranking No. 85 on *The Sporting News's* top-100 players list, compiled in 1999.

Dean was the last National League pitcher to win 30 games in a season (1934; 30–7, 2.66 ERA), and he nearly did it twice, winning 28 the following year. Only six pitchers in the NL have won 26+ games in a season since Dean *averaged* a 27–12 record over *four* seasons, from 1934–36.

Bob Gibson *(1959–75)*: A lifetime Cardinal, Gibson was one of the most dominant pitchers to ever live.

Taken as a whole, his career was impressive—251 wins, 2.91 ERA, 3,117 strikeouts—but he's most famous for his lights-out 1968 campaign.

That year, Gibson was 22–9, with a microscopic 1.12 ERA, winning both the NL Cy Young Award and MVP. The only players with lower single-season ERAs were Dutch Leonard (0.96; 1914) and Mordecai Brown (1.04; 1906), during a time when yearly college tuition was about $150, stop signs were a new thing, and people had awesome nicknames like "Dutch" and "Three Finger."

Of his 22 wins that year, 13 were shutouts—which was more than his home runs and triples allowed, combined (11).

Heck, even his ERA in his nine *losses* (2.24) would have qualified for the sixth-best NL ERA mark overall.

Gibson's historic year is often credited as the main culprit for the mound being lowered the following year, in 1969. Game-changer.

In the postseason, Gibson was just as dominant, posting a 7–2 record, 1.89 ERA, and 0.883 WHIP during 81 World Series innings (earned a ring in 1964 and 1967). He is the National League's World Series leader in wins (seven) and strikeouts (91).

The Glove

Ozzie Smith *(SS, 1982–96)*, the Wizard, had just a .666 OPS during his career—the sixth-lowest among Hall of Fame position players. But, the 15-time All-Star may have been the best defensive player in the game's history.

Not surprisingly, Smith ranks best all-time in defensive WAR (44.2). Sure, he would have to return to baseball and collect 531 straight hits for his average to creep above .300, but, in terms of total WAR, Ozzie actually ranks ahead of the great Derek Jeter, 76.9 to 72.4. Jeter hit .310 in his career, but the Wizard had a whopping 485 more defensive runs saved than the Captain (238.7 to -246.3).

The In-betweener

Yadier Molina (C, 2004–present): Yadi has done a little bit of everything during career—all of which has been played in a St. Louis Cardinals uniform—defense, offense, leadership, you name it.

The nine-time Gold Glove backstop was artfully framing pitches before it was cool (or before PITCHf/x made quantifying it possible) and has compiled 24.4 defensive WAR in his career.

[It is important to remember that WAR is an estimate, especially when talking defensive WAR—double-especially when talking defensive WAR for a catcher.]

From an offensive perspective, Yadi's numbers don't jump off the page. For the duration of his career, his adjusted OPS is actually one percent below average, but when compared to other catchers, he shines. His career .282/.334/.406 slash line is markedly better than that of the average catcher (.250/.316/.392) and his three-year peak, from 2011 to 2013, saw him bat .313/.361/.481 compared to the .246/.314/.392 mark posted by a league average catcher during the same span.

Perennial St. Louis Cardinals catcher Yadier Molina enters the 2019 season with nine All-Star nods, nine Gold Glove and four Platinum Glove awards, a 2013 Silver Slugger Award, and two World Series championships in 2006 and 2011. (Barbara Moore, CC BY-SA 2.0 [https://creativecommons.org/licenses/by-sa/2.0], via Flickr)

Is it enough for the two-time world champion to one day find himself among the immortals in the Hall of Fame?

A catcher has a lot of jobs. Aside from offensive and defensive responsibilities, he's essentially the quarterback of the pitching staff. Molina's leadership through two World Series runs probably puts him over the top.

Stats Incredible!

68: The total amount of home runs hit by the entire Cardinals team in 1991—two fewer than Mark McGwire hit for St. Louis in 1998.

10: The number of MLB seasons in which a player had at least 20 home runs and more homers than singles. McGwire owns half of them. From 1994 to 2001, he had 354 home runs to just 353 singles.

0.98: Bob Gibson's ERA over a 34-game stretch, from September 12, 1967 to September 6, 1968.

.216: Opponents' batting average against Gibson from 1965–70. Gibson batted .224 himself over that span.

16: Johnny Mize's total triples in 1938—the most in MLB history by a player with no stolen bases. Mize's 14 triples the following Cards season is the second-most by a player with no stolen bases.

6: Tied with the Cubs' Sammy Sosa, Mize had the most career three-homer games in history.

7: Lou Brock's record for stolen bases in a single World Series. He did it twice, in 1967 and 1968—including three swipes in Game 7 of the 1967 World Series.

289: Minor-league games played by Randy Poffo—a.k.a. pro wrestler "Macho Man Randy Savage." He slashed .282/.400/.441 in 1973, his final season in the Cardinals organization.

1st: Pitcher Mitchell Harris debuted on April 25, 2015, for the Cards, the first US Naval Academy graduate to play in the majors since Cpt. Willard "Nemo" Gaines on July 16, 1921.

21: Postseason games won by the Cards since Pujols signed with the Angels at the end of 2011. The Angels have won *none*.

3,630: Career hits by Stan Musial—1,815 at home and 1,815 on the road.

21,785⅔: Career innings fielded by Ozzie Smith, all of which came at the shortstop position.

1,129: Stan Musial would have had to go 0-for-1,129 for his lifetime batting average to fall below .300.

50: Vince Coleman stole a major league record 50 consecutive bases without being caught from September 18, 1988, to July 26, 1989.

3: On April 8, 2016, Jeremy Hazelbaker, Aledmys Diaz, and Greg Garcia all hit pinch-hit home runs for the Cardinals. That made St. Louis the first—and still only—team in history to have three pinch-hit home runs in a game.

162: Matt Carpenter is one of just a dozen players in history to play at least 162 games at first base, second base, and third base. The top four among them in OPS are as follows: Jackie Robinson (.883), Carpenter (.847), Paul Molitor (.817), and Pete Rose (.784).

NATIONAL LEAGUE WEST

ARIZONA DIAMONDBACKS

Est. 1998

Triple-feat! Sort of... In Game 1 of the 2017 NLDS, Ketel Marte became the first player in baseball history to triple from both sides of the plate in a postseason game. In that same game, Archie Bradley became the first relief pitcher in history to record a triple during postseason play.

In 1998, the Arizona Diamondbacks were a new expansion franchise. In 2001, they won the World Series. What took the Philadelphia Phillies 97 years to accomplish, the DBacks did in four. FOUR.

It's the fastest championship for a new franchise in the game's history, but it wasn't just beginner's luck. Arizona targeted talented, undervalued veterans—Steve Finley, Luis Gonzalez, Randy Johnson, Curt Schilling, and others—at a time when most new franchises' best hopes would still be hacking away in Triple-A. At the turn of the century, everything the Diamondbacks touched turned to gold...

1999:
- SS Jay Bell, age thirty-three, had a career high in homers (38) his second season with Arizona.

- 3B Matt Williams, thirty-three, also in his second Arizona season, became one of just five third basemen in baseball history to knock in over 140 runs (142).
- OF Luis Gonzalez, thirty-one, during his first season with the team, hit then-career highs in hits (206), batting average (.336), home runs (26), and RBIs (111).
- OF Steve Finley, thirty-four, another newbie, put up the most home runs (34) and RBIs (103) of his career.
- SP Randy Johnson, thirty-five, was a steal in free agency, hitting career highs in innings pitched (271⅔), complete games (12), and strikeouts (364) en route to his first of four straight Cy Young Awards.

2001:
- SP Curt Schilling, thirty-four, recorded his first 20-win season (22 Ws) in his first full year with the DBacks.
- OF Reggie Sanders, thirty-three, had the highest home run total of his career (33)—his first and only season with the club.
- SP/RP Miguel Batista, thirty, a new Diamondback, soared to new personal highs in wins (11) and ERA (3.36).

Arizona defeated the New York Yankees in a thrilling 2001 World Series, and the team did it without a single starting position player in their twenties. It would have been logical to assume that the Diamondbacks would be in for a swift decline thereafter, but it has been a remarkably consistent franchise ever since.

In its 20 years as an MLB club, the Diamondbacks have never had a three-year stretch without at least one second-place finish or better.

The Big(ger) Unit
The Big Unit, Randy Johnson, was, at times, the best pitcher in baseball while with Seattle (1989–98). His six-year stretch with

Arizona, however, put him in the discussion as one of the greatest power pitchers in the game's history.

Johnson, the team's career WAR leader (52.6), also holds the franchise Triple Crown, leading the Diamondbacks all-time in wins (118), ERA (2.83), and strikeouts (2,077). He shares the MLB record for consecutive Cy Young Awards (four, 1999–02) and is the lone Diamondbacks representative in the Baseball Hall of Fame.

With an upper-90s fastball to match his 6-foot-10 frame and menacing scowl, Johnson was the perfect strikeout machine (or potential movie villain).

In 2001, he struck out 372 batters, nearly topping Nolan Ryan's Modern Era mark of 383 set in 1973, despite pitching more than 75 innings fewer than Ryan (249⅔ to 326). Taking a 325-inning stretch from July 9, 2000, to September 2, 2001, Johnson amassed a superhuman 488 strikeouts. And he was still deadly accurate with his pitches.

Ryan led the league in walks the year he set the record (162 BBs), while Johnson, surrendering just 71 walks in 2001, joined Sandy Koufax (1965; 382 Ks, 71 BBs) as the only two players to have 300 more strikeouts than walks since Matt Kilroy in 1886 (513 Ks, 182 BBs) ... when seven balls were required for a walk.

Over the course of Johnson's career, and especially while with Arizona, left-handed batters didn't stand much of a chance. Southpaw legend Steve Carlton, a pitcher, had a higher batting average during his career (.201) than the 22 years' worth of left-handed batters to face Johnson (.199). During his 1999 campaign in which he led the league in batters faced, lefties, incredibly, hit just .103 against him, collecting 11 total bases. Twenty-three MLB batters in 2015 alone collected 11 total bases in one single game.

When Curt Schilling was added to the mix in 2000, things got a little unfair for the opposition.

Acey Deucey

Johnson and Schilling finished 1–2 in the Cy Young voting their first two full seasons playing together. They combined for 43 wins in 2001 and set a new, two-teammate, Modern Era record for strikeouts, with 665.

The duo combined for a 18.9 WAR in 2001, the second-highest combined total for any two rotation mates during the Live Ball Era . . . second only to their 19.3 total compiled in 2002.

Their record over both seasons was 90–24, a .789 win percentage—good for about 128 victories extrapolated over 162 games.

Schill didn't get the Cy Young hardware because of his All-World teammate, but he deserves *something* for being, arguably, the most efficient power pitcher in history. In 2001, beyond just leading the league in wins (22), Schilling became one of just three players in MLB history (Pedro Martinez, 1999; and Justin Verlander, 2018) with at least 290 strikeouts and fewer than 40 walks in the same season—and in 2002, he did it again.

Curt Schilling and Randy Johnson shared World Series MVP honors in 2001. (AP Photo/Elaine Thompson)

Luckily, there was one piece of hardware that Schilling could at least share with Johnson in 2001—World Series MVP. It's the only instance the award has ever been split between two pitchers, and they were worthy recipients.

The Unit was 3–0 with a microscopic 1.04 ERA in the Series, and Schilling wasn't far behind, going 1–0 with a 1.69. Overall, Johnson was 5–1 with a 1.52 ERA in 41⅓ postseason innings in 2001, while Schilling finished at 4–0, with a 1.12 ERA in 48⅓ innings. Schilling pitched the most innings of anyone in history with a perfect postseason record. Not surprisingly, the two sit 1–2 on the single postseason wins list among starting pitchers.

The Other Half

The story of the Dbacks' success goes beyond the pitching mound.

The team was loaded, top to bottom, in 2001, so it's unfair to credit just the offense or just the pitching. As a team, Arizona finished with the fourth-best batting average in the NL (.267), scoring the third-most runs (818). Luis Gonzalez had one of the greatest seasons in league history, finishing third in MVP voting behind Barry Bonds and Sammy Sosa. That was the season Bonds broke the single-season home run record (73 HRs), so even if MVP voting had been exclusive to Gonzalez's blood relatives and D. Baxter the Bobcat, it was still Bonds's trophy to lose.

Gonzalez (.325/57 HRs/142 RBIs) and Sosa (.328/64/160) were the first players since 1938 to register a season with at least a .325 batting average, 50 homers, and 140 RBIs. Gonzo slugged .688 that season playing in the full 162 games, which is the highest slugging percentage ever for a player appearing in all 162.

The plan to acquire talented veterans like Gonzalez paid dividends very early for Arizona—the 1999 squad is the only team in history to have four players with over 74 extra-base hits (Gonzalez, Jay Bell, Steve Finley, Matt Williams)—which also led to a relatively short window for contention.

Jay Bell, who in 1999 (38 HRs) was just the fifth second baseman with a 38+ homer season, was done as an everyday player by 2002.

Steve Finley, still going strong in 2003, was the first player in franchise history to hit double digits in home runs (22), triples (10), and stolen bases (15) in the same season. Stephen Drew in 2010 is the only DBack to match the feat. Finley's last season in Arizona came in 2004, at age thirty-nine.

The young franchise was heavy with older talent, and eventually time caught up with some of Arizona's top veterans. The Diamondbacks have only won one postseason series since capturing its World Series title in 2002 and have not won a division title since 2011.

When the Dbacks dealt Paul Goldschmidt to the Cardinals in 2018, the message was clear: Arizona was decidedly in "win-later mode."

Goldschmidt played eight years for the franchise, his final six as an NL All-Star. In that short time frame, Hall of Fame comparisons can already be drawn. Taking a look at those first eight seasons, spanning 1,092 games, we can compare them to the first 1,092 career games of another five-tool first baseman:

Paul Goldschmidt - .297/.398/.532 with 209 HR, 267 2B, 19 3B, and 124 SB

Jeff Bagwell - .301/.408/.535 with 208 HR, 264 2B, 20 3B, and 124 SB

An uncanny resemblance, and the comparisons do not stop there. Only two first basemen in history have ever had at least 30 doubles, 20 home runs, 20 stolen bases, and 100 walks in a season: Paul Goldschmidt and Jeff Bagwell. Remarkably both have done so multiple times—Goldy in 2015 and 2016; Baggy in 1996, 1997, and 1999.

The oldest team in Major League Baseball in 2018 (29.2 years) clearly saw the writing on the wall, dealing Goldschmidt before his 2020 free agent status could leave the franchise with nothing in return.

Two days after the trade, the Dbacks lost starting pitcher Patrick Corbin to the Nats in free agency, their second-best player in terms of WAR (4.6 to Goldy's 5.9). Then, a month later, the club lost outfielder A.J. Pollock (2.5) to the Dodgers.

Going young was ironically never the young franchise's way. Hopefully, some of their budding prospects will grow up fast.

STATS INCREDIBLE!

9: The number of seasons Randy Johnson had more strikeouts than baserunners allowed.

7/20: Randy Johnson had enough strikeouts on July 20 of both 1999 and 2000 to lead the league in strikeouts for each season.

275: Johnson and Curt Schilling, in 2001, became the first duo with at least 275 strikeouts each since Tim Keefe and Jack Lynch in 1884. They repeated the feat in 2002.

19.3: Combined WAR of Johnson and Schilling in 2002. Highest season WAR total for a 1–2 during the Live Ball Era (post-1919).

.185: The total batting average of opponents that fell behind 0–1 in the count to Johnson. They batted .232

when he fell behind 1–0. Just trying at all was hardly worth their effort . . .

9: Curt Schilling is the only pitcher in baseball history with a 9.00+ K/9 and 9.00+ K/BB in the same season (2002).

40: Johnson's age (plus 251 days) on May 18, 2004, making him the oldest pitcher to toss a perfect game.

448: In 1973, Nolan Ryan had a modern-record 383 strikeouts in 326 innings. From July 9, 2000, to September 2, 2001, Randy Johnson had 488 strikeouts in 325 innings.

.321: Paul Goldschmidt's batting average in 2015, with 33 home runs and 21 stolen bases. He was the second first baseman ever to bat .320 or better in a season with at least 20 home runs and 20 stolen bases (Carl Yastrzemski, 1970).

142: Brandon Webb had a career 142 ERA+, besting Johan Santana (136), Randy Johnson (135), Greg Maddux (132), Sandy Koufax (131), and Roy Halladay (131).

4: On September 4, 2017, J. D. Martinez became the first player to hit a home run off four different pitchers in a game since Joe Adcock on July 31, 1954. He also became the first midseason acquisition with a four-homer game since Pat Seery on July 18, 1948.

8: Curt Schilling had 316 strikeouts, averaging 9.58 strikeouts-per-walk in 2002. The only other pitcher with at least 300 strikeouts and 9.00 or better strikeouts-per-walk is Jim Whitney (Boston Beaneaters) . . . in 1883 . . . when eight balls were required for a free pass.

9: Among the top eight strikeout-per-walk seasons by a pitcher with at least 250 innings, two belong to Curt Schilling (2001 and 2002). The other six occurred between 1875 and 1884, when as many as nine balls were required for a walk and the pitcher stood just 55½ feet from home plate.

COLORADO ROCKIES

Est. 1993

Larry Walker batted .381/.462/.710 at Coors Field and .282/.372/.500 everywhere else. Hall of Famer Chuck Klein batted .395/.448/.705 at the Baker Bowl and .277/.339/.451 everywhere else.

When things don't happen for a while, it's natural to stubbornly think they *can't* happen—like thinking a team can't win a championship. But that's superstitious pessimism; just ask the fan bases of Boston and the North Side of Chicago. With the Rockies, it's oddly scientific.

Playing at Coors Field, almost exactly a mile above sea level (5,200 feet), Denver's Colorado Rockies entered the league in 1993 amid a cloud of skepticism regarding fair playing conditions. The thin, dry air, it is said, creates a climate for (literally) heightened offensive play, making the balls harder and their carry higher and longer. But, as noted in the film *Jurassic Park*—an early name proposal for Coors Field—*life finds a way*.

Stadium designers pushed back the fences at the onset, and the team later installed humidors to control the condition of baseballs put in play. Of course, deeper fences create spacious outfields, ripe for singles and doubles hitters to pick apart, but humidors do nothing to solve the thin-air problem. Coors Field (and the

Rockies franchise itself) is thus a conundrum of both man and nature pushing back at one another. As such, if one were to make a case that the Rockies *can't* win a championship, they could certainly *Bill Nye*-up a PowerPoint presentation that makes a viable case—at least, more functionally than that of some cosmic vendetta against Colorado baseball.

The truth is, Colorado's environment may narrowly impede its chances at winning a championship, but it does not prevent it from pulling it off. If the backdrop is an opponent, it's battled equally by both home and away teams. Sure, even lately, Coors Field has been the highest-scoring stadium in baseball six of the past seven years, and that makes for tough contract negotiations with free agent pitchers. But, the teams that win championships often do so because they make difficult propositions—like wading through thin free agent pools, or finding stars in the draft's later rounds—fruitful. And Colorado has had its chances.

The Rockies made their lone World Series appearance in 2007, after winning 21 of their final 22 contests (14–1 to end the regular season, 7–0 in the playoffs entering the World Series). Beginning that season, they had a four-year stretch averaging 85 wins per season. Not phenomenal, but still proof that sustained success is possible in Colorado, even if the team's biggest names, historically, have been on the offensive side.

Over the years, Rockies superstars such as Larry Walker, Todd Helton, and Troy Tulowitzki lit up the scoreboard and made the game exciting in a city that has (minor league) baseball roots dating back to the 1880s. Denver is a great baseball town, and the game there has always been exciting. Their 1993 expansion mate, the Miami Marlins, may have a pair of titles in hand, but the two clubs share the exact same 162-game average record (76–86). And Colorado has the stronger fan base, routinely finishing in or near the top half in NL attendance.

Inevitably, scientifically, indubitably, this team will win a championship. And at the rate at which they score, it's sure to be one of the most exciting runs in baseball history.

The Hangover Effect

By now, we are all aware of the positive impact that Coors Field has on Colorado's offensive numbers at home. For fans and writers alike, that in and of itself is often enough to credit the "Coors Effect" for any offensive success by Rockies players.

But that is a whole answer to a half-question. Left unasked is: if playing at Coors Field, where the ball carries and breaking balls do not properly break, is there any impact on a player—or his offensive numbers—who plays half of his games in Denver when he comes back down to earth to play on the road?"

Our contention can best be summed up by Newton's Third Law: for every action, there is an equal but opposite reaction.

Though players see a boost in their offensive production when at home, that boost in offensive production is at home and at home alone—and when that player hits the road, his road numbers experience a far steeper decline than a traveling player who plays his home games in, say, Atlanta.

Let's take a by-the-numbers look.

Since 1993, the Rockies have been batting .306/.371/.503 at home as a franchise—good for first in batting average, first in on-base percentage, and first in slugging percentage. But during that same period, they are last in batting average, last in on-base percentage, and last in slugging percentage as a visiting team, batting .242/.307/.382.

Since 2000, the Rockies are batting .301/.367/.494 at home, but .241/.307/.380 on the road. Again, first-first-first at home and last-last-last on the road.

Since 2010, they are .298/.360/.494 at home and .237/.296/.373 on the road; again, you guessed it ... first-first-first, last-last-last.

This should lead one to believe one of two things: either that without the "Coors Effect" the Rockies were and always have been the worst hitting team in baseball, or that the "Hangover Effect" is real and its negative impact is great.

But how great?

Well, since 2010, MLB has slugged, as a league, .405—the Rockies have outperformed that by 21.8 percent at home but undershot it by 7.9 percent on the road, and they have an overall slugging percentage that is 7.0 percent better than league average.

The Yankees, on the other hand, during that same span, have outperformed MLB by 9.7 percent at home and undershot league slugging by less than 0.3 percent on the road, with an overall slugging percentage that is 6.4 percent better than league average. The Blue Jays, as another example, have a slugging percentage that is 9.9 percent better than league average at home, but only 0.2 percent on the road—slugging 4.9 percent better than league average overall.

What we cannot test here, of course, is the quality of these offenses in an economist's dream—an all-else-equal environment. Draw your own conclusions.

Our conclusion?

The "Coors Effect" is definitely real and it certainly has a major impact on Colorado's offense, but so does the "Hangover Effect"— perhaps Newton was a bit off on this one, as the positive offensive impact of playing in Colorado is certainly greater than the negative impact of playing on the road for Colorado. In the end, because of the "Hangover Effect," home field advantage provided by playing home games at Coors Field is really not all that much greater than playing in a hitter's ballpark at or near sea level.

Curing the Hangover: if the "Hangover Effect" is indeed a real thing, and we believe it to be, the Rockies could, in theory, steal wins over the course of a season by platooning one or two positions. It would mean not playing the pitcher matchup, and rather playing the venue matchup, using one or two players only in home games and switching them out when traveling.

No Offense, but These Guys are Future Hall of Famers

Thus far, Larry Walker has seen his name on nine Hall of Fame ballots; 2019 was his tenth and final shot at immortality. He was joined by Todd Helton, who made his first appearance on the ballot; both will look ahead to 2020 to join the likes of Chuck Klein (who also played with a marked home field advantage) in the Hall of Fame.

Baker Bowl and Coors Field vs. everywhere else:

Chuck Klein	.395/.448/.705	.277/.339/.451
Larry Walker	.381/.462/.710	.282/.372/.500
Todd Helton	.345/.441/.607	.287/.386/.469

"Coors Effect," "Baker Effect," "Hangover Effect," whatever . . . all are worthy of enshrinement.

Larry Walker *(OF, 1995–2005):* After a career season in which he batted .322/.394/.587 during the strike-shortened 1994 season with the (world champions that never were) Montreal Expos, Walker signed on with the Rockies.

He batted .295/.367/.594 during his first pair of seasons in Colorado over just 214 games, but broke out in 1997, batting .366/.452/.720 and tallying 9.8 WAR, which still stands as a franchise single-season record. He took home the National League MVP Award as he defied gravity, physics, and all aforementioned effects,

(Ryan Fitzpatrick)

posting a 1.169 OPS with 20 home runs at home and a 1.176 OPS with 29 home runs on the road. That season, he also stole 33 bases, coupled with his .720 slugging percentage; he is the only player in baseball history with a slugging percentage of .700-plus with at least 20 stolen bases in a season.

From 1997 to 2002, he batted .353/.441/.648 with an OPS+ that was 57 percent better than league average—and as a reminder, OPS+ adjusts for ballpark. During that span, in addition to collecting an MVP Award, he added his third, fourth, and fifth Gold Glove Awards, second and third Silver Slugger Awards, made four All-Star Game appearances, and won three batting titles.

Fair or unfair, Walker has four career qualifying seasons in which he batted at least .350 (as many as Ted Williams and Rod Carew, and one more than Joe DiMaggio). He had a higher career WAR (72.7) than Derek Jeter (72.4) and Tony Gwynn (69.2), and a higher career OPS+ (141) than Vlad Guerrero (140) and Ken Griffey Jr. (136).

Todd Helton *(1B, 1997–2013)*: Helton, who never won an MVP Award like Walker (due, likely in large part, to writers' weariness of that pesky "Coors Effect"), but he probably should have. From 2000 to 2005, he batted .344/.449/.626 with an adjusted OPS that was 58 percent better than league average—he added 42.1 WAR during that stretch, averaging just better than 7.0 WAR per season.

In all, it is not wrong—though some may say unfair—to place Todd Helton among some of the greatest players in history. He had two seasons with at least 200 hits, 80 extra-base hits, and 100 walks, joining Stan Musial (two), Babe Ruth (three), and Lou Gehrig (seven) as the only players in history with multiple such seasons. In 2000, he became just the third player in history to have at least 100 singles, 100 extra-base hits, and 100 walks in a season, alongside Jimmie Foxx and Lou Gehrig, who each did it twice.

On the Defensive

Colorado trailed in the NL West by as many as seven games in September of 2007, and trailed the wild card by 4½ with 14 games remaining in the regular season. The team went 13–1 during that final stretch, forcing a one-game playoff with San Diego. After winning the play-in game with the Padres, they swept the Phillies in the opening round (3–0), then swept the Diamondbacks to take the NLCS crown (4–0). They wound up on the wrong side of a sweep to the Red Sox in the World Series (0–4), but it's almost a side note to the incredible 21–1 stretch that got them there.

The Rockies tied a National League record for most consecutive wins to start a postseason (seven), and tied another NL record for most consecutive wins during a combined regular season and postseason stretch (10). The Rockies were showing how dominant they could be with even just-competitive pitching.

The 2007 team, though, was led largely by the offense. Other than Todd Helton, key contributors included batting champion Matt Holliday (who captured two-thirds of the Triple Crown, leading the league with 137 RBIs, but hitting *only* 36 home runs), Garrett Atkins, Brad Hawpe, and up-and-comer Troy Tulowitzki.

Troy Tulowitzki, when healthy, was an offensive and defensive juggernaut; even though he averaged just 112 games per year from 2008 to 2014, he still led all shortstops in baseball with 31.4 WAR and 151 home runs during that stretch. Ipso facto, 112 games of Troy Tulowitzki plus 50 games by a replacement-level shortstop was still the best shortstop in the game.

Since, Nolan Arenado has taken over as franchise centerpiece. He already has three career seasons with at least 35 home runs and 15 defensive runs saved; only Willie Mays has more (five). Arenado's first six seasons have seen him tally 33.1 WAR, the most by a National League third basemen since Mike Schmidt had 36.1 WAR through his first six. Arenado's 186 home runs rank second all-time among third basemen through six years in the bigs, behind only Eddie Mathews (222). As if that were not enough, in 2017, at just twenty-six years old, he had his third career season with at least 130 RBIs—the most in baseball history by a third baseman. His four seasons with at least 110 RBIs are second, behind Mike Schmidt's five.

Colorado Rockies shortstop Trevor Story earned his first All-Star nod and Silver Slugger Award in 2018, after recording a National League second-best slugging percentage (.567), total bases (339), and home runs (37). (Keith Allison, CC BY-SA 2.0 [https://creativecommons.org/licenses/by-sa/2.0], via Flickr)]

Nolan Arenado is complemented by 2017 batting champion Charlie Blackmon and Trevor Story, who in 2018—with Francisco Lindor—became the first shortstops in history with at least 35 home runs, 40 doubles, and 25 stolen bases in a season.

STATS INCREDIBLE!

40/40/30: In 1996, Rockies outfielder Ellis Burks became the game's first player with at least 40 doubles, 40 home runs, and 30 steals in a season . . . in 1997, teammate Larry Walker became the second.

105: Todd Helton's extra-base hit total in 2001, the most in the National League since Chuck Klein had 107 for the Phillies in 1930.

294: Larry Walker would have to return to baseball and go 0-for-294 for his lifetime batting average to dip below .300.

2.85: Kyle Freeland had a 2.85 ERA and 164 ERA+ in 2018, both single-season franchise records for a pitcher with at least 150 innings pitched.

33: Larry Walker, who wore No. 33, batted .393/.485/.571 in 33 career plate appearances against Hall of Famer Randy Johnson.

103: Charlie Blackmon had 103 RBIs batting first in the lineup in 2017, most in baseball history by a leadoff man. Chuck even added one out of the three-hole for good measure.

24: Trevor Story is the first shortstop in baseball history to hit at least 24 home runs in each of his first three seasons.

2.40: Kyle Freeland had a 2.40 ERA at Coors Field in 2018, a single-season mark for a Rockies starting pitcher in his home ballpark. Oddly enough, his road ERA was nearly a run higher, at 3.23.

230: In 2018, twenty-three-year-old German Marquez set a franchise record for strikeouts in a season with 230.

595: Adam Ottavino threw 595 sliders in 2018; opponents had just 17 hits to 90 swings-and-misses. His 112 strike-outs that season are the most ever by a Rockies pitcher without making a single start.

1948: Charlie Blackmon had 35 doubles, 14 triples, and 37 home runs in 2017; the last player with more of each was Stan Musial (1948; 46, 18, 39).

LOS ANGELES DODGERS

Est. 1883

Don Newcombe served in both the US Army and the US Navy. He won both an MVP Award and a Cy Young Award. He is the only player in baseball history who is a US military veteran to win both an MVP Award and a Cy Young Award.

They went by several different names before landing on "Dodgers" in their original home, Brooklyn, NYC.

Along with Bridegrooms, the club took turns as the Atlantics, Grays, Grooms, Superbas, and Robins—without much success, before "Dodgers" became the permanent moniker in 1932. Actually, it wasn't until 1955 that Brooklyn would win its first championship, after coming up short in its seven previous trips to the World Series post-1900. The difference? More than any alteration in nickname or playing strategy, Brooklyn embraced social change more than any club in baseball history.

The most heralded fact attributed to the Dodgers is being the first major-league team in the Modern Era to sign an African American player—second baseman Jackie Robinson. The "Modern Era" qualifier in no way diminishes Robinson's heroically trailblazing accomplishments, but it is true that Robinson was, at best, MLB's fourth black player.

The first credited black player is generally considered to be William Edward White, who subbed into one game in 1879. This was only uncovered within the past decade, though, as White, for most of his life, identified as *white*. Brothers Fleetwood and Welday Walker came five years later, playing a combined 47 games for the Toledo Blue Stockings of the American Association in 1884. Racist influence forced the Walkers from the major-league game almost as quickly as they arrived, and not a single black player would don an MLB uniform until Robinson stood his ground in 1947.

Robinson is justly credited with handling the transition with tremendous courage, but the color-barrier incinerator did so much more. From the very beginning, in the face of tumultuous opposition, Robinson was one of the game's best second basemen, all-time.

He won the Rookie of the Year award in 1947, a league MVP two years later, and was the Dodgers' best player over the course of his career (1947–56), a 10-year stretch during which the team won an average of 95 games, reaching six World Series and winning one. Still, over the same period, the Dodgers were averaging just over 17,000 fans per game.

Dodgers owner Walter O'Malley moved the team to Los Angeles and set new attendance records each of the first three years on the West Coast (per game averages: 23,968; 26,552; 29,271), winning championships in 1959, 1963, and 1965. Really, ever since the move, the Dodgers have been one of the most consistently competitive franchises in baseball, never going longer than seven seasons out west without reaching the postseason.

Some of the best players in baseball history have donned the Dodger Blue uniform, extending the team's proud legacy, and furthering the game's development. After 132 years and counting, though, one player has clearly worn it best.

Fans sit outside the right field wall of Brooklyn's Ebbets Field in 1920. (Bain News Service (LOC))

Same spot nearly 100 years later, the east-end wall of Brooklyn's Ebbets Field Apartments. (Saundi Wilson)

Jackie Robinson

Breaking the color barrier and sticking with a major-league ball club is a great accomplishment in itself. To play at a Hall of Fame level, mostly over the age of thirty, while enduring historical scrutiny, is remarkable. It oozes respect.

Robinson came out of the gate strong, winning the Rookie of the Year in 1947, and receiving MVP votes each of his first seven seasons. He's one of three players all time (Andrew McCutchen and Mike Trout) with at least 200 total bases, 50 walks, and 10 stolen bases in each of his first six seasons. He's one of just seven players in the Modern Era, and the only second baseman, with 170 or more hits in each of his first five seasons. One season, specifically, Robinson had a truly special, all-time great performance.

In 1949, Robinson won the NL MVP and had one of the finest seasons ever for a second baseman. He batted .347 with 66 extra-base hits and 37 stolen bases. No player has had a season in which he batted at least .340 with 65 extra-base hits and 35 stolen bases since. Not only was this the last instance of a player leading the NL in batting average and stolen bases, but 38 of his hits came with runners in scoring position—the most in recorded history. That clutch instinct gave Robinson, by far, the highest single-season RBI total of his career (124), making him just the third second baseman in NL history to reach the mark.

An on-base machine in 1949 (.432 OBP, second in NL), Robinson was second in the league in hits (203) and seventh in walks (86). He's the last second baseman in baseball with a 200/80 season.

To this day, despite having played just 10 MLB seasons, Robinson ranks third all-time in total WAR for the Dodgers (61.4), and his 7.20 WAR per-162 games is the best in team history and 17th most in baseball history.

Jackie Robinson, 1945, with the Kansas City Monarchs of the Negro Leagues, two seasons before his major-league call. (*The Call,* Kansas City, 1945)

Oh yeah, and no one is allowed to wear his No. 42 jersey, ever (except on April 15, each season, when EVERYONE dons the "42" in his honor). *RESPECT.*

Shadow Warriors

Jackie Robinson casts a very big shadow in baseball history. He was a vital part of Brooklyn's success in the '40s and '50s, but a few Dodgers all-time greats played right alongside him.

Pee Wee Reese *(SS, 1940–58)*: Reese was the captain of multiple Dodgers generations, playing 16 seasons (missing three serving in WWII) and appearing in seven World Series. The Dodgers' career WAR leader (66.3) had a keen eye at the plate, but often remarked that he wished he would have swung more.

Reese's .366 on-base percentage outshined his .269 batting average, and despite his laments, is what made him a special player. He only batted over .300 once and never hit more than 16 home runs in a single season, but his walks totals were historic. He owns two of the five total 100-walk seasons for a shortstop in National League history (1947, 104; 1949, 116), and no shortstop in the NL has topped the 100 mark since.

Duke Snider *(OF, 1947–62)*: The Duke is the Dodgers' franchise home run leader, with 389. He hit at least 40 home runs for five straight seasons from 1953–57, and is the only center fielder in NL history to do so.

Snider shined on the big stage too, collecting a .945 OPS in 36 World Series games, with more RBIs (26) and home runs (11) than any other National League player, ever.

Sandy Koufax *(LHP, 1955–66)*: Koufax is well-known for having a too-brief career, but he still played 12 seasons. The late-bloomer was just 54–53 with a 3.94 ERA his first seven seasons —the stretch no one talks about. The next five seasons, he emerged as *The Left Arm of God*, averaging more than 22 victories with 8.16 WAR per season, posting a 1.95 ERA, 2.00 FIP, and 167 ERA+ during one of the most remarkable runs in the game's history.

During the five-year stretch . . .

- Koufax led the league in wins three times, won three Cy Young Awards, one MVP Award, and took home the ERA title in all five seasons. He's the only National Leaguer to win pitching's Triple Crown three times, leading the league in wins, ERA, and strikeouts in the same season (1963, 1965, 1966), and he's the only NL player to do it twice in a row since Grover Cleveland Alexander did it for the Phillies in 1915–16.

- He became the only pitcher in history to toss a no-hitter in four straight seasons, from 1962 to 1965, capping it off with his perfect game on September 9, 1965.
- He tossed three immaculate innings, in 1962, 1963, and 1964, the most in baseball history.
- He became—and remains—the only pitcher in history to win five straight ERA crowns.
- He had three sub-2.00 ERA seasons, which stands as a Live Ball Era record. (Clayton Kershaw came close to tying this in 2016, when he had a 1.69 ERA—it would have been his third, but he missed qualifying by all of 13 innings).
- He had just one more game lost (34) than he had shutouts; over his final four seasons, he had four more shutouts (31) than games lost (27).
- He became the first pitcher to have three seasons with at least 300 strikeouts since Amos Rusie had his third . . . in 1892, a season during which Rusie tossed a mere 541 innings.

Sandy Koufax, over his final two seasons, had 54 complete games, setting the modern record for strikeouts with 382 in 1965—since topped by Nolan Ryan's 383-strikeout season in 1973—and had arguably his best season in 1966, during which he had his career best 190 ERA+ with 10.3 WAR.

And then . . . he was done. Just like that.

Despite long stretches of dominance, Koufax was pitching with severe elbow pain, beginning in late 1964. Following the 1966 World Series, Koufax and his ailing elbow had had enough, and he was forced to retire.

Dr. Frank Jobe, the inventor of Tommy John surgery, had said, "Sandy always says that if I'd thought of the surgery just a couple years earlier, we'd be calling it Sandy Koufax surgery."

Now, we can only fantasize about what Sandy would have done just two seasons later, in 1968, dubbed "The Year of the Pitcher," when Bob Gibson set a Live Ball Era record with a 1.12 ERA.

Bob Gibson and Sandy Koufax were virtually the same age, separated by just 51 days; when Koufax pitched a 1.95 ERA from 1962 to 1966, Gibson had an ERA of exactly one point higher.

Don Drysdale *(RHP, 1956–69):* Drysdale is, kinda sorta, *Koufax-Light.* That's not an insult to the Hall of Fame right-hander—it's just incredible how the two teammates' careers seemed to match up.

Like Koufax, Drysdale had a slow-*ish* start to his career, going 79–64 with a 3.30 ERA his first six seasons, before finishing his last seven full seasons at 125–98 with a 2.68 ERA.

Also like Koufax, Drysdale had a short period of complete dominance . . . only it was much shorter than that of Koufax.

In 1968, Drysdale had a then-record 58⅔-inning scoreless streak, later broken by Dodger Orel Hershiser in 1988 (59 innings). He pitched six straight shutouts, an MLB record that still stands, as part of a franchise-best 1.37 first-half ERA.

Unfortunately, like his lefty teammate, Drysdale entered the league as a teenager and was out before his thirty-third birthday. It wasn't an elbow, but a chronically sore shoulder that forced Drysdale to call it quits.

The Left Arm of God (Act II)

Clayton Kershaw is just thirty-one years old—one year older than Sandy Koufax had been when he was forced to walk away from baseball to save his arm.

Kershaw has, arguably, pitched better over his last eight years than Koufax did over his five-year peak. Since 2011, Kershaw has a 174 ERA+ and a 0.926 WHIP, an adjusted ERA that is seven points better, and a WHIP that is identical to that which Koufax put up during his prime seasons.

Clayton Kershaw throwing his second of a MLB-best three complete-game shutouts during the 2015 season (July 23, 2015). (Arturo Pardavila III, CC BY 2.0 [https://creativecommons.org/licenses/by-sa/2.0], via Wikimedia Commons)

Overall, Clayton Kershaw stands as MLB's all-time leader in adjusted ERA, with a 159 ERA+, and his 2.39 ERA, 1.005 WHIP, and 2.64 FIP are all standards among starting pitchers to pitch the entirety of their career during baseball's Live Ball Era.

Kershaw has already cemented his place in baseball history as one of the greatest pitchers the game has ever seen, and like Sandy Koufax, he could walk away from the game today and waltz right into the Hall of Fame. Fortunately, he will not have to do that.

Stats Incredible!

165: Maury Wills's record for games played in 1962. He won the MVP that season, batting .299/.347/.373 with 104 stolen bases.

.356/.311: Pitcher Orel Hershiser's batting average in 1993 (.356) was higher than the on-base percentage of the batters against him (.311).

417: Times right-hander Kevin Brown was at a platoon disadvantage in 2003 (facing left-handed batters). He did not allow a home run to any of them.

0: Sandy Koufax tossed a shutout in Game 5 of the 1965 World Series, on three days' rest. He tossed another in Game 7, on two days' rest.

123: Hits by Steve Garvey with runners on base in 1975, the most in recorded history. Jackie Robinson is second, with 120 in 1949.

4: Pitchers in history who have had consecutive qualified sub-0.900 WHIP seasons: Kershaw (2014–16), Greg Maddux (1994–95), Christy Mathewson (1908–09), and Mordecai Brown (1908–09).

4: Total seasons in which Kershaw had a sub-2.30 ERA and at least 230 strikeouts. No pitcher in baseball history had more (Pedro, Walsh, and Waddell also had four). He is just thirty years old in 2018.

3.92: Kershaw's career ERA in starts he did *not* win. John Lackey has a career 3.92 ERA through 2018.

21: From July 30, 2013, to May 16, 2014, Zack Greinke had 21 straight starts surrendering two runs or fewer (earned or unearned)—a Live Ball Era record, by four whole starts.

205: Sandy Koufax tossed a 13-inning complete game, striking out 15 on 205 pitches on September 20, 1961.

11: Clayton Kershaw saw his lifetime ERA drop in each of his first 11 seasons, from 4.26 to 2.35. His ERA had its first-ever year-to-year jump in 2018, rising from 2.35 all the way to 2.39.

4: Through his first two seasons, Cody Bellinger has 64 home runs, that is four more home runs than his father, Clay, had hits in his career.

310: Kenley Jansen has 310 more strikeouts than base-runners allowed during his career, the second-greatest differential in history behind only Craig Kimbrel (+342). Amazingly, Jansen still has nearly 1,500 more professional innings caught than pitched.

1/4: In 2017, Curtis Granderson became the first player in baseball history to hit a grand slam batting in both the leadoff slot and the cleanup spot in the same season.

22: Clayton Kershaw has 22 career games with double-digit strikeouts and no walks allowed, which is the third most of all time (Randy Johnson: 36, Curt Schilling: 27).

3.78: Clayton Kershaw has a career 3.78 ERA in his 163 career starts that he did not win; he is 0–69 in those starts. Andy Pettitte had an overall career 3.85 ERA; he was 256–153 in those starts.[1]

1,000,000: General manager Ned Colletti signed Justin Turner for a cool $1,000,000 on February 6, 2014. Since then, Turner has racked up 23.3 WAR, batting .305/.383/.505 over five seasons.

.420: Justin Turner has a .420 on-base percentage during his postseason career. Among players with at least 175 postseason plate appearances, only Barry Bonds (.433) and Albert Pujols (.431) are better.

SAN DIEGO PADRES

Est. 1969

Tony Gwynn ranks 58th all-time in at-bats (9,288), 20th in hits (3,141), and 1,462th in strikeouts (434).

The San Diego Padres entered the league in the 1969 expansion, along with the Montreal Expos (Nationals), Seattle Pilots (Brewers), and Kansas City Royals. To date, the team has five division crowns (1984, 1996, 1998, 2005, 2006), and two National League titles (1984, 1998), but is still seeking its first World Series championship.

The Padres are the only team in Major League Baseball to start with five straight sub-.400 winning percentages . . . and actually had six such seasons at the onset. They had four 100-loss seasons in those first six, which is awkward, because their NL West rival, the San Francisco Giants, have had just one such season in their history (and the Giants are 136 years old and went 102 years before hitting that lone 100-loss season in 1985). But, that's enough hate.

There is a ton to love about Padres history, and they haven't always been basement-dwellers. They finished .500 or better eight times over an 11-year stretch, from 1982–92. If that doesn't sound like a big deal, consider: The Pittsburgh Pirates endured 20 straight sub-.500 seasons from 1993–2012, and the Royals finished over .500 just once from 1995–2012. So, being "not bad" can be a pretty good deal.

Three players, Dave Winfield, Tony Gwynn, and Trevor Hoffman, don the Pads' cap in the Baseball Hall of Fame, after Hoffman's NL-record 601 games saved helped earn him entry in 2018. Plus, the Padres have those sweet camouflage uniforms, and were the first MLB club to regularly honor and appreciate the United States military.

No, it's not a century-old club, rich with old-timey-nicknamed greats, like Babe, Whitey, Lefty, and "Shoeless" Joe. But the Padres can still lay claim to one of the best in the game's history.

Perhaps more than any other team in baseball, the Padres, historically, are defined by one player. The Padres really are the "Club that Gwynn Built." The lifetime Padre was what one may call "OMG great," to put it in modern context—but his game was old school.

Mr. Padre

Gwynn played 20 years, from 1982–2001, and was one of those rare pure hitters that seemingly could have played forever. He actually had a better batting average over his final 162 career games (.343) than his first 162 games in the majors (.321).

He leads a slew of offensive categories for the franchise, and it's not even close. His totals in hits (3,141), singles (2,378), doubles (543), total bases (4,259), extra-base hits (763), and runs scored (1,383) are all more than those tallied by the second- and third-place players combined. And the scope of his greatness extends far beyond just San Diego history.

Gwynn's greatness, by the numbers:

- Batted .338 for his career. No other Padre has hit .338 during any one single season.
- Had a .290 batting average over the WORST 162-game stretch of his career.

NBA, ABA, NFL), and made his debut late in the season for San Diego. Despite a late start to the decade, Winfield was one of just seven NL players in the 1970s with at least 100 home runs and 100 stolen bases.

Only 154 of his 465 career home runs came with the Padres (205 with the Yankees), but they were enough. No Padre has had more 20-plus home run seasons than Winfield (five; 1974, 1977–80).

Trevor Hoffman

The thing with closers is, only the very best seem to get any respect. And the New York Yankees' Mariano Rivera holds just about every relief pitching record there is . . . leaving Trevor Hoffman in the dust. But, while Mariano was the game's best, Hoffman is undoubtedly one of the best relief hurlers of all time and is the third Padre represented in the Hall of Fame.

Hoffman retired with the MLB career saves record (601), and it still stands as a National League record—by a healthy margin.

Hoffman could have retired five years earlier and he'd still have a 12-save edge over second-place NL finisher John Franco (424). He's one of only three pitchers (Francisco Rodriguez, Craig Kimbrel) with 40 saves in four straight seasons, and he's the only player in baseball history to do it twice. Rivera's best 40-save streak was three years (2003–05).

Manny!

San Diego … which of course, in German, means, "Manny Machado."

Yeah, the Padres have had a noticeably famous dearth of marquee talent over their 50 MLB seasons. Time will tell if their signing of Manny Machado (2019; 10 years, $300 million) will help chip away at Tony Gwynn's monopoly on franchise milestones. But as for right now, the message has been sent, and reinforced—the first shoe to drop was the Eric Hosmer signing in 2018 (8 years, $144 million)—San Diego is suddenly a force to be reckoned with. Like an improvised silky-smooth jazz flute solo.

STATS INCREDIBLE!

.410: Rickey Henderson's team-high on-base percentage for the Padres in 1996, despite having the lowest qualified batting average on the team (.241).

75.3: The percentage of career games in which Tony Gwynn hit safely.

1: April 14, 1986, the only time Gwynn struck out three or more times in his career. Dodgers hurler Bob Welch K'd the Pads' hits leader his first three at-bats in the game.

38: Nate Colbert's single-season home run total in both 1970 and 1972. It would stand as a team record for 24 years (40; Ken Caminiti, 1996). Greg Vaughn owns the current record, with 50 in 1998.

31: Saves in Trevor Hoffman's career in which he struck out every batter he faced. Most all-time.

296: Hoffman's career "perfect save" total. Only Mariano Rivera had more.

2014/2007: Jason Lane was the starting pitcher for the Padres on July 28, 2014. His first big-league start was on August 20, 2007, as the Astros' center fielder.

434: Both the career strikeout total of Tony Gwynn and Mark Reynolds's strikeout total from 2009–10.

1,183: Tony Gwynn would have had to end his career on an 0-for-1,183 skid for his career batting average to fall below .300.

69: Times Gwynn batted with men on second and third with two outs during his career. He never struck out.

58: Times Gwynn struck out looking during his final thirteen seasons. He had an idea of what a strike was.

56: What do Tony Gwynn, Deion Sanders, Jose Altuve, Ichiro, Delino DeShields, Willie McGee, and Steve Sax all have in common? Each player had a career-high season of 56 stolen bases.

4.66: Tony Gwynn still owns 4.66 percent of all hits in Padres franchise history.

?: On July 31, 2010, the Padres essentially traded Corey Kluber for Ryan Ludwick. There is no statistical significance here. This was just bad.

.355: Tony Gwynn's batting average over his final 1,000 career games. He retired at age forty-one.

162: Twenty-six-year-old Manny Machado already has two seasons in which he's played all 162 games. No player in Padres franchise history has more than one such season.

677: Manny Machado has 677 batted balls with an exit velocity of at least 100 mph, to 637 games played during the "statcast" era. His 677 batted balls of 100 mph or better are the most in baseball over the past four seasons.

175: Manny Machado led all of baseball with 175 batted balls with an exit velocity of at least 100 mph in 2018. He finished tied for 133rd in strikeouts (104) and tied for 63rd in swings and misses (274).

SAN FRANCISCO GIANTS

Est. 1883

In 2004, Barry Bonds reached base safely 376 times. He had just 373 at-bats. No other player in history has had more times safely on base than at-bats. He turned forty that season.

No matter when or where, the Giants, baseball's winningest team, have seemingly always played well.

Established in 1883 as the New York Gothams, the ballclub got the hang of things quickly, topping .500 in just its second pro season (62–50). Their play emulated their new nickname in 1886, as the "Giants" went 85–27, for an all-time franchise-best .759 winning percentage. They only finished second in the National League that year, but they were closing in on the kind of championship success that would eventually help define the franchise.

The Giants won two straight championships in 1888–89, defeating the American Association's best. But just as those aren't counted as official World Series wins (the AL-NL modern World Series began in 1903), it's probably okay to dismiss the next thirteen years in Giants history, before the first World Series, when the team topped the .500 mark just six times and never finished higher than third in the NL standings.

The dawn of the American League at the turn of the century was also a turning of the page for Major League Baseball. The game had two leagues with staying power, and the Giants would prove to be one of its very best teams. In fact, early on, they probably made the New York Yankees jealous.

After hiring John McGraw as manager in 1902, the Giants quickly became the pride of New York. McGraw had such little respect for the upstart American League (with it, the Yankees), that he refused to play the Boston Americans in the 1904 World Series, which feels so . . . un-American. The club got in line and won its first official Series the following year, beginning a short-term stretch of five straight 90-win seasons, and a long-term run

Christy Mathewson, New York Giants, 1912. (Charles M. Conlon)

of success that has been much more skyline bullet train than roller coaster.

All-time ace Christy Mathewson led a Deadball Era staff including fellow Hall of Famers Joe McGinnity and Rube Marquard, putting up team ERA totals that were routinely under 3.00, collectively. Nine times the Giants had a player win the NL ERA crown, or finish runner-up, from 1903 to 1913. From there, Hall of Fame second baseman Frankie Frisch led a new offensive charge for New York that resulted in four straight World Series trips in the 1920s (1921–24), winning two. By 1924, counting the 1904 abstention, the Giants had played in nine of the 22 total World Series, while their AL-counterpart Yankees had just one win in three trips.

From then, of course, the two teams switched fates a bit, and World Series appearances were no longer an inevitability for the Giants. They managed just one championship over the next 29 seasons ("That's plenty," say Padres fans), despite Hall of Fame play from good ole boys such as Mel Ott, Carl Hubbell, and Johnny Mize. Even with Bobby Thomson's pennant-winning, come-from-behind, "Shot Heard 'Round the World" homer in 1951—before a World Series they LOST—and an all-time great, Willie Mays, leading them back to Series glory in 1954, they weren't long for New York. Their shots may have been heard the world over, but attendance didn't show it.

Mays helped smooth over the transition to San Francisco in 1958, leading the team in WAR each of its first eight West Coast seasons. For 14 years overall, the team never finished below .500. No World Series wins, but also no poor showings. And that was how the Giants would define themselves for decades after—no wins, but no disastrous runs.

Even with the great Barry Bonds destroying home run records, and discovering a beyond-Ruthian dominance in San Fran, all with an upside-down smile on his face, the Giants went 56 years between World Series wins.

The Giants may have already locked up "Team of the Decade" honors (in the NL, at least), having won three championships since 2010 (2010, 2012, 2014).

Big 6

There are only a handful of players in this book (Walter Johnson, Babe Ruth, Ty Cobb, Ted Williams, etc.) that deserve, and likely have, their own stats book. At the very least, they should help push this thing to 1,000 pages with their accomplishments. Alas, we have our limits, even if a few of the players we cover seemingly had none. Christy Mathewson was one of them.

(Willie Mays and Barry Bonds, too, but we'll get to them. . . .)

Mathewson's nickname, "Big 6," was a reference to his stature (six-foot-one), and New York City's famous "Big 6" fire engine. He was one of the greatest players in the game's history, and, by all accounts, one of the greatest human beings.

The two-time Triple Crown winner (1905; 31–9, 1.28 ERA, 206 strikeouts/ 1908; 37–11, 1.43, 259 Ks) won 373 games in his career (third all-time), with a 2.13 ERA (ninth), and a 1.058 WHIP (seventh). During his best five-year stretch (1907–11), he went 139–51 with a microscopic 1.69 ERA. Basically, he put together five straight 2015 Zack Greinke seasons (1.68 ERA). Over that span, he led the league in wins and ERA three times and strikeouts twice.

Since 1920, only Bob Gibson (1.12 ERA; 1968) has had an ERA lower than what Mathewson maintained over a three-year stretch from 1908–10 (1.50).

He was also *big* in the postseason, especially in the 1905 World Series. He tossed a record three straight shutouts in the series, leading the Giants to victory. His 28 scoreless World Series innings to start a career are still a major-league record.

Say Hey!

The "Say Hey Kid" was perhaps the game's greatest all-around talent, and wasted little time getting there. He batted .477 in 149 at-bats in AAA before getting the call-up and winning the Rookie of the Year award for the Giants in 1951 (.274/.356/.472). After a brief call-up by the *United States military*, Mays won the league MVP his next full season, batting .345 with 41 home runs. From there, it seemed there was nothing he couldn't, or didn't, accomplish. He won two MVPs, a batting title, four home run titles, four straight stolen base titles, and was a 20-time All-Star, one shy of Henry Aaron's major-league record. His 660 home runs are now fifth on the all-time list, but, for a brief period until June 10, 1972 (the date Henry Aaron hit no. 649 and pulled away for good), he held the NL home run record.

And then there's everything else:

- He became the NL's first 30–30 player in 1956 (36 home runs, 40 stolen bases). Then, he became the first repeat 30–30 player in 1957 (35 HRs, 38 SBs).
- He had 13 seasons with at least 70 extra-base hits, a major-league record.
- For each season over a 10-year stretch, from 1957–66, Mays finished in the top six in MVP voting, was an All-Star, and a Gold Glove winner.
- Over that same 10-year run, he had a collective .983 OPS—higher than any single-season OPS of Hall of Famer Dave Winfield.
- He's the only player with both a 50-homer season (1955; 51) and a 20-triple season (1957; 20).
- Over a five-year stretch, from 1954–58, he averaged 38 home runs—the exact same number as the Kansas City Royals' single-season franchise record. His 1.019 OPS over

that period is higher than any one single-season OPS of Hall of Famer Reggie Jackson.

- He led the National League in triples (97), home runs (382), and stolen bases (237) during a ten-year period from 1954 to 1963.

B. Bonds

No one had more 30/30 (HR/SB) seasons in baseball history than Bonds.

Bobby? Barry? Take your pick. Father (Bobby) and son (Barry) are the only five-time 30/30 members in baseball history. And while, of course, this section is dedicated to the all-time Home Run King (from here, all "Bonds" references will be to Barry), his father had a heck of a career. In the 1970s, only Hall of Famers Willie Stargell (296); Reggie Jackson (292), who is Barry's cousin; and Johnny Bench (290) hit more home runs than Bobby (280) hit.

A slender Barry Bonds, 1993. (Jim Accordino)

He certainly passed this trait down to his son, as Barry Bonds ended up with an all-time record 762 home runs—586 with the Giants.

Of course, this is common knowledge, along with his much-heralded single-season record (73; 2001), and the alleged steroid-use stench that has, thus far, kept him from Hall of Fame enshrinement. What's left when the basics are peeled away and the asterisks are, in our opinion, fairly set aside, is a fascinating and nuanced career that's a whole lot of fun to look at:

(Deep breath)

- From August 14, 2001, to September 7, 2004, hit 154 home runs over the span of 442 games. He struck out just 153 times during that same span.
- Had 379 intentional walks to just 377 strikeouts in his final 3,700 career plate appearances.
- Had a .514 on-base percentage during his final 1,000 career games.
- Batted .289/.473/.596 with 99 runs, 21 doubles, 39 home runs, 94 RBI, five stolen bases, and just 66 strikeouts over his final 162 career games.
- Batted .303/.387/.655 after falling behind 0–2 in the count from 2002–04.
- From 2000–05, batted .338/.533/.779. No other player ever slashed that in a single qualified season. His 240 OPS+ during that span was only ever matched by Babe Ruth in 1920 and Fred Dunlap in 1884.
- Had 334 home runs and 380 stolen bases through 1996. No other player in baseball history eclipsed both of those totals during their *entire* career.
- Batted .471/.700/1.294 during World Series play, the best batting average, on-base, and slugging percentage of any player with at least 30 World Series plate appearances;

however, he never won a ring. Pat Burrell on the other hand, who batted .037/.235/.074 on baseball's biggest stage, won two—including one with Barry's Giants.

- From 2001–05, had a .559 on-base percentage. No other player in history ever reached base at such a rate in a single qualified season.
- If all of his major league-record 762 home runs were strike-outs, he would still have both a higher on-base percentage and a lower strikeout percentage than Willie Stargell, Reggie Jackson, Mike Schmidt, Sammy Sosa, and Alex Rodriguez.
- Strip Barry Bonds of all seven of his MVP seasons and he still has a total of 90.7 WAR. Ken Griffey Jr. had 83.8 WAR during his career.

Even-Year Magic

The Giants won the World Series in 2010, 2012, and 2014, thanks in large part to Madison Bumgarner. In those three Series Bumgarner allowed a single earned run over 36 innings pitched. His 0.25 ERA in World Series play is the lowest in baseball his-tory, among pitchers with at least as many innings. Sandy Koufax ranks second, with an ERA nearly four times that of Bumgarner (0.95).

Mad Bum is the only pitcher in history with multiple complete game shutouts in winner-take-all postseason games. And, postsea-son aside, in 2016, he became the first player with three seasons of at least 215 strikeouts and three home runs (at-bat) since John Clarkson in 1887.

He is quickly becoming one of the largest Giants in history and as it stands, his bat has been bigger than the batters whom he faces: he has hit home runs at a greater rate (2.82 percent) than he has allowed them (2.43 percent).

STATS INCREDIBLE!

10: Barry Bonds's MLB record number of seasons with at least 25 home runs and 25 stolen bases. From 1990 to 1998, he had as many 25/25 seasons (in a row) as Willie Mays (five), Henry Aaron (two), and Alex Rodriguez (two) combined.

3: The number of starts in a World Series by Giants aces Christy Mathewson and Madison Bumgarner, under age twenty-six, with 0–1 runs allowed—a major-league record.

30/45: Bobby Bonds was the first MLB player with at least 30 home runs and 45 stolen bases in 1969 (32 HRs, 45 SBs). His son did it 21 years later (33 HRs, 52 SBs; 1990).

9: Mel Ott's seasons with at least 25 home runs and 100 walks. Only Lou Gehrig, Ted Williams, Babe Ruth, and Barry Bonds had more.

1.000: J.T. Snow (.429) and Barry Bonds (.609) are the only teammates in history to combine for a single-season 1.000-plus on-base percentage (2004).

2: Grand slams hit by starting pitcher Madison Bumgarner in 2014, the second pitcher ever with two in the same season. Giants catcher Buster Posey hit one the same day as Bumgarner, marking the first time in MLB history a pitcher-catcher battery has combined for two salamis.

136: Consecutive multi-strikeout performances to start RHP Tim Lincecum's career, a major-league record.

80: Home runs hit by Barry Bonds from April 12, 2001, to April 17, 2002, a span of 160 games.

42: From 1992 to 2007, Barry Bonds had one season in which he had a sub-1.000 OPS. It was .9993 in 2006. He turned forty-two that season.

2: From April 25, 1991, to September 26, 2007, Barry Bonds reached base safely 4,516 times in 2,258 games—an average of exactly two times per game.

162.8: Barry Bonds's career WAR. Ken Griffey Jr. and Pete Rose combined for 163.5 WAR, besting Bonds by just 0.7 wins.

232: Barry Bonds's record walk total in 2004. A decade later, in 2014, no player even saw 232 three-ball counts.

188: Willie Mays had a career-high 185 OPS+ in 1965. Willie McCovey maintained a 188 OPS+ from 1968 to 1970.

112: Career non-win quality starts by Matt Cain. He was 0–38 with a 2.39 ERA and a 1.086 WHIP in those starts.

40: Cain had a 104–118 career record. San Francisco's bullpen blew 40 games in which he departed in line for a victory.

171: Buster Posey had a 171 OPS+ during his MVP season in 2012. Only one qualified catcher during the Modern Era has bested that in a single season: Mike Piazza, who did so both in 1995 (172) and 1997 (185).

GLOSSARY OF STATS AND TERMS

Adjusted ERA (ERA+): ERA adjusted by park factor and for league averages. It helps present a more neutral assessment of the performance of players who benefited or suffered from high-scoring parks and leagues or the opposite.

Adjusted On-Base Percentage Plus Slugging (OPS+): An important modification of On-Base Percentage, which adjusts the OPS to account for the ballpark and the league that the player played in. In addition, the number is "normalized" so that the median is 100, with better-than-average scores above 100. A single-season OPS+ performance of 140 or higher could be considered a Hall of Fame level performance for that season. Its formula is OPS+ = 100*((OBP/lgOBP)+(SLG/lgSLG) -1), with lgOBP and lgSLG representing the league average for that statistic in that year.

At-bats (AB): A sub-category of plate appearances that excludes certain outcomes including, but not limited to, a base on balls or hit by pitch. The number of at-bats is used to calculate batting average and slugging percentage, while the number of plate appearances is used to calculate a batter's on-base percentage (noting the afore-mentioned exclusions).

Batting Average (BA): The number of hits gotten by a player divided by his number of at-bats. Batting average has long been viewed as the primary measure of a batter's skill, so that the batting title is awarded to the batter with the highest average, rather than to one who scores or drives in the most runs.

Defensive Runs Saved (DRS): A statistic that measures the number of runs a player saved (or cost) his team on defense relative to an average player. The best fielders typically fall into a range of 15–20 for a season, but any positive number is considered above average.

Defensive Wins Above Replacement (dWAR): A defensive measure of wins above replacement, but given only the defensive stats of the player and his position adjustment. Offensive WAR, or oWAR, uses the same value metrics as WAR, but assumes everyone is an average defender.

Earned Run (ER): A run that is ruled by the official scorer to have resulted exclusively from actions by the batting team and not because of errors by the defense. When the fielding team makes an error or passed ball, the scorer is supposed to "reconstruct" the inning assuming that the defensive miscue did not occur. Only runs that would have scored barring the miscue are considered earned; all others are considered to be unearned.

Earned Run Average (ERA): A primary measure of a pitcher's success. It is expressed as an average number of opponents' earned runs scored per notional nine-inning game. Its formula is (ER x 9) / IP.

Extra-Base Hit (EB, EBH, XBH): A hit that goes for more than one base.

Fielding Independent Pitching (FIP): A sabermetric pitching statistic that is philosophically derived from the concept of Defense-Independent Pitching Statistics (also known as "DIPS"). It's a stat that mirrors ERA but only uses BBs, Ks, and HRs. The formula for FIP is simply: (13*HR + 3*BB - 2*K)/IP + C, where C is a constant term that recenters the league-average FIP to match its average ERA. The weights for FIP were derived from the formula for batting linear weights, setting the DIPS events relative to the average value of a ball in play (essentially zeroing out the runs above/below average from BIP).

Fielding Percentage (FP): A common, though limited, measure of fielding effectiveness. Fielding percentage is calculated as chances accepted divided by total chances, and thus measures how effective a fielder is in avoiding errors.

Home Run Percentage (HR%, AB/HR): A way to measure how frequently a batter hits a home run. To calculate, divide the number of plate appearances by the number of home runs hit.

Isolated Power (ISO): A measure of a batter's ability to hit for extra bases. It is the average number of extra bases beyond first per plate appearance. It can be expressed equivalently as follows: ISO = Slugging percentage - Batting average, or ISO = (Total bases - Hits) / AB, or ISO = (2B + 2*3B + 3*HR) / AB.

Jaffe WAR Score System (JAWS): developed by sabermetrician Jay Jaffe (first at Baseball Prospectus in 2004) as a means to measure a player's Hall of Fame worthiness by comparing him to the players at his position who are already enshrined, using advanced metrics to account for the wide variations in offensive levels that have occurred throughout the game's history. The stated goal is to improve the Hall of Fame's standards, or at least to maintain them rather than erode them, by admitting players who are at least as good as the average Hall of Famer at the position, using a means via which longevity isn't the sole determinant of worthiness.

On-Base Percentage (OBP, OB%): A measure of how often a batter reaches base. Batters are not credited with reaching base on an error or fielder's choice, and they are not charged with an opportunity if they make a sacrifice bunt. It is approximately equal to Times on base / Plate appearances; its formula is (H + BB + HBP) / (AB + BB + HBP + SF).

On-Base Plus Slugging (OPS): The sum of on-base percentage and slugging percentage.

Per-162 Stats: An attempt to condense each batter's career into a single season's worth of stats. To calculate for a batter, divide his total number of career games played by 162, then divide his career totals by that factor.

Plate Appearances (PA): Every time a batter completes a turn batting, he is credited with a PA. A player is considered to have completed a turn batting when he reaches base safely via a hit, fielder's choice, or an error, is awarded first base via a base on balls, hit by pitch or interference/obstruction (including catcher's interference), or is retired before reaching base. If a turn at the plate is interrupted by an inning ending on a caught stealing or other similar event that prevents the completion of the batter's turn at the plate, then no PA is charged and the batter leads off the following inning with a fresh count. Similarly, if a game ends on a balk, the player who was batting at the time of the balk is not credited with a PA. If a batter is replaced during time at the plate, the count at the time he is replaced is used to determine whether or not he is charged with a PA. For statistical purposes, plate appearances that result in a batter reaching base via obstruction or interference are ignored when calculating OBP.

Qualifying Player: For a player to qualify for league awards and single season records–
Batters:
Prior to 1920, 60 percent of team games to qualify, rounded to nearest integer:
  1920–37, 100 games.
  1938–44, AL - 400 ABs, NL - 100 games.
  1945–56, 2.6 at-bats per team game. However, from 1951–54, if a player came up short, a player could still qualify for a batting title if they led after the necessary number of hitless at-bats were added to their at-bat total.
  1957–present, 3.1 plate appearances per team game. However, after 1967, if a player came up short, a player could still qualify for a batting title if they led after the necessary number of hitless plate appearances were added to their plate appearance total. Case in point . . . Tony Gwynn, in 1996, hit .353 in 498 plate appearances, but tack on an 0-for-4 (needed four plate appearances to qualify) and he still reigns at .349. Moreover, Willie McGee won the 1990 NL batting title, despite finishing the season in the American League. He qualified after the necessary number of hitless plate appearances were added.
  In 1954, Bobby Avila won the AL batting title. He bested Ted Williams, despite Williams having a higher batting average. By today's standards, Williams would have won the batting crown, but he had so many walks that he did not have enough official at-bats to qualify. This inspired the change to plate appearances, instead of at-bats, as the qualifier shortly thereafter.
Pitchers:
ERA, per nine starts: one inning pitched per team game played that season, rounded to nearest integer. In most cases, this will require 162 innings pitched.
  Win Percentage—Minimum number of decisions is the number of team games that season multiplied by 0.098 rounded up to the nearest integer. Example: 162-game season, 16 decisions.

Quality Start: A game in which the starting pitcher pitches six or more innings and allows three runs or fewer. The implication is that a quality start allows his team a much better than even chance to win the game and is a credit to the starting pitcher, whether he ends up with a win, a loss, or a no-decision for his efforts.

Slash line: The most commonly used short listing of a player's key offensive statistics. In the 1990s, it replaced the former Triple Crown stat usage, as it more aptly describes a player's offensive contributions. A player's batting average is listed first, then OBP, and finally slugging percentage. For instance, R. J. Reynolds hit .288/.354/.344 for the 1990 Pirates; he had a .288 average, .354 OBP, and .344 slugging percentage.

Slugging Percentage (SLG): The number of total bases divided by the number of at-bats. Its formula is ([Singles] + [Doubles x 2] + [Triples x 3] + [Home Runs x 4])/[At-Bats].

Strikeout Percentage (K%, K Rate): A statistic for either a pitcher or a batter. For a pitcher, it represents the number of strikeouts per batter faced. For a batter, it represents how many times he walks or strikes out per plate appearance.

Strikeout-to-Walk Ratio (K/BB, SO/BB): The measure of a pitcher's ability to control pitches, calculated as: strikeouts divided by bases on balls. A pitcher that possesses a great K/BB ratio is usually a dominant power pitcher.

Walks and Hits per Inning Pitched (WHIP): Walks plus hits, all divided by number of innings pitched. It is one of the standard measures of a pitcher's efficacy, noting how well they prevent base-runners. It became prominent in the 1980s and 1990s.

Weight On-base Average (wOBA): wOBA is a version of on-base percentage that accounts for how a player reached base—instead of simply considering whether a player reached base. The value for each method of reaching base is determined by how much that event is worth in relation to projected runs scored (example: a double is worth more than a single).

Weighted Runs Created Plus (wRC+): wRC+ takes the statistic Runs Created and adjusts that number to account for important external factors—like ballpark or era. It's adjusted, so a wRC+ of 100 is league average and 150 would be 50 percent above league average.

Win Probability Added (WPA): A statistic that attempts to measure a player's contribution to a win by looking at each of the player's plays within a game, and how that player has altered the outcome.

Wins Above Replacement (WAR): An attempt to measure a player's value—expressed in wins—over that which would have been contributed by a fictional "replacement-level player" (essentially a AAA-quality player who can be readily acquired by a team at any time for the league's minimum salary) in the same amount of playing time.

Effort Above Replacement (EAR): New arbitrary stat we invented, akin to participation trophies for the athletically challenged. Still haven't worked out all the kinks.

Most definitions provided by

INDEX

Note: Illustrations and photographs are indicated by page numbers in *italics*.